The Unknown

This book fills up a significant gap about the information available on the life of the illustrious Buddhist scholar, Hsüan-tsang, who visited India in the seventh century AD. While his experiences and observations from these travels are well documented and easily accessible to the English-speaking world, there is a silence on the years that followed his return to China in AD 645. Works that translated Chinese and Uigur texts on the life of Hsüan-tsang into German and French were in print as early as the 1850s, but have not been available to a wider audience.

This book brings together a selection of the available material, freshly translated into English. Devahuti's introduction and summary of life bring out, in sharp focus, the contributions and impact of Hsüan-tsang. This work stands out for its in-depth research and use of original sources. It will be a valuable addition to the existing literature on Hsüan-tsang and Buddhism of the time, and opens new areas for further research and analysis.

The late **D. Devahuti** (1929–88) specialized in ancient Indian and early South-east Asian history. She taught at the universities of Malaya and Queensland. Her last teaching assignment was with the history department of University of Delhi. Some of her other works include *Harsha: A Political Study, India and Ancient Malaya, Problems of Indian Historiography,* and *Bias in Indian Historiography.*

The Unknown Hsüan-tsang

Edited by
D. DEVAHUTI

OXFORD
UNIVERSITY PRESS

OXFORD
UNIVERSITY PRESS

YMCA Library Building, Jai Singh Road, New Delhi 110 001

Oxford University Press is a department of the University of Oxford. It furthers the
University's objective of excellence in research, scholarship, and education
by publishing worldwide in

Oxford   New York

Auckland   Cape Town Dar es Salaam Hong Kong Karachi Kuala Lumpur
Madrid   Melbourne Mexico City Nairobi New Delhi Shanghai Taipei Toronto

With offices in

Argentina Austria Brazil Chile Czech Republic France Greece Guatemala
Hungary Italy Japan Poland Portugal Singapore South Korea Switzerland
Thailand Turkey Ukraine Vietnam

Oxford is a registered trademark of Oxford University Press
in the UK and in certain other countries

Published in India
by Oxford University Press, New Delhi

ISBN-13: 978-0-19-568349-3
ISBN-10: 0-19-568349-8

Printed in India by Pauls Press, New Delhi 110 020
Published by Manzar Khan, Oxford University Press
YMCA Library Building, Jai Singh Road, New Delhi 110 001

Contents

Preface

Professor Devahuti, the author of *Harsha: A Political Study*; *India and Ancient Malaya* and numerous other articles in learned journals, was engaged in exploring the nature of interaction between India and its neighbouring civilizations of Central Asia, China, and Southeast Asia. She has left behind several finished and partly finished manuscripts and voluminous notes on a variety of subjects. *The Unknown Hsüan-tsang* is part of a considerably larger work on Central Asia. This study was undertaken by the author, as she herself said, ' . . . to rediscover links with civilizations which interacted for centuries with India's own. As I discovered by my study, these links continue to exist in Southeast Asia even in areas predominantly animist, Muslim or Christian. The same is true for Central Asia whether in the medieval or modern context.'

Indian scholars in general, and historians in particular, are aware of the fact that the Chinese have made a significant contribution to the modern reconstruction of ancient Indian history and culture. However, such an awareness remains largely without purpose until employed in an in-depth study. Devahuti, when she did her Ph.D. and later published the dissertation as *Harsha: A Political Study* (Oxford University Press, 3rd revised edition, 1998, originally published by Clarendon Press, 1970), had embarked on that course.

Unearthing Devahuti's personal archives we found many manuscripts. *The Unknown Hsüan-tsang*, now being published by the Oxford University Press, shall give readers access to hitherto unknown material.

The indepth enquiries and research in this book can lay the foundation for future scholars to study the exploits of this great cultural ambassador between India and China so that everything unknown about him may be learnt, well-preserved and perhaps provide a model for future interactions.

Devahuti's major field was ancient India, but her canvas extended to inter-continental, inter-civilizational, and inter-disciplinary dimen-

sions. She was not a China scholar by training, but various circumstances aroused in her a keen interest in Chinese history and culture.
As far back as in the 1950s, during her doctoral research at the School
of Oriental and African Studies, University of London, she met and
interacted with many Chinese scholars, particularly Professor Lau.
Later a teaching stint at universities in Australia and visits to Malaysia
and Singapore for academic exchanges brought her into contact with
more Chinese scholars. Southeast Asia became for her a window to
the ancient Chinese civilization and culture, one she peeped through
off and on. She had examined—often with the help of experts and
language specialists in their specific fields—original literary sources
including formal compositions and folk literature, archaeological finds
and art objects, in libraries and museums in Delhi, Dharamshala,
(former) East and West Germany, the former USSR, and China.

More important was Devahuti's acquaintance with Professor Tan
Chung, from the late 1960's. Devahuti joined the Department of History,
Delhi University while Professor Tan Chung was in the Department of
Chinese and Japanese studies. This new department used the History
Department as a platform to popularize Chinese studies among graduate
students of the university. Devahuti and Tan Chung enjoyed a close
personal friendship. In 1978, Tan Chung joined the Jawaharlal Nehru
University. Devahuti and Tan Chung continued their academic association and they had even planned to take up a joint research project
together. However, all plans for the future were cut short by her
untimely death in 1988.

Apart from Tan Chung, Devahuti also had many good friends in China,
one of whom was Professor Huang Xinchuan, former Director of the
Institue of South and Southeast Asian Studies (later renamed as the
Institute of Asia Pacific Studies) of the Chinese Academy of Social
Sciences (CASS), Beijing. Huang was introduced to Devahuti in 1979
when she first visited India. The two regularly exchanged correspondence and writings. Devahuti learnt many things from Huang about
contemporary studies in China on ancient Sino-Indian contacts. Xuanzang (the new spelling of Hsüan-tsang) was a common academic interest
between them. Both Huang and Tan Chung greatly miss Devahuti now
that there is a renewed interest, both in China and India, in Hsüan-tsang.

I have alluded to Devahuti's strong spiritual ties with Tan Chung; they
treated each other as friends, philosophers, and guides. Tan is the son of
the luminous Chinese scholar, Tan Lun-shan, who was invited by the
Nobel Laureate, Rabindranath Tagore, to India from Singapore, and who

helped Tagore establish the renowned Cheena-Bhavana at Viśva Bharati, laying a strong foundation for Sino-Indian studies. Tan Chung has since been, like his father, working ceaselessly in promoting India–China understanding. Devahuti had always had a great admiration for the work done by Tan Chung's father, whom she described as the 'modern Hsüan-tsang'. Devahuti, her husband Damodar, Tan Chung and many others have all been quiet workers for the promotion of friendship and understanding between the two great civilizations. *The Unknown Hsüan-tsang* is a reflection of Devahuti's efforts towards this lofty end.

Research is like a chain reaction. It can lead the inquisitive mind from one area to another, to yet another, endlessly. Devahuti's journey from Harshavardhana, an ancient north Indian ruler, to Hsüan-tsang, the talented Chinese monk-scholar, is the result of such a chain reaction. Both Devahuti and her husband, Professor Damodar Prasad Singhal, were great travellers and path-finders. In her meticulous attention to detail, Devahuti would be unmindful of time, effort, and expense. She tracked the forgotten traces of Hsüan-tsang by visiting libraries and museums in a number of countries. Travelling thus, she was only emulating the shining example of Hsüan-tsang himself.

I have just mentioned Damodar, my brother-in-law, and I know how greatly my sister Devahuti loved and admired him. They were symbiotic in their scholarship. He authored a dozen well-known books on historical subjects, the best-known being *India and World Civilization* (Michigan State University Press, 1969). In the concluding paragraph of this work, Professor Singhal spells out the universal outlook of a modern Indian mind:

> In an era of increasing scientific and technological advancement the cultural isolation of one region could scarcely be possible. Without the impediment of colonial rule, Indian response to the West might have been even more unrestrained. Even so, although her choice of western learning was somewhat limited by British imperial needs, the initiative to select from what was offered was mainly her own. India elected to absorb voluntarily. She resisted western domination, but not western learning. (vol. 2, p. 313)

This was Devahuti's perspective too. It was this mindset that made her voluntarily travel beyond the west, beyond the western studies on China, to swim in the 'unknown' waters of the 'orient'. *The Unknown Hsüan-tsang* was meant to be her first break-through in her larger endeavour of making known the 'unknown China'. That she had evinced keen interest in Hsüan-tsang much earlier than many Chinese academia reveals her perceptiveness in seeing Hsüan-tsang's greatness from a trans-civilizational perspective.

Hsüan-tsang holds special interest for us. Our historical discourse, for quite some time, has been informed by a body of literature on and by Hsüan-tsang. But some of this primary source material for the study of Indian history and culture has been either largely neglected or dissatisfactorily used. Professor Devahuti felt the need to have a fresh look at it for reasons which become clear in her Introduction. During Harsha's reign, Hsüan-tsang travelled to India and recorded his experiences. Shortly thereafter I-tsing also visited the country and left a record of his visit. Devahuti studied their writings closely and had focused her research on the broader subject for the last seven years of her life. Her sudden and untimely death has not only delayed the publication of her work by several years but also requires that an explanatory note on the contents of this work be provided. Though the portion of Hsüan-tsang's biography that covers his stay in India has been translated in full and studied in detail, his life and activity after his return to China have been neglected as a source of information on India. The present work addresses and fills this lacuna to a considerable extent.

The first chapter of this book, which is a summary of chapters VI–X of the pilgrim's biography by Hui-li and Yen-ts'ung, is a fresh translation of this less-known but very interesting and informative section of that work. The letters exchanged between the pilgrim and the monk scholars Prajñā-deva and Jñāna-prabha of Nālandā are the subject of the second chapter. We have here the English translations of both the Uigur and the Chinese versions, which have been checked with the help of language experts. These letters first appeared in English as an appendix to the 2nd edition of the author's book on Harsha and are included here with extensive and expanded notes. A comparison of the two versions is very interesting, especially as there is a mention of the *Ṛg Veda* in the Uigur version, which is missing in the Chinese. Dr A. von Gabain's original work on the Uigur letters in German—consisting of an Introduction, Observations and an Index—has also been translated from German to English (chapter two). The importance of Gabain's work lies in the wealth of detail about the original manuscripts, the language and style of the letters themselves, and the peculiarities of their translation. Stanislas Julien translated Hui-li's biography of Hsüan-tsang into French in 1853, but chapters VI–X of the book, which dealt with the pilgrim's life in China on his return from India, were rather imperfect. Chapter three of the present work is an English translation of Julien's French rendering of the above mentioned chapters, with copious notes and comments by Devahuti, which to a large extent takes care of the shortcomings of Julien's translation. The portions of Hsüan-tsang's account of his Indian travels that are relevant to and important for the study of Ancient India have been translated anew, and with the author's comments comprise chapter four of this book. The Korean edition of the *Tripiṭaka* (no. 778) contains very useful material on the Chinese pilgrim's works. A descriptive list of these writings compiled by Lancaster has therefore been added as an appendix at the end, which should provide valuable information to researchers.

This book is not only important for its contribution to the history of Ancient India, Buddhist religion and as a biography of the learned Buddhist pilgrim, it also provides a glimpse of the mutual influence of the civilizations of India, Central Asia and China. The significance of this work can be appreciated in the light of the much discussed and totally contrasting views of Professor Samuel P. Huntington on the impending clash of civilizations. Professor Devahuti would not have shared this vision at all. She looked at civilizations in terms of their mutual enrichment and a healthy, fulfilling give-and-take relation, in contrast to Huntington's thesis. Religion provides the key in her research works. Here is an excerpt from her unpublished manuscript on Central Asia.

> The Central Asian frontier did not constitute a boundary; with the introduction of Buddhism, it becomes an area which united the three regions of India, Central Asia, and China. The diverse ethnic elements such as the Saka and Sogd, the Hunnic and Altaic, and the varied religious beliefs—Hindu, Zervanistic, Tao, Confucian, Manichaean and Nestorian—brought about qualitative changes in Central Asian Buddhism without violating it. They introduced new folk traditions and proverbs; incorporated fresh artistic motifs; accentuated specific aspects of the faith, such as the celebration of the Buddha of the future, Maitreya; laid emphasis on the penance-and-forgiveness kshanti prayers, dharanis; combined shamanic and magical practices; brought about linguistic changes; and introduced new elements in the form of historical texts. In the political realm, Buddhism led to fresh alignments; indeed it gave a different turn to Chinese history. It strengthened economic contacts, trade often being placed at the service of politics, and politics at that of religion—a condition as natural to the medieval, predominantly agricultural societies as its reverse is to their modern industrialized counterparts.

In another place, she wrote:

> Eastern Turkistan was the crossroad of many vigorous cultures. This factor, and the Uigurs' adoption of sedentary, even urban way of life, led to the development of the first Turkic literature on a considerable scale, mostly in translation, but yet of a creative nature. Largely religious in character, the works relate to Nestorian Christianity, Manichaeism and Buddhism, particularly the latter. Uigur Buddhism was reinforced by that of the Saka-speaking people of the southern oasis belt with their centre at Khotan; further influences came from Bamian and Bactria, possibly also from Bukhara and Samarkand.

What is significant to note in Devahuti's approach is her recognition of the positive aspects of the interaction while accepting the trauma, which is in sharp contrast to Huntington's focus and emphasis on hostility and conflict. Here is what she had to say about the Turks who have been termed the 'scourge of humanity':

> The Turks of Central Asia were amongst those peoples who initiated the process of equalizing among the great civilizations of the world; they did so with a force which reflected the severity of their own environment. On account of their physical closeness to China they affected its history more than that of India, Iran or the Roman Empire. That they themselves were influenced by all these civilizations is attested by the religions that flourished in their various kingdoms together with their own shamanism: a limited Tao and Confucianism, Indian and Tibetan Buddhism, Mazdaism, Manichaeism, Nestorian Christianity and finally Islam.
>
> While the Turkic invasions were a traumatic experience for the established civilizations, they prevented cultural inbreeding. Not only did the Turks provide a stimulus in themselves, they also carried the seeds of one culture to another in the form of objects and ideas.

The geographical setting of *The Unknown Hsüan-tsang* is the vast arena that had been covered by Hsüan-tsang's footsteps. Known variously and ambiguously as Central Asia, the more romantic and fashionable 'Silk Road', the politically contentious term of Eastern Turkistan, and the official Chinese Hsin-Chiang / Xinjiang (meaning new territory), here is the 'Unknown' Hsüan-tsang standing at the fertile point of interculturalness. Devahuti liked Tan Chung's description of the Silk Road as the *Dharma-ratna-marg* (road transporting the jewel of truth). From her archives we discovered that she had already started work on a manuscript titled 'India and Central Asia', along with the *The Unknown Hsüan-tsang*. The following paragraphs from this unpublished work place Hsüan-tsang's life and work against the backdrop of the spread of Buddhism and its scope of activity, and provide a glimpse of the vast body of literature in Turkic languages with an emphasis on Uigur. This background will give an indication of the scale and type of material available for further study and research and will put the activities of this illustrious pilgrim in perspective.

The Uigur played a very important part in the preservation and transmission of Buddhist texts. To a relatively early time belongs the *Maitri-simit*, the theme of Maitreya Buddha, which is an adaptation of a Tokharian example. The *Suvarnaprabhasottama-sūtra*, which is based on a Chinese version of the *I-tsing*, was frequently copied. An Uigur translation (of the *Life*) from the tenth century comes from Bišbalïq and a later version is available from Kansu. The almost complete block-print version preserved at Leningrad also has a commentary which is not to be found on the six fragments of the text in the Berlin collection. The translation of the biography of Hsüan-tsang was undertaken not only because of the great esteem in which the pilgrim was held but also because of its special interest for the region. A superb manuscript has survived of the *Yogāchāra-bhūmi-śāstra*, the main text of the Vinayavadins, in which the chapter on the forms of appearance of Avalokiteśvara has been copied from the Saddharmapundarīkasūtra. A manuscript of the *Abitaki* from the Chinese *Amitābhasūtra* and a treatise on *Shraddhā* testify to the prevalence of the Pure Land School and the increasing popularity of the *Amitābha* cult. A number of manuscripts have been discovered with formulae of confessions for lay people.

The sūtras are Uigur commentaries on the Chinese texts. The twenty-fifth chapter of the Saddharmapundarīkasūtra, in praise of Avalokiteśvara, receives the most attention. The Turkic version corresponds with Kumārajīva's translation of this work in Chinese, but has been reworked to a great extent. The *Suvarṇaprabhasottama*, of which an almost complete block-printed edition is extant in Leningrad, is of special interest. The translator of the biography of Hsüan-tsang, Singqu Säli of Bišbalïq, also rendered this work into Uigur Turkic in AD 930, using the Chinese version of I-tsing. A portion of the *Prajñāpāramitā* has survived. According to Gabain, it could be part of another text. The Maitreya and Amitabha cults were popular in Central Asia. We have a *Maitri-sudur* as well as *Abitaki* (A-mi-to-king) or *Amitābhasūtra*. The Sakiz Yukmak, in addition to praising the Buddha, also contains much material of secular interest. The *Yitikan-sudur* or *Sūtra of the Seven Stars* is a Tantric text which has survived in many manuscripts and block-printed forms, and was translated into Uigur in 1328. In good Turkic is the relatively more recent *Aryarājāvavādakasūtra*. An interesting colophon tells us that the two upadhyayas in India, Jinamitra and Sailendrabodhi, have had it translated by an interpreter named Jnanasena, probably in Tibet, on the instruction of the king of the family of Bodhisattvas. Qoludi Sanghasri had retranslated it into Uigur from Tibetan.

There are small fragments in Uigur of the *Mahamayurisūtra*. There is a printed fragment in good Turkic in the style of the second half of the *Suvarṇaprabhāsasūtra*, in which the repentance, forgiveness or *kshānti* (skt. *ksham*) prayers have an important place in Central Asian Buddhism. The Turkic monks who met for this purpose once a month, like their Theravada counterparts in Sri Lanka, probably recited these prayers in Sanskrit, as the laity was not present on these occasions. Long prayers of penance in old Turkic were, however, available for the laity who were strongly encouraged to purge themselves of past, present, and potential sins (owing to belief in rebirth), in community prayer sessions. The *Ksānti qilgulug nom*, a translation of the Chinese *Ts'u-pei tao ch'an fa*, is dated as early as the first century (Nanjio, 1980: 1106). The Chinese translation was done by An Shih-Kao of Bokhara.

Following a period of spontaneous changes in the language to accommodate new ideas and thoughts there came a phase of planned development when key words and technical terms were accurately translated from the Sanskrit, and from Buddhist as well as non-buddhist sources. Sanskrit equivalents in the Brahmi script were inserted against the Uigur equivalents in handwritten and block-printed texts. From the time of Hsüan-tsang, old Turkic renderings became more accurate due to the exactitude and punctiliousness with which the gigantic task of translation was conducted. In Central Asia, scholars and religious experts, stylists and phoneticians, Sanskritists, Tocharists, and Uigurists combined their efforts, and their Uigur expertise was later used by the Chinese and Mongols.

It is with satisfaction but trepidation that I hand this work to the editors at OUP without whose help and support it could not have been published. I do this not only in fond memory of my sister, but also to make available that which I feel deserves to be known, read, and commented upon rather than letting it fade into oblivion.

Yet it is not just the information and insight of Devahuti that should be preserved; her faith in human communication, cultural interface, and synergy, and a respect for differences should also be widely shared.

When death overtook her, the manuscript was ready for publication and had been delayed by Professor Devahuti only for incorporating new material that had been located by her on her latest trips to museums and libraries. I soon discovered that even a 'finished' manuscript requires painstaking effort to bring out posthumously. Such was her personal and professional life that I was able to draw upon the help of her friends, and they gave of their time and expertise unstintingly and unhesitatingly. The deficiencies, that are bound to be there, are due to my inexperience in handling such a complex work. Annoying as they are, I hope they will be overlooked by the scholars as also by my meticulous but indulgent sister.

Professor Tan Chung has helped right from the start to the completion of this work, and indeed, even with this preface. That the foreword to this book is by him is appropriate not only because of its subject but also because of his long friendship with Devahuti. Professor Lokeshchandra, who has had a long association with Devahuti and her work, gave generously of his time, expert advice, illustrations, and access to his library to double-check references and clarify marginal notations. Professor Ramchandra Gandhi helped me in a better understanding of the civilizational context of this book. Professor U.S. Pathak and Professor D.N. Panigrahi were extremely encouraging and helpful in resolving problems. Professor A. Rahman's sustained interest and support in the preparations for the publication have helped me carry on. The contributions of Professor J.N. Tiwari and Mr. P.S. Dwivedi have been unquantifiable and inexpressible. Musée Guimet has to be suitably acknowledged for the permission to again use the pictures we had for *Harsha*. I would like to express my warm thanks to Avinash Pasricha for his expert help with the illustrations. Anshu Dogra's participation in this project started with the search through Devahuti's archives for all material relevant to its preparation for publication, and continued every step of the way. For his time and generosity, I wish to thank Praveen Mehta. Ms Neeta has helped with typing and proof-reading. The patience, consideration, empathy and trust that have been shown to me by Bela Malik, Rasna Dhillon, and Gaurav Ghose at the Oxford University Press will ever remain with me. It is not possible to name everyone, and there will also be those whose help Devahuti would have liked to acknowledge but about whom I do not know. I cannot thank all these people enough.

New Delhi   VEENA SACHDEV
January 2001

Foreword

Even if Oxford University Press had not asked me to get involved with this publication, I would have invited myself into it, because it offers me a special privilege and pleasure in keeping my spiritual reunion with one of my dearest friends, Devahuti, and one of her favourite research themes—Hsüan-tsang. Like Devahuti, I, too, am endeared to Hsüan-tsang (or spelled as 'Xuanzang'), because not only is he an inspiration to me, he is also an icon that off and on smiles on a Chinese family settled in India—an icon that symbolizes a 'cultural envoy' or 'people's ambassador'.

When Veena, younger sister of Devahuti, showed me the unfinished manuscript of *The Unknown Hsüan-tsang* many years ago, I could not suppress my sense of loss that such an important project was left unfinished, and I was keen to see its completion. Partly because I was in the thick of a project absolutely unrelated to Hsüan-tsang, and partly because of a lack of confidence on my part, I could not undertake the work to complete it. The 'Hsüan-tsang scholarship' that Devahuti had attempted to build up requires one to have a mastery over history, geography, sociology, culture, and literature, and an ease with Chinese, English, Sanskrit, ancient Central Asian languages, and even Japanese, French, and other European languages so that one can incorporate the latest findings of Hsüan-tsang experts all over the world. I felt I was an intellectual pygmy before the height of such a scholarly challenge. I turned the manuscript to a very senior scholar of Sanskrit and archaeology, who was also conversant with Chinese, and particularly, Central Asian history. Having initially agreed, this scholar later gave up. All this reflects the height of the academic level of Devahuti's project, which deserves to be published as she had left it. It is like the magnificent wall paintings of the Dunhuang (or Tun-huang) caves illustrated by innumerable Chinese and foreign artists from the fourth to the fourteenth centuries spread in 492 grottoes. Some of these masterpieces are also 'unfinished', but they shine as magnificently as the finished ones.

Devahuti was a pioneer, and therefore, a loner in her Hsüan-tsang project. She had asked for my companionship in this vital academic pursuit. Much as I felt embarrassed to decline her request, I was at that time facing a number of challenges both in teaching and in research, in addition to academic administration duties in a university that I had only recently joined. Her acknowledgement of my help in the manuscript has put me to shame, as I regretfully reminisce about having left her alone in what she was doing. Devahuti started her quest for the 'unknown Hsüan-tsang' almost half a century ago, when she was treading a lonely path. Now, when the path is no longer lonesome, one laments that Devahuti is not with us to embark on it.

No description is more profound for the understanding of Hsüan-tsang than the word 'unknown' used by Devahuti. In Buddhist and also in Taoist logic, there is little that divides the known from the unknown. Even in Confucian thinking, the more you want to know, the more you find that you don't know. Like William Shakespeare, Hsüan-tsang has the dimension of a 'national industry' in the pursuit of wisdom, information, and understanding. Researchers can exhaust themselves, they cannot exhaust the now more or less established 'Hsüan-tsang Studies'.

Much scholarly work has been done in the name of 'Xuanzang (Hsüan-tsang) Studies' after Devahuti left our world. A common friend of her and mine, Professor Huang Xinchuan, a leading Chinese scholar on Indian philosophy, has become the driving spirit in the last several years to mobilize scholarly enthusiasm on Hsüan-tsang. He established a research institution—The Institute of Xuanzang Studies—in 1992, and organized an international seminar in 1994, commemorating the 1,330th anniversary of the birth of the pilgrim at his birth place, Luoyang, and the place of his major work and death, Xi'an (the modern location of the ancient imperial capital, Ch'ang-an). Had Devahuti lived several years longer, she would have presented her *The Unknown Hsüan-tsang* to this unprecedented international gathering of more than a hundred eminent admirers and spiritual disciples of the ancient pilgrim, where over sixty research papers on Xuanzang/Hsüan-tsang were presented.

Even before this event took place, many scholars from the renowned Beijing University had carried out significant research on Hsüan-tsang, synthesizing his 'travelogue' and 'biography' (as mentioned by

Devahuti) and various other well-known, not-so-well-known, and un-known sources in Chinese and other languages. Their annotated volume of *Xiyuji* (Hsi Yü chi) is the most comprehensive research done so far on the pilgrim's historic travels to the Buddhist countries inside and outside India. (Ji Xianlin et al., *Da-Tang Xiyuji Jiaozhu* or 'The Annotated Version of Xuanzang's "Records of the Western Regions" ', Beijing: Zhonghua Bookshop, 1985.) Yet, none of the contributors of this masterpiece would disagree with my conclusion that much work still should and can be done to carry the significance of Xuanzang further afield.

Ji Xianlin, Life Professor of Beijing University, is the doyen of Chinese scholars specializing in Indian and Sino-Indian studies. He has summarized the achievements of Xuanzang in four aspects. First, the translation of Buddhist scriptures from Sanskrit into Chinese. In total 1,335 fascicles (a fascicle is about a score of pages) were rendered into Chinese with great mastery by Xuanzang. As Professor Ji puts it: 'While China occupies a unique place in the history of translation in world literature, Xuanzang occupies a unique place in the history of translation in Chinese literature. Professor Ji also sees three stages in the evolution of translation techniques in China's gigantic and magnificent *Sūtra*-translation (*yijing*) feat. The early pioneers from the first century onwards used the method of 'direct translation' (*zhiyi*), producing works which were not so readable, if not difficult to comprehend. Then arrived Kumārajīva in the 4th century who inaugurated a new stage of 'concept translation' (*yiyi*), making the end-products very readable, but a little too free to be faithful. Xuanzang combined the advantages and forte of both the above approaches, a method what we now call 'transcreation'.

Second, Xuanzang helped to establish a new school of Buddhist disciples known as the 'Weishi' (*Vijñānamātra*) or 'Faxiang' (dharma-lakṣaṇa) sect, although the School did not endure. Third, Xuanzang had the marvellous achievement of getting diplomatic relations established between India (under king Harshavardhana) and China (under the Tang Dynasty). The pilgrim made Harsha (another one of Devahuti's favourite research topics) admire the Tang emperor, Taizong (or T'ai-tsung) who, in turn, was convinced by Xuanzang's accounts that India was a marvellous country. Several embassies were exchanged between these two rulers, which was unprecedented in the annals of India-China relations.

Fourth, Xuanzang made the Chinese begin to enjoy a marvellous

Indian invention known in ancient China as 'shimi' (stone honey), *i.e.*, brown cane-sugar. It was according to Xuanzang's information that the Chinese ambassador, Wang Xuance (or Wang Hsüan-ts'e), got two sugar-making workers and eight Buddhist monks from the Mahabodhi Temple in Magadha to go to Yangzhou in eastern China to convert cane into 'stone-honey'. Finally, the pilgrim's 'travelogue' has been a great source book of information for the studies of both India and China. According to Professor Ji, Xuanzang is a 'household name in India'. This may seem exaggerated. But, at least, those Indians who have visited ancient Buddhist monuments at Ajanta, Ellora, Nalanda, and other places, would have seen the name of Xuanzang in the introductions put up by the Archaeological Survey of India (ASI). Modern tourists are unaware of the initial difficulties faced by the ASI in identifying the ancient monuments at the time they were unearthed a century ago. Xuanzang's writings were a godsend. It was Xuanzang (and many others, of course) who made it possible for modern Indians to rediscover their own ancient cultural heritage. As an eminent historian of the Aligarh Muslim University told Professor Ji, ancient Indian history cannot be satisfactorily reconstructed without the accounts of Xuanzang. (Ji Xianlin, *Zhong-Yin wenhua jiaoliu shi* or 'History of Sino-Indian Cultural Intercourse', Beijing: Xinhua Publishing House, 1991, pp. 72–8.)

How much of Professor Ji's conclusion is known to the readership of this book I cannot gauge. It is equally unknown whether Professor Ji has exhausted all the dimensions of this wonder pilgrim's exploits. An affirmative information available in the volume on 'Religion' (*Zongjiao* or 'Tsung-Chiao') of the modern 'Great Encyclopaedia of China' (*Zhongguo dabaike quanshu* or 'Chung-Kuo ta-pai-ke Ch'üanshu') says that Xuanzang was ordered (by the emperor) to translate *Laozi* (Lao-tsŭ) and *Dacheng qixing lun* (Ta-ch'eng Ch'i-hsing lun) into Sanskrit to be circulated in India. (*Zhongguo dabaike quanshu*, the *zongjiao* volume, Beijing & Shanghai, 1988, p. 440.) The book *Laozi*, also known as *Daode jing* (Tao-te Ching or Tao-te King), written by a mystic philosopher of the times of Confucius, was widely regarded as the holy book of Taoist philosophy, while *Dacheng qixing lun* is a treatise which was originally authored by the ancient Indian philosopher Aśvaghoṣa, *i.e.*, the *Mahāyāna śrāddhotpāda-śāstra*. This Indian text has had many Chinese versions and a host of annotations making it almost a separate genre in Chinese Buddhist literature. If this information about Xuanzang's retranslation is to be believed (many scholars are sceptical about it), then Xuanzang was the pioneer of a feat—a reverse-engineering of rendering the translated Chinese Buddhist scriptures back into their original languages of Sanskrit and Pali— which my late father, Professor Tan Yun-shan, founder-director of Viśva-Bharati Cheena-Bhavana, had initiated at Śantiniketan in late 1930 with the blessings of Gurudeva Rabindranath Tagore. Though the experiment has yielded little, it indirectly proves the marvellous genius of Xuanzang in translating almost the entire Mahāyāna literature from Indian languages into Chinese.

Tagore and Nehru firmly believed that India and China were linked together by thousands of years of spiritual bonds and thousands of 'golden links'. Tan Yun-shan likened the spread of Mahāyāna Buddhism to China to India's marrying off her daughter. There is little doubt that this marital tie has contributed to the longevity of both these great civilizations. Xuanzang was one of the chief match-makers of this civilizational marriage. To quote a Chinese saying that is obviously steeped with Mahāyāna logic: 'There is you in me, and I in you' (*Nizhong you wo, wozhong you ni*). The symbiotic relationship between the Indian and Chinese civilizations cannot be ignored if we want to study Xuanzang in a proper perspective.

Like great saints who do not cross our paths very often, a versatile genius of Xuanzang's calibre is a rarity in life. When he was 13 years old, there was a rush among young intellectuals in the imperial capital, Luoyang, for the entrance to Buddhist priesthood. Several hundred candidates lined up for only 27 seats. The 13 year old boy was a curious bystander to the scene of the open recruitment. He was singled out by the recruiting officials for his unusual personality and intelligent appearance. This was how Xuanzang donned the robe. The next time a similar surprise came his way was when he was 46, having distinguished himself as a successful pilgrim from India. The all-powerful Tang Emperor, Taizong, was overwhelmed by the monk's unique personality and scholarly accomplishment. He wanted Xuanzang to take off the robe and take up high imperial positions to help reign the country. Xuanzang's excuse was: 'If I return to laymanhood now, it is not different from taking a boat out of water and ground it. Not only will it cease to be useful, but it will rot away.' (Huili and Yanzong, *Da-Ci'ensi sanzang fashi zhuan* or 'Biography of Hsüan-tsang', reprint, Beijing: Zhonghua Bookshop, 1983, p. 129.) Xuanzang had to overcome an equally powerful persuasion when he was in India. His colleagues in the Buddhist University at Nālandā did not wish him to return to

China, arguing that working in the motherland of the Buddha was more important than working anywhere else. Xuanzang then asked his friends: 'Why is the sun going on travelling over Jambudvīpa (our world)?' The answer was: 'To erase the dark spots [of the world].' 'This', said Xuanzang, 'is exactly my intention of returning [to my country].' (*Ibid.*, p. 103.)

Such anecdotic evidence help us to size up a versatile genius, a holy man, a thinker, an idealist, a missionary, a diplomat, a patriot, and an internationalist all rolled into one. His intellectual universe encompasses religion, philosophy, history, geography, sociology, economics, horticulture, literature (including oral literature, *i.e.*, legends, folklore, etc.) and linguistics. As this universe combines the quintessence of two great civilizations, Tagore invented the term of 'Sino-Indian Studies'—a separate interdisciplinary subject to be expounded within and outside Viśva-Bharati Cheena-Bhavana. Tan Yun-shan carried the torch of Sino-Indian Studies further afield after Tagore's demise (in 1941). I am doing the same after my father passed away (in 1983). In this effort I miss Devahuti who was a natural comrade in Sino-Indian Studies— Xuanzang Studies is only a part of it.

Tagore saw two mainstreams in the modern world: 'progress' and 'civilization'. He said: 'Progress which is not related to an inner ideal, but to an attraction which is external, seeks to satisfy endless claims. But civilization, which is an ideal, gives us power and joy to fulfil our obligations.' (From his opening address at the Viśva-Bharati Cheena-Bhavana on 14 April 1937. See Tan Yun-shan, ed., *Twenty Years of the Visva-Bharati Cheena-Bhavana 1937–1957*, Śantiniketan: The Sino-Indian Cultural Society, 1957, p. 44.) While admiring modern 'progress', Tagore also saw the danger of its ruthless development, the divorce of 'civilization'.

I congratulate Oxford University Press for bringing out *The Unknown Hsüan-tsang*. It will set off a new thinking process to inquire into the many dark areas of our knowledge about the ancient times. Xuanzang was not unknown to many Indian scholars of Devahuti's times or earlier, but most of them who made use of the name Xuanzang to augment their writings and their academic standing did so only by scratching the surface of the Xuanzang phenomenon. Devahuti was, perhaps, the first Indian who never took Xuanzang for granted. She first established the 'unknown Hsüan-tsang' and only after that embarked upon getting to know him. This is the right spirit to dig deep into the bramble-ridden ground of ancient India, ancient China, and ancient Sino-Indian relations. Those who read this book may not get all their answers about Xuanzang, but if they imbibe the Devahuti spirit of tackling the unknown to get into the known, the gate of wisdom, information, and insight would be instantly open.

I also congratulate Oxford University Press in its endeavour in promoting 'civilization', forsaking the 'attractions' of 'progress' that have already overflooded the mass media. The more readers are drawn towards Xuanzang and the great epics he and others have unfolded between the Indian and Chinese civilizations, the better it is for humankind to preserve the purity of 'civilization' and develop it, not towards Huntington's course of a 'clash', but along the highway of peace, harmony, compassion, nobleness, spiritual values, and humanitarianism.

Furthermore, since Xuanzang belonged to both China and India, Devahuti was in the vanguard in embracing Xuanzang as an Indian heritage, calling upon the Indian academia to exploit this Indianness of Xuanzang. *The Unknown Hsüan-tsang*, I am sure, will greatly enhance the awareness among Indian historians and other intellectuals about the importance of this cultural ambassador. And this Indian awareness will join its Chinese counterpart to put the civilizational studies in both countries on a sound footing. When humanity marches into the 21st century and the third millennium of our common era, not only India and China, but the entire world needs a civilizational perspective and understanding to make our globe less commercialized so that we have a place easier and more comfortable to live in with dignity, decency, and dedication—not destabilization and destruction.

New Delhi
May 2001

TAN CHUNG

Introduction

Hsüan-tsang, whose family name was Ch'ên (Ch'in), was born in AD 602 at Chin-liu near the town of Kou-shih in the Honan province of China. He died at the age of 62 in the Yuh-fa (Jade Flower) Palace Monastery near the main capital Chang-an in AD 664. Hsüan-tsang spent fourteen years of his life, from AD 630–44, in India as a Buddhist pilgrim. The length of his sojourn at various places in the country was determined by what they had to offer by way of Buddhist lore and learning. He stayed in Kashmir for two years (631–3), at Chīna-bhukti in eastern Punjab for fourteen months (633–4), at Nālandā for five years (637–42), and in what may be described as Buddha country, in and around Magadha, for two years (636–8). He spent the remaining years in other places, including the Deccan and the South. He left India in early 644, and after a few months' stay in Khotan reached the Chinese capital in April 645.

Hsüan-tsang carried back with him some relics and images of the Buddha, several hundred copied texts, some notes on the immense amount he had seen and heard, and much more besides, in memory. For the next two decades, until his death in AD 664, he worked ceaselessly on this material, carried out multifarious duties and catered to the genuine but often ostentatious Buddhist fervour of his royal patron.

In addition to the prodigious translation work—740 Sanskrit texts of various sizes with the help of amanuenses—Hsüan-tsang also copied scriptures, moulded and painted images of the Buddha, initiated novices into the Saṁgha, instructed the student monks of the monasteries and sometimes the imperial officers who visited him, and even carried bricks and stones for the construction of the Tayen pagoda. He instructed the emperor in the subtleties of Buddhism, translated into Sanskrit Tai T'sung's letter to the thaumaturge/alchemist Nārāyaṇa-svāmin seeking youth and longevity, blessed the empress who was expecting a baby and then the new-born whom he temporarily ordained a monk, led grand processions to the palace and the monastery, wrote endless letters seeking the emperor's calligraphic messages as prologues for his writings and epigraphs for the monasteries, and sought royal decrees in favour of Buddhism when it was pitched against Taoism. He arranged for a decent reinterment of his parents' mortal remains in new tombs. He attended to his Indian guests and also translated some diplomatic papers.

However, details of Hsüan-tsang's life and activity from AD 645–64 are not sufficiently known to the English-speaking world. This is not for lack of material on the latter part of Hsüan-tsang's career but rather due to its neglect by the pioneer translators and commentators.

The two major sources on Hsüan-tsang's life are his biography: *Ta T'ang Ta Tz'ŭ-ên Ssŭ San-tsang Fa-shih Chuan* (*Life of the Master of the Law, Tripiṭaka of the Great Monastery of Motherly Love*) by Hui-li and Yen-Ts'ung, and his travelogue, the *Ta T'ang Hsi Yü Chi* (*Records of the Western Lands of the Great T'ang Period*). Two lesser known sources which supplement the biography are a notice in the *Hsü Kao Sêng Chuan* ('Continuation of the Lives of Eminent Monks') by Tao-hsüan (Takakusu 50, 446) and *Ta T'ang Ku San-tsang Hsüan-tsang Fa-shih Hsing-chuang* ('Report on the Career of the Late Master of the Law, Tripiṭaka Hsüan-tsang of Great T'ang') by Ming-hsiang (Takakusu 50, 214). We shall provide some essential data about these sources, working backwards from the latter-most.

The 'Report' by the monk Ming-hsiang was sent to the Bureau of History for entry in the official records, which probably explains the inclusion in the *Chiu T'ang Shu* (Old T'ang History, chapter 191) of the brief but inaccurate accounts of the lives of three monks, one of whom is Hsüan-tsang. The 'Report' (*c.* 664) which is known through two early manuscripts preserved in Japanese monasteries contains many details not found elsewhere.

The monk Tao-hsüan (d. 667), who wrote the notice in the *Hsü Kao Sêng Chuan*, was closely associated with Hsüan-tsang. He appears to have used some of the same sources as the 'Report'. Additions to this work, the first part of which appeared in AD 645, range between that year and AD 667 and also include a later notice by another hand about the reinterment of Hsüan-tsang's remains in AD 668 or 669. Among other details, the *Hsü Kao Sêng Chuan* provides brief information for the year 647 which should have been dealt with in chapter VI of the *Life* (biography of Hsüan-tsang by Hui-li and Yen Ts'ung) but is missing for some reason.

The *Hsi Yü Chi* or the account of Hsüan-tsang's pilgrimage was compiled by his assistants under his supervision, in just over a year after his return to China. The emperor had asked him to write this account. In the eighteenth century, an abridged version of this work, entitled *Chen-po Than Gu Duskyi rGya-Gar ZhinGi bKod Pahi Kar Chag bZhugs So*, was prepared in Tibetan by Mgon-po-Skyabs (*c*. 1690– 1750). This was published in 1973 in Ulan Bator in Mongolia by Š. Bira. In modern times Stanislas Julien translated the *Hsi Yü Chi* in French as *Mémoires sur les contrées occidentales* . . . in 1857–58, and Samuel Beal in English as the *Buddhist Records of the Western World* in 1884. In 1904–5, Thomas Watters published *Yuan Chwang's Travels in India* in which he paraphrased, translated and commented upon the *Hsi Yü Chi*. Each succeeding writer made extensive cross-references to earlier translations. These pioneering attempts made between 125 and 75 years ago are very valuable, but there is room for improvement in them from the viewpoints of linguistic proficiency and methodology.

We have selected for fresh translation[1] the general account of India as given in chuan II of the travelogue [chapter 4 of this work]. It carried the following subheadings: The names of India, measures of space, measures of time, cities and houses, dress and personal characteristics, written and spoken language, Buddhism, castes, army, social and legal matters, acts of salutation and reverence, sickness and death, revenue and taxation, and general products. Also included is a fresh translation of the section on Kānyakubja (Kanauj), the centre of power of the greatest contemporary Indian ruler Harsha, whom Hsüan-tsang visited twice. In fact Kanauj, the pride of the Maukharis and later the chosen capital of Harsha, continued to be the prime city of northern India under Yaśovarman, the Pratīhāras and the Gahaḍavālas almost until AD 1200.

Ta Tz'ŭ-ên Ssŭ San-tsang Fa-shih Chuan (*Life of the Master of the Law, Tripiṭaka, of the Great Monastery of Motherly Love*) is the biography of Hsüan-tsang which supplements the travelogue. It was written by two of his disciples, Hui-li and Yen-ts'ung. Hui-li, who was on the board of amanuenses for the 'Records', was in close touch with Hsüan-tsang while writing the biography and completed the first five chapters on the Indian years between the end of AD 648 and the summer of AD 649. Chapters six to ten dealing with Hsüan-tsang's career after his return to China [a

[1]Grateful acknowledgements to Professor D.C. Lau, Professor Wang Ling and his colleague Mr. Tamotsu Sato, and to Professor Tan Chung.

summary is provided in chapter 1 of this work] were written by the monk Yen-ts'ung who continued and perhaps to some extent edited the work of Hui-li. The latter died in *c*. AD 670, or a little later, and all ten chapters were published by Yen-ts'ung in AD 688.[2]

So inspiring was the career of Hsüan-tsang and so devoted were his disciples that another biography of the Master was written by the monk K'uei-chi, a little earlier than the better-known one by Hui-li and Yen-ts'ung. Discovered at Tun-huang, the work is in the process of being edited.[3]

Recounting the life of the pious pilgrim was almost an act of religious merit and in the tenth century AD one Tutung Singqu Säli, a monk from Bišbalïq in Central Asia, translated the work of Hui-li and Yen-ts'ung in Uigur-Turkish. [The English translation of parts of Anne-Marie von Gabain's German translation of this work is produced in chapter 2 here. —Ed.] This work has some details which are not in the original, a matter which deserves careful investigation. Did the translator make arbitrary insertions or did he have some Chinese or Sanskrit monastic sources—written or oral—at his disposal? We have studied in some detail a reference to the Rgveda in connection with the Buddha which occurs in the exchange of letters, in AD 652–4, between two Indian monks and Hsüan-tsang. The correspondence forms part of chapter VII of the biography. [Translations of some sections are produced in chapter 2 of this work. —Ed.]

In modern times, French and English scholars have performed acts of historiographical merit by translating Hsüan-tsang's biography into their respective languages, although with insufficient or no attention to the latter half of his career which is narrated in the last five of the ten *chuan* (chapters) of Hui-li and Yen-ts'ung. Stanislas Julien translated it into French in 1853 as *Histoire de la vie de Hiouen-thsang et de ses voyages dans l' Inde* with a sixty-page 'résumé' of the last five chapters, and Beal into English in 1888 as the *Life of Hiuen-tsiang* with a four-page summary of the same material. Useful in their own time, the translations are in definite need of replacement. Arthur Waley described Julien's work as 'very imperfect'[4], and the same may be said of the five chapters by Beal.

---

[2]For the composition of the *Ta Tz'ŭ-ên . . . Chuan*, see K. Utsunomiya, in *Shirin* 12.4 (1932).

[3]We are grateful for this information to Professor Huang Xin-chuan of Peking University.

[4]*The Real Tripiṭaka*, p. 11.

We have provided an English rendering of Julien's résumé of the last five chapters [chapter 3 of this work] and have checked it against the original Chinese for faults of mistranslation which have been listed in footnotes. We have also retransliterated the proper names (according to the Wade-Giles system). This was considered necessary so as not to lose the benefit of the earlier writers' insights.

In 1952, Arthur Waley wrote the *Real Tripiṭaka*, an eminently readable account[5] of Hsüan-tsang's life in 120 pages (China years, 53 pages) based not only on the Master's biography by Hui-li and Yen-ts'ung but also on the 'Report' in the *Chiu T'ang Shu* (Old T'ang History) and the 'notice' in the *Hsü Kao Sêng Chuan* mentioned earlier. However, his work makes no mention of Tutung Singqu Säli's version of the *Life*. In 1959, the Chinese Buddhist Association published an English translation of the *Life* by Li Yung-hsi as part of the commemorative activities in honour of Hsüan-tsang. This is meant more for the general reader, yet is very difficult to obtain.

---

[5]Waley's sense of fun spills through the work. A characteristic example is the following passage describing the conversion of a bird, in itself a fully acceptable happening when faith, unity with nature, and belief in incarnation characterized the times. Says Waley (p. 120): 'If the Refuges were properly administered the bird must have repeated, after the Tripiṭaka, the words: "*Buddham śaraṇaṁ gacchāmi, Dharmaṁ śaraṇaṁ gacchāmi, Saṁghaṁ śaraṇaṁ gacchāmi*" (I go to Buddha for refuge, I go to the Law for refuge, I go to the Community for refuge), or their equivalent in Chinese or indeed in bird-language.'

1

The Life of Hsüan-tsang

*A Summary of Chs. VI–X of Ta Tzŭ-ën Ssŭ San-tsang Fa-shih
Chuan (Life of the Master of the Law, Tripiṭaka of the Great
Monastery of the Motherly Love) by Hui-li and Yen-ts'ung*

CHAPTER VI

Hsüan-tsang arrived in the Chinese capital of Ch'ang-an (modern Sian)
in the spring of AD 645. He brought with him from India a total of 657
texts bound in 520 cases loaded on twenty horses. They included the
following: Mahāyāna *sūtras* (224), Mahāyāna *śāstras* (192), *Hetu-vidyā
śāstras* (36), *Śabda-vidyā śāstras* (13), and Tripiṭaka texts of the six
'Hīnayāna' schools—*Sthavira* (22), *Kāśyapīya* (17), of Dharma-guptaka
(42) and *Sarvāstivādin* (67).[1] Hsüan-tsang also brought with him 150
grains of *se-li* (*śarīra*, relics) of the Buddha and several images of the
Buddha in gold, silver, and sandalwood.

Upon orders from the emperor, T'ai Tsung, of T'ang, carried out by
the Lord-lieutenant at Ch'ang-an, different monasteries sent out ceremonial processions to the Hung-fu Monastery (constructed by T'ai Tsung
in AD 634 in memory of the queen mother) to receive the sacred items
brought by the pilgrim. For several tens of *li*,[2] the roads were crowded
with people including scholars, and imperial and local officials who
participated in the pageant. Along the whole length of the route one
could see sailing a sweetly scented cloud (of incense) and hear the
rythmic chant of hymns.

Within a few days, Hsüan-tsang travelled to Loyang to report to the
emperor (where he was making preparations for battle against Liao-tung
in Manchuria). The pilgrim was received kindly but was asked why he

---

[1]The total is in fact 14 short of 657
[2]See p. 104, note 49

had not obtained permission before leaving for India. Hsüan-tsang offered an apology and was readily granted pardon. T'ai Tsung then put to him many questions about the geography, climate, products, and customs of India, the ancient monuments of the eight Kings[3] and the sacred remains of the four previous Buddhas[4]. Hsüan-tsang's replies were so clear and precise that the emperor asked him to write a history of his travels, adding that such details had not been put together by historians such as Pan (Pan Ku), and Ma (Ssŭ-ma Ch'ien).

Impressed by his ability, T'ai Tsung invited Hsüan-tsang to accept a government appointment. The latter humbly declined, saying that such a commission for him would be like grounding a boat that was riding the waves. He would (like such a boat) not only become useless, but would also rot and decay. Nor did the Master agree to accompany the emperor on the eastern campaign. He would be unserviceable on such an occasion, he said, in addition to being guilty of transgression of the *vinaya* rules by witnessing a military campaign.

The pilgrim then sought the emperor's permission to settle down for the translation work at the relatively remote Shao-lin Monastery in his native town of Loyang where Bodhi-ruchi had also stayed to render the Sanskrit Buddhist texts into Chinese. But the emperor wanted Hsüan-tsang to live at the Hung-fu Monastery in the western capital of Ch'ang-an. The pilgrim agreed but requested the emperor to appoint guards who should strictly keep out curious and inquisitive visitors wanting to have a glimpse of the monk who had returned from the holy land of the Buddha. Upon the emperor's orders he was also provided with a large staff of assistants. They included twelve monks, well-versed in Theravāda and Mahāyāna, nine 'phrase-connectors' (*chui-wen*) who looked after the synthetical connections of the sentences (a difficulty posed by translation from Sanskrit into Chinese), a lexicographer and a Sanskrit expert, apart from many others who helped with the more tedious tasks such as copying and proofreading.

In the autumn of AD 646, Hsüan-tsang informed the emperor that the narrative of his travels to the western countries was complete. Although he had not reached the limits of the great Chilicosm, he had written about all the countries beyond the Ts'ung-ling mountains. They were 128 in number, those that he had seen for himself and those that he had enquired about. He had written in a straightforward and authentic manner, treating his facts

---

[3]That is, the eight Bodhisattvas: Vajra-sattva, Mañjuśrī, Ākāśa-garbha, Maitreya, Avalokiteśvara, Kṣiti-garbha, Āryāchala-nātha, and Viśva-bhadra.

[4]Krakucchanda, Kanakamuni, Kāśyapa, and Gautama.

with respect, and not daring to embellish them. He had divided his work into twelve chapters, he said, and given it the title *Ta T'ang Hsi Yü Chi*.[5] The emperor graciously praised the work and its author.

In the summer of AD 648, T'ai Tsung again invited Hsüan-tsang to assist him in state affairs but the latter declined the offer as politely as he could, saying that the emperor already had several very competent ministers in his service. Commenting on the importance of ministers, Hsüan-tsang remarked that even the great emperors of old depended on sagacious advisers. Confucious had also said that a Lord might neglect, his minister may remind him. A lord is, therefore, compared to a man's head and the ministers to his limbs. When one of T'ai Tsung's ministers, who was present on the occasion, modestly remarked that the minister's advice to a great emperor was like a glow worm to the moon or a candle to the sun, his master observed

> No, it is not so. A precious fur coat is not made with the fur of a single fox, and a mansion must be built with a large quantity of wood. How can I do anything alone without you . . .

The emperor once again graciously allowed Hsüan-tsang to devote all his time to the service of Buddhism. He asked him which works he had translated.

> Hsüan-tsang informed the emperor that he had completed the translation of the following texts: the *Bodhisattva-piṭaka Sūtra*, the *Buddha-bhūmi Sūtra*, the *Shanmukhi-dhāraṇī Sūtra*, the *Prakaraṇ-ārya-vācha śāstra*, the *Mahāyān-ābhidharma-samyukta-saṅgītī śāstra*, and the *Yogāchāra-bhūmī śāstra*.[6] He petitioned the emperor to write a preface to these works.

T'ai Tsung wanted Hsüan-tsang to enlighten him about the contents of the *Yogāchāra-bhūmi-śāstra*. The Master briefly explained the seventeen stages of Bodhisattvahood detailed in the text. The emperor was highly impressed and remarked:

> . . . the Buddhist scriptues are as unfathomable as the height of the sky

---

[5] Records of the Western Regions (made) under the great T'ang dynasty, K 1065, N 1503.

[6] The Chinese titles of these works and references to them, in the same order, are: *P'u-sa-tsang-ching*, K 22 (12), N 23 (12); *Fo-ti-ching*, K 460, N 502; *Liu-men t'uo-luo-hi-ching*, K 447, N 493; *Hsien-yang-sheng-chiao-lun*, K 571,N 1177; *Ta-ch'eng-a-p'i-ta-mo-tsa-chi-lun* K 946, N 1178; *Yu-chia-shih-ti-lun*, K 570, N 1170.

One of the major works of Asaṅga, founder of the mystic school *Yogāchāra* or *Vijñāna-vāda*. I-ching records the existence of the *śāstra* in Śrī-vijaya as well. It is surprising that all modern editors and translators of works related to Chinese Buddhism spell it as *Yogāchārya- bhūmi śāstra*. Probably this is traceable to the mistake or misprint in Bunyiu Nanjio's *Catalogue*, pp. 257–8.

or the depth of the sea ... Compared with the Buddhist scriptures, the texts of Confucianism and Taoism and the Nine Schools are but a small island in a great sea. It is ridiculous that the people should say that the three religions of Confucianism, Buddhism and Taoism are of equal value.

Upon being reminded by Hsüan-tsang that he had promised to write an introduction to the translated scriptures, the emperor found time to compose a preface of 781 characters which he copied out himself.

CHAPTER VII

In the sixth month in the summer of AD 648, the crown prince (Kao-tsung) too wrote a preface for the holy scriptures. He had ordered the construction of a grand new monastery, the Ta Tz'ŭ-ên Ssŭ, in the memory of his mother. This meritorious act, he prayed, might cause her to be reborn in the Trayastriṁsa heaven.[7] The monastery was built in the style of the Jetavana vihāra.[8] It had 'storeyed pavilions and double halls, lofty towers, and spacious chambers'. They were spaced out in ten courtyards consisting of, 1897 rooms, all fully furnished with bedding, utensils, and so on.

The emperor continuously sought the Master's guidance on Buddhism. He was so impressed by the *Bodhisattva-piṭaka sūtra* which Hsüan-tsang had recently translated that he asked the crown prince to write an epilogue for it. He gave instructions that the Master be supplied with more personal amenities. Hsüan-tsang was presented with a religious robe worth a hundred pieces of gold so finely made that not a single stitch was visible on it. He was also given a razor.[9]

In the autumn of AD 648, the emperor, on Hsüan-tsang's request, ordered all the 3,716 monasteries of the realm to ordain five monks/nuns each (making a total of 18, 580) while the Hung-fu monastery was allowed to take fifty of them.

The emperor was keen that the *Vajra-chhedikā Prajñā-pāramitā sūtra*[10] should have an excellent translation, for 'listening to it gives

---

[7]Of the six *Kāmāvachara*, divine kingdoms of pleasure, the *Trayastriṁsa* is the second in ascending order. Those who have *kuśala* (*puṇya*, meritorious) acts to their credit in the world enter this heaven after death. The Buddha continued to visit this *deva-bhūmi* for three months in order to impart *dhamma* to his mother.

[8]Of Anātha-piṇḍika at Śrāvastī. The Chinese description gives us a good idea of the Jetavana vihāra in India.

[9]Apart from its practical use for a monk, it is also a symbol of wisdom which cuts away the meshes of ignorance.

[10]*Neng-tuan-chin-kang-p'an-jo*, K 16, N 13.

more merit than ... donating as many gems and jewels as the sand-grains in the Gaṅgā'. Upon being asked if the existing rendering of this work was satisfactory, Hsüan-tsang told the emperor that the important word *chhedikā* was missing in the title. There were also other omissions although 'Śrāvastī as rendered by Kumāra-jīva, and Bhagavān by Bodhi-ruchi are acceptable'.[11]

He was therefore asked to retranslate the *sūtra* on the basis of the Sanskrit text he had brought. On completion of the work a report was presented to the emperor.

In the winter T'ai-Tsung returned to the capital along with Hsüan-tsang. So keen was he on religious discourses that the Master could return to his translation work only in the evenings. He rendered into Chinese the Mahāyāna-*saṃparigraha śāstra*[12], with commentaries respectively by Aśva-bhava bodhi-sattva and Vasu-bandhu, each in ten volumes, the *Pratītya-samutpāda sūtra*[13] and the *Sata-dharma-vidyā-nikāya śāstra*.[14]

In the winter of AD 648, in the tenth month, the crown prince issued an order that the Ta Tz'ǔ-ên monastery[15] be occupied by monks; the

[11]Different commentators defined the terms differently. The renderings and their acceptance depended, among other factors, on the understanding of the languages involved, the school of thought of the person/s concerned and the time (age) at which the work was written and evaluated.

[12]*She-ta-ch'eng-lun*, K 594, N 1171 1 and 4.

[13]*Yuan-ch'i-sheng-tao-ching*, K 736, N 279.

[14]*Pai-fa-ming-men-lun*, K 644, N 1213.

[15]This monastery of Maternal Love in the Chinese capital of Ch'ang-an was visited in the autumn of AD 752 by Ts'ên Shên, a Chinese poet-administrator in Central Asia, together with some of his friends including the poet Tu Fu. Each wrote a poem to commemorate the visit. Ts'ên Shên's poem captured the majestic beauty of the monastery where a century earlier Hsüan-tsang had worked on his Buddhist texts:

> Like a jet of water this tower springs from earth,
> Lonely and high, brushing the palaces of Heaven.
> As we climb the steps we leave the World of Men;
> The stone stairway winds in an open void.
> Its looming presence daunts our holy land;
> Its storeyed heights seem made by demon skill.
> Its four corners block the light of the sun;
> Its seven storeys brush the vault of the sky.
> I look down, to point at the highest bird;
> I raise my head to listen to the startling wind.
> Mountain chains like wave on wave of the sea,
> Hurry forward, bearing their tribute to the West.
> Green sophoras flank the Imperial Road;
> Faultless in beauty stand the mansions of the great ...
>
> (Arthur Waley's translation in
> *The Secret History of the Mongols*, p. 34)

emperor had specified that 300 monks should be ordained and fifty monks renowned for their virtue should be invited to settle down there. A beautiful and costly house had been specially constructed for carrying out translation work. The crown prince invited Hsüan-tsang to occupy it and also to accept the headship of the monastery, but the Master declined the offer.

However, on the 22nd day of the twelfth month (AD 648), a grand procession 'of which one could see neither the beginning nor the end', was organized on the emperor's orders to escort the holy scriptures and the Buddha's images and relics, as well as the Tripiṭaka master, from the Hung-fu Monastery to the Ta Tz'u-ên Monastery. Tens of thousands of people watched a dazzling pageant of sight, sound and smell consisting of chariots, *chhatras*, pennants, banners, tapestries and paintings of the Buddha's image, bells, drums, incense, flowers, chants and acrobatics. Nine palace orchestras provided the music.[16] Eminent monks, civil and military officials and royal bodyguards, on foot and in carriages, accompanied the precious objects which were received at their destination by members of the royal house.

The monks were ordained on the 26th day. On the same occasion amnesty was granted to all prisoners in the capital, their heads shaved for monkhood and food provided to them.

The emperor wanted to keep the Master as close to him as possible and took him back to the imperial palace. He continued to take instruction from Hsüan-tsang until his (T'ai Tsung's) death after a brief illness in the summer of the following year (AD 649). Kao-tsung ascended the throne and after one year, in AD 650, the title of the reign was changed to Yung-hui.

Hsüan-tsang devoted himself fully to translation work. If he could not complete a self-assigned task during the day, he worked into the night until after the end of the second watch. When he encountered a difficulty he paused and engrossed himself in worship and religious observances. Then he allowed himself some sleep. At the fifth watch (2 am) he arose and read the Indian texts aloud, marking in red ink the portions he had to translate at sunrise.

Hsüan-tsang was now also head (abbot) of the monastery and gave full attention to his duties in this regard. In the mornings after a brief meal, he expounded the newly translated texts for two (four of our time) hours. Student monks from different regions would come to have their

---

[16]Of these, all but one or perhaps two normally played the foreign music of India, Central Asia and Korea.

doubts resolved by him. In the evenings he patiently and clearly replied to the queries of the monks of his monastery, over a hundred of whom might fill the galleries around his chamber. Often he would talk to the monks about different theories of the various schools founded by the sages and saints of the western countries, about his travels and other experiences. From time to time he instructed and advised the imperial officers who visited him. Calmly and methodically, he carried out a multitude of tasks and duties everyday. He discussed aloud and spoke with warmth, never appearing fatigued or in need of rest, so great was the strength of his body and soul.

In the spring of the third year of Yung-hui (AD 652), the Master decided to have a 300-foot stone pagoda built in the Ta Tz'ŭ-ên Monastery to store the scriptures and the images of the Buddha which he had brought back with him. He wanted to protect them against the ravages of time and the risk of fire. When he reported his intent to the palace, the emperor obliged by arranging for the construction at royal expense, but reduced the height and ordered the use of bricks instead of stone. Indian, rather than Chinese, architectural design was followed in the building of the Tayen—Wild Goose—*Vanahaṃsa*[17] pagoda. The base measured 140 feet on each side and the five storeys to the top of the spire reached a height of 180 feet.[18] At the centre of each storey provision was made for the preservation of the relics. The top storey contained a stone chamber with two slabs on the southern side inscribed with the two prefaces to the holy scriptures composed by the former emperor T'ai Tsung and the reigning monarch when he was crown prince.

The Master contributed physical labour to the building of the pagoda by carrying stones and bricks for it. The Tayen pagoda took two years to complete.

On the twenty-third day of the fifth month in the summer of AD 652 Hsüan-tsang received letters from two monks from the Mahā-bodhī monastery (or Bodhgaya; Waley, p. 100) in *madhya-deśa* (Central India).[19]

[The letters that follow here in the *Life* appear in chapter 2 in this book. See p. 17.]

---

[17]It was modelled as well as named after the *Vanahaṃsa stūpa*, east of the *Śakrendra* grotto in Magadha: Lokesh Chandra and Sudarshana Devi Singhal (eds), *Acharya Raghuvira Ka Cheena Abhiyana*, New Delhi 1956 /69, p. 98.

[18]About 130 English feet (Waley, p. 100).

[19]The original Mahā-bodhi; see p. 24.

CHAPTER VIII

Hsüan-tsang had translated the *Nyāya-praveśa*[20], a text on logic, in AD 647, and the more difficult *Nyāya-mukha*[21] in AD 649. Several of his disciples, including the monk Ch'i-hsüan, wrote commentaries on the latter work. A versatile lay scholar, Lu Ts'ai, who had proficiency in fields as far apart as medicine, music, astronomy, chess and Taoist philosophy, was provoked in a friendly way by Ch'i-hsüan to attempt a commentary on the *Nyāya-mukha*. Lu Ts'ai did so in AD 655, causing a long and acrimonious debate between Buddhists and Taoists.

Finally, it is said, Lu Ts'ai's commentary was discussed and demolished in the presence of Hsüan-tsang.

In the following year, the first of Hsien-ch'ing (AD 656), the then crown prince Chung chose to accept another position and Chih, the prince of Tai, was installed in his place. A feast for 5,000 monks was held at the Tz'u-ên Monastery to celebrate the event. Two imperial officers were deputed to attend the function and ask the Master if he required additional assistance to further the work of translation; also to enquire as to how it was promoted in earlier times. Hsüan-tsang took this opportunity to ask for the help of scholars in imperial service. He could not assert anything about the Han and Wei times, he said, but in the fourth and sixth centuries, Dharma-nandi[22], Kumāra-jīva[23] and Bodhi-ruchi[24] respectively, had been assisted by capable and important government officers and personages such as chamberlains, counts and princes. In more recent times, at the beginning of the Chen-kuan period (AD 627), Prabhā-ratna received the collaboration of a minister, a prince, a steward of the royal household and a treasurer. Hsüan-tsang also requested through their favour a commemorative inscription by the emperor for the Tz'u-ên monastery.

The officers made their report to the court. Almost immediately, more than six important imperial officers, among them the tutor to the crown prince, the left premier of the secretariat, the head of the board of ceremonies, and the secretary of the board of administration were ordered to be attached to Hsüan-tsang's translation bureau. The emperor

---

[20]*Li-men-lun*, K 607, N 1216.

[21]*Yin-ming-lun*, K 604, N 1224.

[22]For details see Nanjio, 1883, Appendix II, no. 57.

[23]Ibid., Appendix II, no. 59.

[24]Ibid., Appendix II, no. 114. He had translated thirty or more works by AD 535. There was also a Bodhi-ruchi (originally Dharma-ruchi) during the T'ang dynasty who did translation work between AD 693–713.

also promised to compose the inscription for the Ta Tz'ŭ-ên Monastery. Hsüan-tsang expressed his profound gratitude for these favours.

In the next month of the same year (AD 656), a talented and scholarly lady, Pao-cheng, who had taught the emperor in his young days, was ordained a nun along with some others to serve as her attendants. The ceremony was held in a special nunnery, the Ho-lin (later Lung-kuo) which had been specially constructed for the purpose within the palace precincts. It was spring. Peach flowers blossomed beyond the green willow leaves and blue pines hid behind a purple fog. Hsüan-tsang, accompanied by nine monks renowned for their virtue, each attended by a novice, made such an elegant and stately entry into the palace grounds that they resembled the monks of the Jetavana *vihāra* going to Rājagṛha. With Hsüan-tsang as the *āchārya* and the other monks as witnesses, Pao-cheng was ordained with others, over fifty in all. The ceremony lasted three days. Pictures were painted of the ten teachers to be kept in the nunnery for worship.

On the same occasion, the Master initiated into Bodhisattva rules the several hundred nuns of the Teh-yeh nunnery which was also within the palace precincts. He was then escorted back with great honour, a *chhatra* held over his head, to the Ta Tz'ŭ-ên Monastery.

CHAPTER IX

The emperor Kao-tsung composed the inscription for the Ta Tz'ŭ-ên Monastery for which Hsüan-tsang, accompanied by the resident monks, went to thank him personally in the court. Upon his return he sent a letter to the emperor imploring him to lend it beauty and authenticity in his own calligraphy. The emperor finally obliged in the spring of the first year of Hsien-ch'ing (AD 656). To show his gratitude, Hsüan-tsang went to the palace to receive the epigraph. He led a huge procession of monks and nuns holding banners and tapesteries, accompanied by the royal band. A thousand carts carried musicians alone. The return was delayed by heavy rain but when they eventually made their way back, over a million people watched the pageant. The epigraph was ceremoniously brought to the Ta T'zŭ-ên Monastery and later placed in a *stūpa*-like hall specially constructed for the purpose.

In the summer of the same year, the Master had a serious relapse of an old illness caused by glacial cold when crossing the Ling mountain, but he quickly recovered with the help of the best medical attention from the court physicians.

In AD 637, an imperial decree had been issued to the effect that on ceremonial occasions Lao-tzu's name be placed before those of the Buddha as he was an ancestor of the imperial line. The question had been debated in court by monks and others, but the decree had not yet been rectified. Hsüan-tsang had been executing the order rather harshly to the great humiliation of the monks. Hsüan-tsang appealed to the emperor to look into these matters.

The emperor replied that the question of the status of Lao-tzu in relation to the Buddha would be reconsidered and the decree regarding the trial of Taoist and Buddhist clergy at par with laity would be annulled. A royal order was then promulgated saying:

> Taoism is pure and noble, Buddhism sublime and great. They are both like a bridge for the common man to cross the ocean of rebirth. They are both highly honoured in the three worlds . . . As for the common law for clergy and laity the intention is not to belittle religion. It is only because it is the termination period of dharma, and people are more prone to commit offence that worldly laws are applied to priests and monks. However, as the religious orders have their own disciplinary rules it would be cumbrous for them to abide by two sets of laws. Uniformity of punishment for clergy and laity is therefore abolished and those belonging to the religious orders of Taoism and Buddhism are to be dealt with according to their own disciplinary rules.

Hsüan-tsang was overjoyed with the decisions and wrote a letter of thanks to the emperor.

Soon afterwards the Master was invited to carry out his work from one of the courts within the palace complex. He was so busy that he came out of the court only every twenty or thirty days.

In the winter of AD 656 a son was born to the emperor, and upon Hsüan-tsang's request was dedicated to the Buddhist order. The Master gave him the name Fo-kuang-wang (Buddha-prabha, meaning of the Buddha's brilliance) and performed all the ceremonies such as the first robing, tonsures, and so on, and kept him under his close watch.

In the spring of AD 657, the emperor decided to visit the eastern capital, Loyang. Hsüan-tsang accompanied him along with a few assistants for translation work which they had lately been carrying out in the Chi-ts'ui palace. The baby prince, Buddha-prabha, was also taken to Loyang. Two months later, the emperor decided to go to the Ming-teh palace, and took Hsüan-tsang with him. In the following month he asked the Master to return to the Chi-tsui palace, but the latter excused himself. Hsüan-tsang was in the middle of translating a long text, the *Mahā-*

vibhāṣā śāstra (no more than half of which had been translated earlier, and very poorly at that) when the emperor issued orders that the Master should concern himself with only such work as had not been handled before. The Master submitted that he had already completed thirty volumes of the *Abhidharma-jñāna-prasthāna*[25] and seventy of the *Maha-vibhāṣā*[26] when in the capital and should be allowed to complete the rest. The emperor finally gave his consent.

Loyang was Hsüan-tsang's native place and he asked for royal permission to return there for a visit after a long time. His only surviving relative now was an elderly sister. He visited with her the dilapidated tombs of their parents and was overcome with sorrow and regret. The times were troubled when they had died nearly four decades earlier in the last years of the Sui. He wanted to give them a decent burial, in fact one that should impress the Indian guest(s) he had with him at the time. He wrote to the emperor stating his intent and purpose.

The emperor responded generously and an imposing ceremony was held, attended by high personages of the empire and more than 10,000 monks and lay people from Loyang. The city contained the beautiful Shao-lin Monastery built by the emperor Hsiao-wen of the later Wei dynasty. This was where Bodhi-ruchi[27] had worked and Buddha-śānta[28] had meditated. Their remains were buried there. The Master again asked for permission to live at Shao-lin but the emperor did not agree.

In the winter of the eleventh month (AD 657), the first birth anniversary of the prince was celebrated in Loyang with the presentation by the Master of a religious vestment and other objects to him. Around this time Hsüan-tsang suffered from an illness caused by overwork.

In the 12th month Loyang, the eastern capital, was given the same status as the main capital, Ch'ang-an. Its area was increased by taking some territory from the surrounding districts and it now included the birthplace of Hsüan-tsang. Hsüan-tsang was delighted at the distinction bestowed on his home town even though it had happened coincidently. In the spring of AD 658, the emperor returned to the western capital, with Hsüan-tsang accompanying him.

[25]*Fa-chih-lun*, K 944, N 1275.
[26]*Ta-pi-p'o-sha*, K 952, N 1263.
[27]See pp. 5, 10 and note 24.
[28]For details see Nanjio, 1883, Appendix II. no. 115.

CHAPTER X

The Master had returned to the capital (Ch'ang-an) with the emperor in the spring of AD 658. In the autumn of that year he was asked to move into the Hsi-ming Monastery which had been ordered to be built two years earlier.[29] The construction of a Taoist temple elsewhere was also ordered at the same time, but the monastery was completed first—in the summer of AD 658.

The grandest and the most beautiful monastery in the capital, it was 350 *pu*[30] wide on each side and several *li* in circumference. It had ten courtyards with more than 4000 rooms. The buildings were so tall that 'they would frighten a flying bird' and the golden painted pillars were 'as dazzling as the sun'. There were green pagoda trees outside the buildings and streams of clear water flowed through its compound.

The procession on the occasion of the ordination ceremony of the monks, supervised by the Master, was as grand as that which was organized to welcome Hsüan-tsang and the imperial inscription into the Ta Tz'ŭ-ên Monastery.

In the tradition of his father, and even more than him, the emperor Kao-tsung showed consideration and respect to the Master. He showered him with honours and gifts so that Hsüan-tsang once had over ten thousand rolls of silk and brocade, not to speak of several hundred *kāshāyas* (religious vestments). But the Master never kept anything for himself. He donated all for religious causes such as the building of *stūpas*, the copying of scriptures, and the making of images. He also distributed them as alms to the poor and as presents to his foreign (Indian) *brāhmaṇa* guests.

In the tenth month of the fourth year of Hsien-ching (AD 659), Hsüan-tsang was, on request, permitted to move into the Yu-hua (Jade Flower) Palace Monastery to concentrate on his work without the distractions of life in a capital.[31] Hsüan-tsang now wanted to translate the massive *Mahā-*

---

[29]One of the most famous in the history of Chinese Buddhism, the Hsi-ming monastery was built in western Ch'ang-an at the site of the palace of Prince T'ai of P'u, the fourth son of T'ai-tsung. Patron of an important geographical work, the *Kua Ti Chih*, the prince died at the early age of 34 in AD 652. It was contemplated to build two monasteries there, one Taoist and another Buddhist, but Hsüan-tsang, who inspected the site, reported that there was room for only one.

[30]*pu* is approximately 5 feet.

[31]In a month he retranslated, with the help of his favourite disciple K'uci-chi, his most popular contribution, the *Vijñapti-mātratā-siddhi*, a work of thirty stanzas by Vasubandhu with commentaries by ten different people. Hsüan-tsang and his disciple depended mainly on the commentary of Dharma-pāla, the teacher of Śīlabhadra.

prajñā-pāramitā sūtra. The translation had been attempted earlier but was incomplete. At first, on the advice of his disciples, Hsüan-tsang thought of abridging the text in the fashion of Kumāra-jīva (who would expunge the tedious and the repetitive in his translations. But ominous dreams made him give up the idea. The *Prajñā-pāramitā sūtra* was indeed considered to be the most holy in the eastern country (China). The Buddha is said to have preached this sūtra at four places: Gṛdhra-kūta in Rājagṛha, Jetavana vihāra, the abode of the *Paranirmita-vaśavartins*, and the Veṇuvaṅa vihāra at Rājagṛha. The original Sanskrit text had 200,000 *ślokas* and was in 16 parts. Hsüan-tsang had brought with him three copies of the work from India. Before undertaking the translation, he carefully went through them several times and compared and collated the material. No one had ever been so faithful to the original. Whenever Hsüan-tsang had an insight into a profound idea, or resolved a difficult point, or restored a corrupt passage, he attributed it to divine intuition, his heart abloom and his mind clear as if lit by the bright sun which had pierced the clouds. Distrusting his own intelligence, he ascribed his success to the spiritual guidance of the Buddha and the Bodhisattvas.

The translation of the *Mahā-prajñā-pāramitā sūtra*[32] was begun on the first day of the first month in the spring of the fifth year of Hsien-ching (AD 660). It was completed on the twenty-third day of the tenth month in the winter of the third year of Lung-shuo (AD 663). Upon the Master's request the emperor agreed to write a preface to the great work.

With the completion of this task, Hsüan-tsang felt that his life's work was done. At the insistence of his disciples he commenced the translation of the *Mahā-ratna-kūta sūtra* but felt too exhausted to continue. He then decided to devote his remaining days purely to religious devotions.

In the spring of AD 664 on the eighth day of the first month, a disciple of Hsüan-tsang dreamt that a tall and magnificent *stūpa* had suddenly collapsed. When told about it, the Master interpreted it as a portent of his imminent death. The next day Hsüan-tsang happened to lose his balance when crossing a ditch and suffered a slight injury on his shin. This was the beginning of his last illness. During the next few days, Hsüan-tsang dreamt wonderous dreams and had beautiful visions. He helped compile a list of his meritorious deeds which was read out to him on his sick-bed. He had translated into Chinese seventy-four Sanskrit-Buddhist texts consisting of 1335 *chuan*,[33] painted a thousand images each of the Buddha and

---

[32] *Ta-p'an-jo-ching,* K 1, N 1.

[33] Rolls of paper used as measure, not necessarily corresponding to chapters in the case of Sanskrit texts.

Maitreya, moulded one (ten?) million statues of the Buddha, and finally made a thousand copies each of the *Vajra-chhedika-prajña-pāramitā-sūtra*, *Ārya bhagavatī-bhaishajya-guru-pūrva-praṇidhāna-nāma-mahā-yāna sūtra*,[34] the *Śatamukha-dhāraṇī sūtra*, and some other *sūtras*. More than ten thousand *bhikshus* and the same number of poor people had received alms from him. He had lit a hundred thousand sacred lamps and saved the lives of tens of thousands of living creatures. Hsüan-tsang listened to this with gratification. Then he formally donated all his personal belongings to the Saṁgha for the promotion of religious causes.

He asked the sculptor Sung Fa-chih, who was engaged in making a replica of the Buddha after the Bodh-gayā statue, to place the full-scale clay model in the Buddha hall of the monastery where he was lying. In its presence he shared all the merit of his good deeds with all living beings so that they may be re-born in the Tushita heaven with him to serve Maitreya Bodhisattva; and when the future Buddha should descend to the human world, they may all accompany him to live in the ways of the Buddha under his guidance until the attainment of supreme enlightenment.

Having said his farewell, Hsüan-tsang meditated in silence, reciting from time to time the Buddhist doctrine:

> Form is unreal.[35] Perception, thought, action, knowledge—all are unreal. The eye, the ear, the mind are unreal. Consciousness through the Five Senses is unreal. All the twelve causes, from ignorance to old age, and death, are unreal. Enlightenment is unreal. Unreality itself is unreal.

In the next few days, Hsüan-tsang's disciples had dreams and visions of the Master being welcomed into the blessed world of the Buddha. On the midnight of the fifth day of the second month, Hsüan-tsang passed away. For seven days his body showed no signs of decay. On the night of his death a monk of the Ta Tz'ŭ-ên Monastery saw four white rainbows in the sky just as twelve such rainbows had appeared on the night of the Buddha's *nirvāṇa*.

The Master was seven *chih*[36] tall, with pink-white complexion, big (or wide-apart) eyebrows, and bright eyes. His bearing was grave and dignified, and he was as handsome as a figure in a painting. The timbre of his voice was pure and resonant, his language impressive, elegant and agreeable, so that people were never tired of listening to him.

---

[34] *Yao-shih-ju-lai-pen-yuan-kung-teh-ching*, K 177, N 171.
[35] *Anupalambha*, unverifiable.
[36] *Chih* is more than a foot, but the old measure would have been much smaller.

Whether amidst his disciples or in the presence of an illustrious host, he always sat erect and without moving for a long time. He liked to wear a Gandhāra robe made of fine felt, neither too loose nor too tight. His gait was easy and graceful and he always looked ahead without any side-glances. He was majestic, like a great river . . . , and of brilliant wisdom like a lotus rising out of water. He observed monastic rules strictly... till the end of his life. *Vinaya* rules were more important to him than a floating aid for crossing a river... He loved solitude and simplicity and shunned social life. Once he entered a monastery it was only an imperial decree which could make him leave his pious retreat.

The emperor had, on being informed of Hsüan-tsang's illness, sent royal physicians to attend on him, but they had arrived too late. When Kao-tsung learnt of the Master's death on the ninth day he was deeply grieved and repeatedly said, 'I have lost a national treasure'.

On the sixth day of the third month an imperial order was issued that the translation work should be suspended. The texts already rendered into Chinese should be copied by government staff as usual and the rest be safely stored in the Ta Tz'ŭ-ên Monastery. Only the monks belonging to the Yu-hua palace might remain there, others should return to their respective monasteries.

According to his wishes, Hsüan-tsang's body was placed on a bier of bamboo matting and brought to the capital to be placed in the Ta Tz'ŭ-ên Monastery. Thousands of people paid him homage.

The funeral, at state expense, was fixed for the fourteenth day of the fourth month (AD 664). The monks and nuns and the people of the capital prepared more than 500 items: white *chhatras*, banners and standards, *nirvāṇa* screens, a gold coffin in a silver case and *śāla* trees,[37] all appropriately arrayed along the streets to be traversed. Mournful music resounded in the air. The inhabitants of the capital and of districts within a radius of 500 *li* who formed the procession numbered more than a million. The silk dealers of the eastern market used 3000 rolls of thick coloured silk, flowers and garlands for making a marvellous *nirvāṇa* coffin to carry the Master's body, but Hsüan-tsang's disciples placed on it only his three garments and the expensive religious robe that had been presented to him. The bier of coarse matting carrying his body followed the decorated hearse.

More than thirty thousand people, monks and laity spent the night at

---

[37]Śāl or śāla, the teak tree, the *Shorea* (or *Vatica*) *robusta*; Śāla-rāja, a title of the Buddha; the twin trees in the grove in which Śākya-muni entered nirvāṇa.

the cemetery. The next morning the grave was closed. A religious assembly was held and there was a great distribution of alms before the people dispersed. The sky darkened at that time and the earth changed its colour. Birds and beasts uttered cries of lament. If nature and animals so grieved, how great was the pain of human beings over the great loss? . . . It was as if a mountain had collapsed, a great tree had fallen.

It was so painful to the emperor to be constantly reminded of the fact of Hsüan-tsang's death that in AD 669 he ordered the Master's remains to be transferred to a pagoda, specially built for the purpose on the plain to the north of the Fan river.

The procession on that occasion rivalled the first one in splendour and solemnity.

2
Hsüan-tsang, Prajñā-deva, Jñāna-prabha Correspondence

A. FROM THE CHINESE TEXT OF THE LIFE OF HSÜAN-TSANG*

1. *Prajñā-deva to Hsüan-tsang*

Mahā-sthavira Prajñā-deva who is surrounded by the well-known in the Mahā-bodhī Monastery at the *vajrāsana* of Mañjuśrī Loka-jyeshṭha (the Buddha) sends his greetings to the Moksh-āchārya of Mahā-chīna who has achieved a subtle understanding of the boundless Tripiṭaka, and wishes Your Reverence good health and happiness.

I, Bhikshu Prajñā-deva, have composed a hymn in praise of the great divine power of the Buddha, as well as the *sūtras* and *śāstras*, and the comparative merit of Buddha dharma (to other

*Our sincere thanks to Professor Tan chung for translating (in idiomatic English) the above section from the *Ta T'ang Ta Tz'ŭ-ên Ssu San-tsang Fa-shih Chuan* (*Life of the Master of the Law*, etc.) by Hui-li and Yen-ts'ung published by Chih-na nei-hsueh-yuan (China Academy), 1923, reprint, Taipei, 1963.

[1]The Uigur has dirgadrmi > Dīrgha-dharma.

[2]Professor Tan Chung says that the grammar of the sentence in question as we have it in the extant editions of the *Life* does not permit the translation found in the Uigur version. He also observes that the Chinese characters 讚 for hymn(s) of praise (the literal meaning of the Ṛg-veda. —ed.) cannot be used twice to mean the *śloka* in praise of the Buddha composed by Prajñā-deva, as well as Ṛg-veda, the Buddha's views on which are said to be the subject matter of the *śloka* in the Uigur version. Moreover, Hsüan-tsang's biographer who chose to transliterate the word Veda as 吠陀 (Fei-t'uo) in another context a few pages earlier may be expected to have transliterated and not translated the Ṛg-veda by using the characters for hymns of praise. According to Professor Tan Chung, the Uigur translator read too much into the Chinese characters if he used this text of the original.

For the literal meaning of *Ṛg* see Monier-Williams, *Sanskrit-English Dictionary*, p. 225a; E.J. Eitel, *Handbook of Chinese Buddhism* (a Sanskrit-Chinese Dictionary), 1888, p. 131a.

faiths). I have entrusted Bhikshu Dharmārūḍha (Fa-ch'ang)[1] to bring the hymn to you.[2]

The profoundly learned āchārya Jñāna-prabha here also sends his regards, and Upāsaka Sūrya-labdha[3] also salutes you. We jointly send you two rolls of white cotton cloth[4] to show our affection.

As the distance is great, we pray that you will accept them without minding the meagreness.

If you require any scriptures, kindly send a list, and we shall make copies and send them to you.

Regards to the Moksh-āchārya.

2. *Hsüan-tsang to Prajñā-deva (dated the 2nd month, AD 654)*

Bhikshu Hsüan-tsang of the great T'ang Empire begs to address this to the Venerable Tripiṭaka Master Prajñā-deva of the Mahā-bodhī Monastery.

Your Reverence, it has been quite long since we parted, which enhances my longing and admiration for you. The non-communication between us all the more leaves the thirst of the yearning unquenched.

Bhikshu Dharmārūḍha arrived here with your very kind letter which brought me delight. There were also two rolls of fine cotton cloth and one fascicle of a hymn. I feel rather embarassed as my want of virtue does not deserve such kindness.

The weather is getting warmer now, and I don't know how you have been keeping since you last wrote.

I can imagine how you have assimilated the theories of all the schools, pondered over all volumes of the scriptures, hoisted the flag of the right *dharma*, led the straying people to the correct path, and beat back the discordant preachers. You surely maintain your spirit in front of princes and nobles, and compliment or criticize at will in a galaxy of talented people. All this contributes to your highly pleasant demeanour.

As for me, my incapacity is compounded by the decline of vigour. This all the more increases my yearnings when I

---

[3]Waley, p. 101, has Ādityadatta
[4]Ibid., 'pair of white cotton sheets', Waley, op. cit., p. 102, 'two lengths of white cotton'.

remember the virtue of Your Reverence.

During my sojourn in your country, I had the honour of meeting Your Reverence. In the convocation of Kānyakubja, we also engaged in a debate and argued out our respective viewpoints in the presence of the princes and thousands of devotees. As one of us expounded the tenets of the Mahāyāna school, the other advocated the aims of Hīnayāna. In the course of debate, our arguments unavoidably got heated up. In order to defend the truth, there was scant regard for personal feelings. Thus there were clashes. But, as soon as the debate was over, we did not take each other amiss. Now, you have sent word through the messenger apologizing for the past. How scrupulous you are!

You, holy sir, are profound in scholarship, eloquent in speech, firm in belief, and superb in cultivation. Your knowledge is greater than the expanse of the water in the Anavatapa Lake, and your purity is greater than that of the purest *maṇi* (jewel). Your Reverence set an example for emulation by the juniors among whom Your Reverence stood like a giant.

I wish you all the best in your endeavour in promoting the noble tradition and disseminating the true *dharma*.

Mahāyāna Buddhism surpasses all other schools in its perfection in reasoning and in its meridian level in argument. It is regrettable that Your Reverence has reservations about it. It is like preferring a sheep-drawn or deer-drawn cart to a bullock-drawn carriage, or preferring crystal to beryl. Enlightened as Your Reverence is, why such persistence in unbelief? Our mundane life is ephemeral. It is advisable that Your Reverence makes an early resolution to embrace *Alaṁkāraka-saddharma* (Mahāyāna Buddhism) so that there is no regret at the end of life.

Now, there is a messenger returning to India, I send you my sincere regards and a liittle memento as a token of my gratitude. It is too inadequate to express my deep feelings for Your Reverence. I hope Your Reverence would appreciate this.

When I was returning from India, I lost a horse-load of scriptures in the river Sindhu. I attach herewith my list and request that they be sent to me. This much for the present.

Yours
Bhikshu Hsüan-tsang

3. Hsüan-tsang to Jñāna-prabha (dated the 2nd month, AD 654)

Bhikshu Hsüan-tsang of the Great T'ang empire begs to address this to the Venerable Jñāna-prabha, the Tripiṭaka Master of Magadha in Central India.

More than ten years have elapsed since I bade farewell to Your Reverence. My yearning for Your Reverence increases with the passage of time, as we are separated by great distance, and with scarce communication between each other.

The arrival of Bhikshu Dharmāruḍha brought your kind inquiries, and news of your good health, which suddenly opened up the vistas [of memory]and brought the ecstasy of that moment. The weather is getting warmer now. I don't know how things have been [at your end] since you last wrote to me.

Years ago, our envoy returned [from India] and told us that the Great Dharmākara Master was inquiring about me at his deathbed. On hearing this, I felt my heart deeply stabbed, and could not recover from such a wound. Oh, it was as if a boat had capsized in the *dukha-sāgara* [ocean of sorrow that the worldly life is] or a celestial being lost the light of his eyes. How unexpectedly soon had come the pain of our bereavement!

The Great Dharmākara Master had cultivated virtue in the past, and accumulated merits for a long time to come. This was why he was endowed with a harmonious and noble nature and uniquely outstanding talent. He inherited the virtue of the Buddha, the Āryadeva, and extended the brilliance of Nāgārjuna. He rekindled the torch of wisdom and re-hoisted the flag of *dharma*. He extinguished the volcano of heterodoxy, and stopped the river of untruth from flooding. He led the exhausted travellers to the spiritual treasury, and opened up new vistas for those who had lost their bearings. He was at the same time a vast ocean and a lofty mountain, and a pillar of the edifice of *dharma-paryāpa*. He was thoroughly conversant with the teachings of all sects of *Triyāna* [the three schools of Buddhism], whether they were deficient or perfect; and even with the writings of heterodoxy which propounded theories of *Uchchheda-darśana* and *Nitya-darśana*. They not only permeated his mind, but also liquified in his heart. His literary style was circuitous while thoroughly expressing his ideas. His reasoning was allusive while clearly putting across his message. All this led to a mass following of his teachings from both the religious and secular, hailing him as a spiritual leader of India.

On top of it, he was skilfully persuasive, preaching day and night without fatigue. He filled the minds of the folks like street urns, providing inexhaustible drinks for them.

When I was seeking truth [in India], I had the honour of association with His Reverence and of benefiting by his teachings. Much as I was mediocre and unintelligent, I became amenable in his noble company.

When I bade him farewell to return to my country, he offered me deep and sincere advice which is still ringing in my ears. I had wished that he would live long to provide a noble example for emulation. Never had I imagined that he would one day depart from us eternally—how unbearable!

Your Reverence had, for long, received his noble teachings, and risen in status in the *āśrama*. It must have been difficult for you to suppress your longing for the departed guru. What can we do? I wish you could overcome your sad feelings.

In the past, after the *nirvāṇa* of the Enlightened One, the Buddha, his cause was carried forward and made to thrive by Mahā-kāśyapa. And after Śāṇakavāsa had passed away, Upagupta expounded his doctrines. Now the *dharma* is returning to its right path, and the great task [of disseminating it] devolves on Your Reverence. I pray that your fine speech and debating skills flow eternally along with the waters of the four seas; and your blessedness, sagacity and moral adornments stand eternally along with the five sacred hills.

Of the scriptures (*sūtras* and *śāstras*) which I have collected, I have already translated thirty odd works like the *Yogāchārya-bhūmi śāstra*,[5] etc. The *Abhidharma-kośa śāstra* and the *Abhi-dharma-Nyāyānusāra* are now being translated, and the work will be completed this year.

Now, the Son of Heaven of the Great T'ang empire enjoys the best of health, and tranquility reigns throughout his kingdom. With the compassion of a *Chakravartī-rāja*, he is disseminating

[5]See p. 30 in text and n. 12.

the teachings of the Dharma-rājā (the Buddha). His majesty has so kindly penned with his sacred hand a preface to the scriptures translated by me and ordered them to be transcribed by the clerks and circulated within the country. By and by, they are also being studied in the neighbouring states.

Your Reverence would be glad to hear that working, as we are, at the end of the period of *Saddharma-Pratarūpaka*, the brilliance of *Buddha-dharma* is still as magnificient as when it was first propounded in the Jetavana Garden in Śrāvastī.

One more thing: when I was crossing the river Sindhu, I lost a horse-load of scriptures of which I am enclosing a list herewith. Kindly send them to me when you write next.

I am sending a small memento which, I wish, Your Reverence will condescend to accept. The long distance which separates us prevents me from sending more things. Please forgive me for the meagreness of the thing.

Yours
Bhikshu Hsüan-tsang

B. From the Uigur Text of the Life of Hsüan-tsang[6]

We have tried to minimize to the best of our effort and ability the accuracy risks involved in a third or fourth rendering of the letters which were originally in Sanskrit. Their first paraphrase and translation were undertaken in the seventh century by Hsüan-tsang's Chinese biographers. Thence an excellent Uigurish Turkish version in the tenth century by Singqu Säli Tutung of Bishbalïq. (For a bibliography of Singqu Säli Tutung's works see P. Zeime, 'Singqu Säli Tutung— Übersetzer Buddhistischer Schriften ins Uigurische', *Tractata Altaica*, Wiesbaden, 1976, 763–75.) For the identification of Bishbalïq (in Turfan area) with Pei-t'ing, see A. Stein, *Innermost Asia*; II, p. 555; also see Watters I, p. 47). This has, with equal excellence, been critically annotated and translated into German by Dr Annemarie von Gabain. We translate the letters and the relevant notes from this study. The crucial passages, however, have been rechecked directly with the help of a scholar of Uigurish. We have also provided, in these limited cases,

---

[6]For a comparison see the translation from the Chinese text, pp. 17–22
[See translation of (Introduction) by Dr A. von Gabain, pp. 34–37. —Ed.]

an English rendering from the Kyoto edition of the Chinese text (used by Gabain) which may be compared with their counterparts translated from the Uigur Turkish.

Old *pothi* pages of the Uigur version of the seventh chapter of the *Life* (biography of Hsüan-tsang by Hui-li and Yen-ts'ung) which contain the letters are partly in Peking and partly in Paris. Our references to these pages and lines are those used by Dr A. von Gabain.

Standard Chinese editions of the *Life* provide somewhat less information than does the Uigur. How do we explain it? In the first place the Chinese might have deliberately paraphrased the material for reasons of literary style, imperial etiquette, etc. Indeed some element of paraphrase and stylistic changes may be expected to have taken place in the Uigurish as well, whether directly from Sanskrit or from Chinese.

In what form did the Uigur translator obtain his material? The pace of life being slow, memories were long in those times, and the *guruśishya* tradition was very much alive. Singqu Säli, therefore, might have obtained his information from oral monastic sources. Or perhaps he had access to a copy of the original Sanskrit which he used with the flair of a philologist, belonging as he did to a region where several languages were spoken. He may also have been a more zealot Buddhist than his Chinese counterparts as he worked under certain handicaps for which he had to make up. For instance, Buddhists had to compete with Manichaeans and Zoroastrians among the Turkish people of Central Asia. Singqu Säli was two stages removed from the land of origin of the text, and he did not have the kind of imperial patronage that the Chinese team enjoyed.

Perhaps the Uigur translator had at his disposal a Chinese version with information in colophons, and in the form of interlinear transcriptions in *Siddham* Brāhmī, as in the case of the term Ṛg-Veda which he transliterated as Ritivid whereas the Chinese monks had translated the word literally as hymn(s) of praise, not suspecting that this generalized description would fail to evoke the memory of the specific composition in the minds of annotators and translators of later times not in touch with the living monastic tradition. Or was it Singqu Säli who was guilty of reading too much in the Chinese characters—if that is all that he had at his disposal—which, because of a difficult conversion situation from Sanskrit into Chinese, were used without sufficient discrimination both for ordinary hymns of praise and the specific composition, the Ṛg-Veda, literally, the hymns of praise? In any case the word Ritivid occurs three times in the Uigur version, in ll. 1809, 1831 and 2047 and the phrase 'four Vedas' once in l. 1774. 'Four Vedas' also occurs in the Chinese version.

It may be remembered that the greater faithfulness of the Uigur, or for that matter of the Tibetan or the Singhalese, to a Sanskrit original is not peculiar to this text. The Uigur rendering by Singqu Säli Tutung of the Chinese version of the *Suvarṇprabhās-ottamma sūtra* by I-tsing, for example, has the same distinction.

It is apparent that a number of points have to be borne in mind before determining the precise significance of the Ṛg-Veda passage in the letters.

The Mahā-bodhi monastery where Hsüan-tsang's correspondents lived is to be located at Bodh Gayā although the contents of the letters, especially long passages about Śīlabhadra and the reference to the Kanauj debate organized by Harsha which was attended by approximately a thousand monks from Nālandā, may give the mistaken impression that it was situated there. However, Hsüan-tsang, his biographer, and I-tsing, in their respective accounts, give a prominent place to the Mahā-bodhi Monastery at the *vajrāsana* of the Buddha. Collation of information from these and some other Chinese and Tibetan sources may help us arrive at a fairly accurate location of the monastery—approximately twenty-eight miles south-west of Nālandā.

Manuscript no. Y16
(Reverse—8th line)

p. 373[7] (1763) In summer in the fifth month, on the day *ir-Hase* (in AD 652), letters came to the Tripiṭaka master from the two great wise men Jñāna-prabha and Prajñā-deva, the great virtuous (Skt. *bhadanta*) monks living in the monastery of Mahā-bodhī (or Bodhgayā) in Middle India (*madhya-deśa*). The contents of one letter are as follows:

(Jñāna-prabha to Hsüan-tsang)[8]

(1772) 'Tripiṭaka master, you have illumined the great vehicle (Mahāyāna), and the small vehicle (Hīnayāna); and also the
p. 374 four Vedas belonging to the "outer" [heretical] works, and the teachings which are known as "knowledge of the five wisdoms"

---

[7]Page numbers in the margin refer to Dr A. von Gabain's paper 'Briefe der Uigurischen Hüen-tsang-Biographie' and page numbers in parentheses refer to the Uigur text.
[8]It is a kind of covering letter for the letter and gifts sent by Prajñā-deva.

are by no means unknown to you.[9] You are the leader best among the students of the great teacher and wise master Śīla-bhadra. You are loved and honoured equally by all the teachers who live in the *Five Indias*.

Manuscript no. Y17 (front)

(1783) Prajñā-deva completely understands and has thoroughly imbibed the teachings found in the eighteen classes of Hīnayāna, and he is skilfully competent to teach and show the path. Also by such a teacher and wise man you are being honoured. (He too sends you his respectful compliments through this letter or through an accompanying letter.) When you stayed in India this teacher had discussions with you for long and. . . Although he was versed in Hīnayāna you teacher and master, admonished and disapproved of him constantly because of his one-sided views as his heart was not with Mahāyāna.

(1799) At the time of the congregation of the group of the teaching in the city of Kānyakubja you had defeated him with p. 375 extraordinary decisiveness. He had felt very much ashamed of himself and had announced himself as defeated. Since he has separated from you, this Master has longed for you with a heart full of respect, never forgetting you. Therefore, he appointed the monk Dīrgha-dharma, who belongs to the same monastery . . . [as messenger] and sent with very deep respect of . . . a poem about the Rg-Veda and two pieces of cotton.'

(reverse)

(1813) 'The "undamaged" letter of the *Sāmgha-sthavira* Prajñā-deva, who is surrounded by numerous, wise people living in the lovely, blessed monastery of Mahā-bodhī on the *Vajrāsana*.'

(1819) 'To the master Moksha-deva [or Moksh-āchārya. It is significant that this title was applied to Buddhist monks of distinction at this time and perhaps earlier], who is living in the blessed land of Tawqac mentioned to be in *mahā-chīna-deśa*

---

[9]This refers to the curriculum of Nālandā which consisted of the teachings of the Theravāda, Mahāyāna, four Vedas and the *Pañca-vidyā*, namely *sabda, hetu, adhyātma, cikitsā* and *śilpa-karma-sthāna*, i.e. grammar, logic, esoterics, medicine and artistic/technical.

and who has finely and completely seen through (mastered) the numerous, uncountable *sūtras* and *śāstras* and the *kleśas.*'

(Prajñā-deva and others to Hsüan-tsang)

(1824) (Through the messenger) 'With deep respect we ask after your well-being and we ask with our whole heart. How might he have fared in peace in times of even minor sickness and on the occasion of even small worries.

After I, the monk, Prajñā-deva have composed a verse (Uigur, *ślokin*) about the view which the god of gods, the Buddha deigned to have with regard to Ṛg-veda, and further a sign for all *sūtras* by way of the measure called comparison (Skt. *anumāna?*)[10] (I use) monk

Manuscript no. Y18 (front)

Dīrgha-dharma . . . you which (comes from) them all one pair of undyed cotton (to bring it to you).

(1837) The masters . . . and the *bhadanta*, the master Jñāna-prabha, ask (after you) with their whole heart. I, the lay brother Sūryadatta (probably a well-to-do devotee who donated the cotton) also make myself prostrate in obeisance. Now, I most

---

[10]The Buddhist system admits two means of right knowledge, *pratyaksha* (perception), and *anumāna* (inference). The Saṃkhya admits three by adding *upamāna* (comparison). Although the Uīgur *tänglä mäk* is translatable as comparison, it is apparently *anumāna* that could have been meant by it. The last sentence of the text (from and to comparison) may be understood to mean as follows: . . . the view (of the Buddha regarding the Ṛg-veda) served as a sign (post) or yardstick for all *sūtras* through being used as *anumāna*, a method of proof or of obtaining knowledge.

Thus, the Buddha's world-view became the point of reference for later Buddhists.

In spite of the insertion of Ṛg-veda and many other words which make the Uigur text quite different from the Chinese, the two basically have, I think, the same import, i.e. the views of the Buddha, which also served as a guide for later Buddhist literature, were superior to those of Hinduism.

We give below a word for word break-up of the crucial sentence:

Uigur	English	Uigur	English
nın	I	tagšut yaratïp	have composed, made it anew
prtyadiwi	Prajñā-deva	yana	and further
toyïn	monk	qamaγ	all
tngri tngrisi	god of gods	sudur-larïγ	*sūtras*
burkhan-nïng	Buddha, of the	tänglä mäk	comparison (Skt. *anumāna?*)
ritiwid	Ṛg-veda	atlγ	entitled, named, termed
körünč qïlu	insight, perception, view	ülgü	measure
yrlïqamïšïn	condescended, deigned	üzä	by means of, through
šlok	*śloka*, poem, verse	bilgü-sin	sign (signpost), mark

humbly present the gift to honour you which (comes from) them all. One pair of undyed cotton brought so as not to appear with empty hands. In view of the long way, he (the master) may not consider the negligible quantity strange. This is my wish: if there is any need for the necessary *sūtras* and *śāstras* may he write down their names and send here. We will most subserviently (as subject would to master) send them to the master Moksha-deva. This is our wish. He (respectful substitue for 'you') shall know that our love for you the noble one, here, far away is such,' so a letter arrived.

p. 377

(1855) In the fifth year (of the title *Yung-huei*, i.e. AD 654) in the spring in the second month, Dīrgha-dharma asked to be allowed to leave for India. And he asked to be allowed to take away a letter of reply. The Tripiṭaka master tied up (?) a return present and he also wrote a letter to the master Jñāna-prabha. The matters contained in the letter are as follows:

(Hsüan-tsang to Jñāna-prabha)

(1862) 'Undamaged letter by me, Hsüan-tsang living in Mahā-chīna.'

(reverse)

(1864) 'To the master Jñāna-prabha of Magadha in the empire of Middle India (*madhya-deśa*), who understands the Tripiṭaka.'

(1866) 'Since we parted ten years have passed. Because of the distance of the countries it has not been possible for us to hear good news of each other (but) our concern, love and good wishes grow from day to day to bind us (together).

(1873) (Now) the monk Dīrgha-dharma came and arrived safely. When we heard of the well-being of the . . . physical elements of the master, at that time the invisible got illumined as if (we) had seen the honourable one (personally). Our heart . . . and danced (with joy); it isn't possible to attempt to express this with brush and ink.

p. 378

(1880) After he (Dīrgha-dharma) had arrived, the times had become gradually warm (pleasant). In this pleasant time we do not know whether (Jñāna-prabha also) after the (sending of) the present might be moderately well?

(1885) Furthermore know: when we learnt last year from the messenger coming from India that the master Dharma-guptaka (Śilabhadra), our teacher is different (deceased) we could not overcome our state of feeling broken (hearted) and shattered.

Manuscript no. Y 19 (front)

(1891) Oh, the ship sailing on the sea of suffering has sunk. The eyes of the gods and people are blinded. When we thoughtfully reflect: How astounding and swift is the pain of the arrival of the law of *puṇya*! So (but we have to consider:) p. 379 Because the master Dharma-guptaka, in his earlier existence had [sown] love, because he in many epochs had performed good and meritorious deeds, therefore he has been chosen among the . . . as generous and fine . . . , and among all he has been distinguished as the lovely (?), wonderful *bhadanta* . . . .

(1904) His ability to continue the teaching was like that of Bodhisattva (Ārya-deva), his efficiency to continue its radiance was like that of Bodhisattva Nāgārjuna.

(1909) He lit the flame of *bodhi* anew. Anew he planted the banner of the teaching. He beat out the burning fire on the mountain of false views. He blocked the mighty stream in the sea of false teachings. He drove the exhausted students to the Jewel Island. To the erring community

(reverse)

he showed the great means (Skt. *upāya*). O (thou) most wonderful of the wonderful! the greatest of the great! He was the rafter and the support of the portal of true teaching. And futher it was not at all so that he did not take into his breast and into his heart for example those "half" and "full" teachings which are in the *Triyāna* and the writings of the heretics which assume a "destruction" or "eternity".

(1929) He openly preached to those who had been confused by the letter (form); he deigned to preach illuminatingly to those who were in darkness in relation to the meaning. Therefore, he deigned to be the hope and refuge of those who were in the "inner" and "outer" teachings and to be the most honoured master of the p. 380 whole of India. Further "he guided and led (the people) skilfully and in a way worthy of the greatest respect and untiringly day and night". Crosslegged they sat on the cross roads; by themselves (their beakers) were filled; without pause they poured the rice wine. Earlier I have Hsüan-tsang, . . . ask . . .

Manuscript no. Y20 (front)

(1945) I could pay my respects (to the master Śīlabhadra) from close by. And I have been able to partake of the wise teaching. Although I was stupid, I was like the salt-herb which could make itself stand straight against the hemp as a rafter.[11] And he had asked (me) to come to my own land. Finally there have been (i.e. are still with me) to this very day very many words of (his) sympathy and love. I hoped and wished that he [has finished] his life in peace. I praised and paid honour to his profound goodness. How is it possible that he deigned to depart on a single (one) day to join the innumerable number of those who have been?

p. 381 When I ponder over (the fact) that he has gone finally to the long striven for undiscoverable (Skt. *nirvāṇa*), (and) when I consider that the master led us in the nights and evenings to beneficial studies (and) that he, (nevertheless, would already) be up early in the mornings and go to the Great Hall, then I find no peace in my tormented heart. What shall I do in order to. . . (fulfil) the law (rules) of the *Saṃskṛta dharma*.

(reverse)

I shall do.

(1972) I wish that my life would not continue.

When previously the Mahābuddha had deigned to go [into] *nirvāṇa*, the Arhat Mahākāśyapa had propagated the teaching; and when the Arhat Śaṇavāsa had attained *nirvāṇa*, the Arhat Upagupta had explained and illumined the benefits of (the teaching). When now the continuing of the teaching to seek the truth has deigned to go (i.e. master Śīlabhadra has died) then the master Jñāna-prabha is left (now) (to continue it).

(1983) In the succession he is suitable to do the work of teaching. I wish he would always let flow [stream] his pure eloquence

p. 382 which is akin to the four oceans of the world; and that he would

---

[11]Waley, p. 101. 'Commonplace and stupid though I am . . . even tangleweed must perforce lose some of its kinks when it grows among hemp . . .'.

always, and for long, let his possessions of (religious) merit (*puṇya*) and spiritual wisdom (*jñāna*) which resemble the five mountains be effective.

(1990) By the way, I Hsüan-tsang have translated, more than thirty chapters [works] of different lengths, [starting] from the beginning of the *Yogāchāra-bhūmi-śāstra*[12] that I brought. While we are now translating the *Abhidharma-kośa śāstra*, we are at the same time translating the [*Nyāyānusāra śāstra*] We have not yet finished it. Doubtless it will not (?) be finished this year. [The emperor]

Manuscript no. Y21 (front)

(1999) has with his blessed person, given peace with immeasurable blessings to his country and empire (Hend.). With goodness akin to that of *Chakravartī-rājā*, he has spread teaching like that of *Dharma-rājā*. The recently translated texts, he at once had copied and personally composed the prefaces and has distributed them far and wide in the empire and the country. In this way the neighbouring kings also behave . . . (according to the texts). Even though these are matters which belong to the "time of the left behind, outer form" when one considers that the teaching and the instructions (Skt. *śāsana*) shine and radiate, multiply and enlarge, (then one has to admit that) it is really absolutely nothing else but the teaching in the city of Śrāvastī in the Jetavana Monastery. We would like him to know this exactly.

p. 383

(2020) By the way, when we arrived from India a load of books was left in the water (drowned) when we crossed the river Indus. We have noted their names and have sent them (herewith) so that a messenger coming (here) later (can bring the books to us).

(2025) Then we have sent a very minor gift, (a token) of our respect.

(reverse)

We wish that he would be kind enough to accept it. The way is long. One could not send much. May he not have contempt

---

[12]Gabain has *Yogāchārya-bhūmi-śāstra* which we believe is a mistake stemming perhaps from a misprint in Nanjio's *Catalogue* (pp. 257–8) followed by all sinologists and those depending on them.

for it because it is too small. Daily I bow in reverence upto the ground.'

(2031) Furthermore, he (Hsüan-tsang) sent a letter to the master Prajñā-deva. The words contained in the letter are as follows:

Hsüan-tsang to Prajñā-deva

(2035) (From) 'the monk Hsüan-tsang living in the empire of Mahā-chīna; (a) complete letter.'

(2036)   '(Delivered) at the feet of the great master Prajñā-deva in the monastery of Mahā-bodhī, who knows the Tripiṭaka'.

p. 384   (2039)   'It has been quite a long time since we parted. As no news came through we were left with much immeasurable wilting and thirst sadness and longing . . . The monk Dīrgha-dharma arrived safely and when we took from him, with deep respect, the undamaged letter, our joy (Hend.) was intensified.

(2047)   By the way you have sent two (bales) of cotton and a parcel with the Ṛg-veda *sūtra* poem*, and they have arrived. About this respectful (or respect-worthy) generosity I, the monk Hsüan-tsang who is poor in virtue, am deeply ashamed (embarrassed). . . .

Manuscript no. Y22 (front)

[The times] have

(2053)   become/been made calmer gradually (but it could be: the weather has improved, an epistolary formula). We have not learnt how, after your present has been sent to us, your honoured self might be.

(2056)   With this thought you let your meditations work in hundreds of *śāstras*. With wisdom you think about the nine different texts; and you are the one who gathers the visitors (that is those who are still outside the teaching) [not of the faith] [but] who put their trust into the veneration (of the three jewels),

p. 385   [you gather them by beating the victory drum (Hend.). (But) you demolish the strangers (i.e. the enemies of the teaching), who have become strengthened through their stomachs [reference to the Jainas?].† You confuse those who stand before the

*The German *Gedicht* (English Poem) is *Slokin* in Uigur.
†See Gabain, l. 2064, p. 406. But there are other versions.

kings.-You are the highest . . . among the wise men who have passed through thousands and ten thousands (of generations). In view of these circumstances and for this reason I am feeling very joyous and happy. I, Hsüan-tsang have been worried. I have become bad [unwell]. My power and strength has completely declined. But still when I think (Hend.) of you, (I have to note:) your fully deserved venerability (Hend.) multiplies and increases; there is no decline there.

(2076)   When I, at one time travelled in India, I came across your radiant life/conduct. In the congregation which was gathered in the city of Kānya-kubja.

(reverse)

One was allowed to have discussion with you and in the presence of all the kings and a crowd of hundreds of thousands find out the profundity or shallowness of [views]. There we had brought forth for acceptance the basic principles of the Mahāyāna teaching. But you had given the impression as if you wanted to do that for the veneration of the half teaching (of the Hīnayāna). Between the coming and going [exchange of words and arguments] there was in the power (Hend.) of the words no . . . [solution].

(2091)   With acts [heated arguments in this case] which are contemptuous of the true meaning one does not care for the heart [feelings] of man. Therefore developed that passionate, enraging fight. After the going away [of the incident], right there, that became known by itself. The messenger who has now arrived has come to tell me that you are full of regret and in repentance are asking for forgiveness (*kśānti*).

(2001)   (*sic.*) (2100) Indeed how strong, steady and true is your heart. You are the master of Teaching. Of you it is said: his word is pure, his heart is strong. You are [like] the remote water of the Anupadat lake, hard to reach (profound). One can compare absolutely (no one) with you.

Manuscript no. Y23 (front)

(2107)   You are a (shining) jewel and treasure; one cannot compare anything with your splendour. The teachers of a later day will have to recognize you as well as the highest among those who are (setting) an example (Hend.). Longingly we beseech (you). Try hard. Praise the true teaching and reveal it p. 387 (to us). When one has attained the truth and has fathomed its meaning, (one has to confess that) the basis of the teaching does not surpass the Mahāyāna. (But) our heart is (now) full of [sorrow] because you, master, who is not capable of believing deeply belong to the "wagon drawn by ram/sheep or *maral*"[13] and reject the "great wagon drawn by a white bull". It is as if you highly prize rock crystal but reject the beryl"[14]. The most shining one, the most praiseworthy (*bhadanta*). How could you have allowed yourself to be held back by such error? By the way, it is said that the length or shortness [of the existence] of this human body, as that of a good scent,[15] is hard to protect. [The body may or may not live long.] But here is the right thing to do. Awaken early a broad-minded sentiment or way of thinking[16]. Adorn and grace yourself with true teaching. When death comes may one not have to repent (any longer). The [messenger] who is going forth now . . .

(reverse)

(2134)   When (we) now try to show our true sentiment through a few objects we can by no means convey sufficiently the sentiment or intention which results from it.

(2138)   With great force we wish to convey that when we came to India and crossed over the river Indus, a load of books was left back in the water [drowned]. We have written down the names of those books and have sent them [to you]. Please let them be brought here (later some time) through a messenger coming here. It is impossible to report everything else. The monk Hsüan-tsang, my letter'.

(2149)   In the blessed great empire of Chīna, the master Hui-li, who understands the Tripiṭaka, has received instruction and has written down in Chinese; the master called Yen-ts'ung has expanded; and from the Chinese language the Tutung Singqu Sali of Bišbaliq has translated again in the Turkish language:

[13]duck, goose, flamingo; horse, elephant. Monier Williams' *Sanskrit–English Dictionary*, 1899, p. 789 c.
[14]Uigur *sparir* > Skt. *sphaṭika*.
[15]'. . .We are but vessels of unbaked clay . . .', Waley, p. 104.
[16]German *gesinnung*, Uigur *Kọngülü*; also see below (2134).

the *kāvya* book called the 'teaching the life of the Boddhisattva master Tai-T'ang San-tsang' or '*Ts'ŭ-ên-ch'uañ*.

The seventh chapter has ended.

Veneration to the Buddha! Veneration to the Teaching (*dhamma*)! Veneration to the congregation (*saṁgha*)!

[*Note*: In the original *Life* these letters follow the last paragraph of Ch.VII. In *Summary of Life* by D. Devahuti see p. 8, Ch. VII.]

LETTERS OF THE BIOGRAPHY OF HSÜAN-TSANG IN UIGURISH*

English translation of parts of BRIEFE DER UIGURISCHEN HÜEN-TSANG BIOGRAPHIE
by Annemarie von Gabain: Introduction, Observations and Index

Introduction

After the fragments of the fifth chapter which I published in *SBAW* in 1935, a further sample of this interesting biography now follows .

All sheets (pages) of the seventh chapter are preserved partly in the possession of Peking (with the marking Y given to it after its finder Mr. Yüan) and partly in the possession of Paris (the marking G given to it after its possessor, the Musée Guimet). The page numbering is largely missing, but, by means of a comparison with the Chinese original and on the basis of its contents, it is possible to determine with certainty that the pages belong to this chapter and their sequence.

I wish to publish here four letters which form the end of this chapter. They begin on the 33rd page on the 8th line of the verso. As every page has 27 lines and every sheet therefore 54 lines, the 33rd page must begin with line $32 \times 54 = 1728 + 1 =$ no. 1729. The verso of this page begins (then with the line 1756; the 8th line with which I wish to begin) is therefore the 1763rd of the whole chapter (while quoting from this treatise one would say VII 1763 etc., for practical reasons).

The corresponding Chinese text begins in the Kyoto edition of the Tripiṭaka in volume number 30, book no. 3, page 239 of the front page below line no. 13.

*'Briefe der Uigurischen Hüen-tsang biographie', Deutsche Akademie Der Wissenschaften, Berlin Philosophisch-historische Klasse. Stizungsberichte (SBAW), 1938, pp 371–415.

In consideration of the strange, peculiar punctuation of this manuscript and the unusual word-sequence in this text, I have added, as my own explanations, full stops or commas in round brackets, as in the previous work, they are therefore to be considered critically. Points in the square brackets indicate restorations in corrupt passages.

The first letter (lines 1772–1812) originates from *Jñāna-prabha*, from Central India,[17] and is addressed to Hsüan-tsang. As an accompanying present are mentioned two bales of cotton and a poem on the Ṛg-veda.

The second letter (lines 1824–1854) is likewise from India from Prajñā-deva and a band of wise men and is sent in like manner, to Hsüan-tsang. Since these senders also mention as presents a couple of bales of cotton, a text from/by Prajñā-deva on the Buddha's observations (*Bemer Kungen*) on the Ṛg-veda and a further text, we can assume that both these letters were brought with him by the Dīrgha-dharma, who is mentioned in line 2042 and that we are dealing with the same cotton gift.

In reply, Hsüan-tsang writes the 3rd letter (lines 1866–2031) to Jñānaprabha and also the 4th letter (lines 2039–2146) to Prajñā-deva, from China to India. The thanks expressed for the presents (two bales of cotton and the Ṛg-veda poem) one finds only in the last letter.

The letters 2 to 4 with respect to their form show us a definite pattern—one begins with the mention of the sender's name upon which there follows, unconnected and in a formulaic manner, the annotation, *äsängü bitig*, 'complete letter'. That should certainly be an expression on the outside of the letter, perhaps on the seal?

Furthermore, there naturally belongs to the address the name of the addressee, which is only given after this and which stands in the dative of the end aimed at.

The ending of the letters contains no special or typical turns of speech. The accompanying presents are mentioned at the end.

The first letter uses the address 'Ihr', 'you'[18] and the sender does not name himself. In spite of the Turkish 'Ihr', 'you', which does not appear in the Chinese version, we must therefore regard this letter as a paraphrase.[19] This is indicated also by the fact that before its (i.e. of

---

[17]*Madhya-deśa*, literally Central India, traditionally central part of northern India. The letters were from Bodh-gayā.

[18]*Aap* in Hindi

[19]This and footnote 21 on the next page partly explain the difference between the Chinese and the Uigur-Turkish versions.

line 1772) beginning, the statements which are customary in the other
letters about the sender, the addressee and the characteristic notice
äsängü bitig are here missing. The second letter addresses Hsüan-tsang in the third person and as
'master Moksha-deva'. The senders refer to themselves as 'we', 'I' or
'monk Prajñā-deva'. Although on one occasion (line 1838) a 'master
Jñāna-prabha' appears, I think that he is only indirectly the sender; the
author is the man who modestly describes himself as 'monk Prajñā-
deva'.

Probably the first two letters were composed in Sanskrit and thus
were preserved in the monastery archives, perhaps provided with a
more or less correct Chinese translation , that is why there is the
inconsistency of forms. Hsüan-tsang's letters are written in the artistic Chinese style[20]. By
contrast, those of the Indians are simpler and also considerably shorter.
This also hints at the fact that the former are not reproduced word for
word.[21]

In the third letter the address is 'the master' and 'he'. The sender
calls himself 'we' or 'I'.

And finally the fourth letter: it uses the address 'you' and the personal
designation as 'we' or 'I'.

The formula *äsängü bitig* is not in the Chinese text; it might
therefore have been typically Uigurish.[22]

At the begining of the Mongolian letters, we find after the mention
of the name of the sender, the formula—'my word'. Compare Ramstedt,
Mongolian Letters from Idiqut-Schähri, SBAW 1909, XXXII, page 843:
Öljeitemür. üge manu. 'Öljeitemür; Mein Wort' (my word). Further the
(two famous letters from the kings of Persia to Philip the Handsome)
(Prince Roland Bonaparte *Documents de l'epoque mongole*, tablet 14,
line 3 and 1). *Arγun üge manu* and *Öljeitü sultan üge mnu: 'Arγun*; my
word', *'Öljeitü*; my word'.

This usage is also abundantly present in our biography: **G 58 r 20**
toyïn huintso sawïm. **Y 38**, 10 *toyïn huintso ötügüm.* **Y 78**, 9 *toyïn
huintso ulatï acarïlar saw(ï)mïz.* **G 11 r 19** *bügü ilig ymä süü yaratu
yrlïqamïšqa, toyïn huintso sawïm.*

---

[20]It may be expected that the letters were translated for Jñāna-prabha and Prajñā-deva
by resident or visiting Chinese monks at Bodh Gayā or Nālandā of whom there must have
been several all the time.

[21]See footnote 19 of this chapter.

[22]Perhaps because the Uigur version, made directly from the Sanskrit, is 'complete',
it is not a paraphrase.

If Hsüan-tsang at the end of a letter addressed to the emperor says occasionally (**G 13**, 5) *uqmïš bolu yrlïqazun* 'If he would condescend to look at' (Chinese 236 v.o.2), the form of politeness on the part of the emperor towards Hsüan-tsang is (for example **G 13**, 26) *körü ämgänzün* 'he would be glad to take the trouble of seeing for himself'. 月关 Chên is used for 'I' in Chinese for the emperor; Uigurish (e.g. **G 46** r 11) renders it as *bizing qut* (*äšid-tük-ümüz bar*) which means 'Our majesty (we have resolved)'.

[Dr. Gabain concludes with formal thanks to those who have assisted her.]

This time also I have to thank Mr. Privy Councillor Lüders for the checking of the Sanskrit expressions.

For the—as usual—careful set [of the composition] I thank the Government Press, and especially the proof-reader, Mr. Pagel, who over and above his duty, has actually given several scholarly suggestions.

Futher, at the close of the chapter, I give the colophon *Anmerkungen* [Observations] to follow on the four Letters.

Observations

1764. The month as a common (time factor) chronology, appears in Instr., as *ol ödün* 'in those days' and (Kāš) *bu tïδïn* 'at present'; compare Schinkewitsch p. 45. The day, as an exact point in time has the dative ending (ibid. p. 22). Of course the common chronology can appear indefinitely in Kas. Line 1855 *bišinč yïl , yaz ikinti ai*.

1764. *ir* < Chinese 乙 *i*, B. Karlgren 176. i̯ĕt, is the second

sign of the cycle of ten (Chinese 十 干 *shĭ kan* < B. Karlgren 876 and 296 *z̯i̯əp-kân* > Uig. *šipqan*); compare Rahmeti in *TT VII* p.20 no. 10 and 98, table 1. *tawišqan* 'Hase' is the 4th part of the cycle of 12 (*TT VII* p.98). This combination means the 52nd day of the cycle of sixty. The days are, as is well known, counted without regard to months and years.

1765. *-kä* is dittography.

1766. *mkha bodiram sangram* < Skt. *mahābodhī ārāma saṅghārāma*. This monastery arose, according to tradition, (lines 1813–1815) above the *Vajrāsana*, the 'diamond' throne, that is, at the place where the Buddha achieved Enlightenment, a place where alone, in all eternity complete enlightenment can be achieved. It lay in Magadha in Urubilvā near modern Gayā. Not very far away was also the famous monastery of Nālandā, where for a long time Hsüan-tsang had dwelt, and wherefrom he had sought out the display (Austellung) of the Buddha relics in the Mahābodhī Monastery (see S. Julien, *Life*, pp. 216–17)[23]

1767. *inan* / /; 1859 *inanprbi* = Chinese 智 光 *Chĭ-kuang*. The glory of knowledge Skt. Jñānaprabha (As Julien had rightly recognized; Beal's *Prajñāraśmi*—he proves himself wrong through the Uigurish) a student of Śīlabhadra. In the monastery of Nālandā he had been Hsüan-tsang's teacher.

1768. *prtyadiwi* = Chinese 慧 天 *Huei-t'ien* 'the god of knowledge' = Skt. Prajñā-deva. (Eitel 94 b:) A monk from the monastery of Mahābodhī famous for his scholarship and piety. Through which linking language would the Skt. -*jñ*- become -*ty*- in the name? Mr. Pagel reminds of the Bengali *jñ*, which has approximately the same pronounciation as the German *dnj* (B. Bonnerjea, *Prakt. Grammatik der bengal. Umgangssprache*, p. 1, The Practical Grammar of the Bengali Colloquial Language, p. 1), Professor Weller shows us a similar composition in *Tib: Mélanges chinois et bouddhiques*, IV, 137 § 3 tib. *dña-na* < Skt. *Jñāna* (?) Another Turkish text (SBAW 1907, page 959) writes against it *pratnay-* or *pratani-arakš(i)t ačari*.

1773. *taš bitiglär* 'The outwardly Books' is a word to word translation of 外 書 *wai-schu*. Because of that the 外 道 書 *wai-tao-shu*, the 'books of outside, i.e. foreign teachings' is meant.

1774. *bĭš bilgä bilig bilmäk* 'The knowledge of the five (kinds

[23]In this same moon, in accordance with the practices of the kingdoms of the West, one brings out of the monastery of intelligence (*Bodhivihāra*) the *che-li* (*śarīras*) relics of the Buddha. The clergy and the laity of the other kingdoms come in crowds to see them and worship them.

of) wisdom' = Chinese 五 明 *wu-ming*. 'The five fold understanding (recognition, knowledge)' are after *Mahāvyutpatti* ed. Sakaki § 76 the *pañchavidyā*: 1. *śabda* = 聲 *shêng* '*Grammar*', 2. *hetu* = 因 *yin* 'logic', 3. *adhyātma* = 內 *nei* 'esoteric', 4. *cikitsā* = 醫方 *i-fang* 'Medicine'; 5. *śilpa-karmasthāna* = 工巧 *kung-k'iao* 'artistic' (technical). Exact explanation is in *Ta-Ming san-tsang fa-shu*, p. 169b, which cites the *Hua-yen-king-shu-ch'ao*.

1778. *tïtsï*, not *titsi* for it is in line 1914 as *tïtsï-larïγ*. This word also appears in the form of *tïsï* (*M III* 12, 10) and even *taisï* (line 2151 and *U III* 75, 6). The last one is not a normal sound crossing, it is possibly a contamination of 太師 *t'ai-shĭ* 'Great master'.

1783. *siošing säkiz ygrmi nikai* 'The eighteen classes of Hīnayāna' (*nikai* < skt. *nikāya* 'Classes, Groups') = 十八部 *shĭ-pa-pu*. Refer C.F. Köppen, I, p. 151.

1785. *widis birmäk* = 誘 *yu* 'to awaken / to incite / to encourage'. The same sign in line 1938 is translated through *yirčilä-uduz* as lead, conduct (guide)[24]. **Y 8** r. 23 *yüz tïtsïlarqa widis birür ärdi* = Chinese 238 r.o. 10. 弟子百餘人咸請教誡 'the more than 100 students beg for instruction / advice and prescription'. **Y 14** r.17 *widis bošγun (almaq)* = Chinese 239 v.o. 19 授 *shou* 'instruct / teach'. **G 75**, 23 *widis bir-*.

For the explanation concerning 'sound' I thank Mr (Dr) Hansen:

---

[24]This gives us some idea of the style of the Chinese-to-Uigur translation, which we regard felicitous rather than indicative of license. On our part we have maintained literalness, freedom being the prerogative of the original author, not of the interpreter. See for example Gabain's and our translation of a word in ll. 2131, 2135, and 2137.

parth. *'bdys* (about) *abdēs* 'instruction'; np. dial ـبـدس 'instruction' (Ivanow, *IRAS*, 1923, p. 367) proofs: Andreas-Henning, *Mitteliranische Manichaica II* (Medieval Iran's Manichaica *SBAW*, 1933, p. 301, n. 2), and the same (*Mir. Man III SBAW*, 1934, p. 892); here also the verb *'bdyštn'* 'to prove / show / demonstrate / to instruct'.

1786. *uzan-* means 'to be skilled in … ' already proved in *U II* 28, 4. It is a construction of *uz*, 'capable / adept' as *il + än-* 'to rule' (*A. Ind.*) *boš + un-* 'to become free' *U II* 88, 71 and *köz + ün-* 'to appear' *U* 37, 15. This meaning also suits the examples in *A. Ind.* and it is to be preferred to the derivation that is there, from **uz-* 'to continue for a long time'.

1790. *ärkän*, which never appears in the inscriptions and rarely in the manuscripts concludes as 'adverbial statement'. I consider the *kän-* to be for the same purpose as (*kän*) in *amtï + qan*, *ärtägän < ärtä + kän, tükämäz + kän*. Since it appears to be joined only to nouns, *ärkän* must surely be explained from **är-ür + kän*; compare **bar-ïr > bar*.

1792 *tüšär, -ö-* ? *-s-* ? In Chinese it is 磋 *ts'o* 'to polish / to perfect / improve oneself'.

1799. *kanyakubči* < Skt. Kānyakubja. About the gathering, King Śīlāditya for Hsüan-tsang's sake had collected together in the presence of king Kumāra and sixteen other kings, 3000 Hīnayāna and Mahāyāna monks and 2000 Brāhmaṇas and Nigranthas; compare S. Julien *Life*, pp. 242–7. Śīlāditya was so impressed by Hsüan-tsang's Mahāyānish expounding, that he let himself take part in the extra-ordinary worship accorded to Mahāyāna already at the opening of the gathering. For eighteen days no one dared to oppose (challenge) the thesis of the wise pilgrim, so that he was finally declared the winner, he did not even have to debate with them. At that time, the Mahāyāna acquired many new followers from the members of the Hīnayāna. When the followers of the 'great vehicle', after this success of Hsüan-tsang, bestowed upon him the reverential title of Mahāyānadeva, the followers of the 'smaller vehicle' also

p. 391

recognized his knowledge and called him, admiringly, Moksha-deva.[25]

It was furthermore reported that in the heat of the debate a plot was hatched behind the scenes by an agent against the sovereign power owing to whose favour Hsüan-tsang had come. To this are related the lines 2091–2095.

1805. *üzäki, i.e. üzä-k-i,* I believe it to be an intensive in -*k*-as *alq-* 'to exhaust', to *al-* 'to take'; *ök-* 'to think', *U II* 11, 8 to *ö-* 'to think'; *könük-* 'to burn up' *M I* 17, 12 to *kön-* 'to burn' (Kāš: *Arγu*-dialect). There could thus lie **üzä-* at its base, from which having been derived Kāš recognizes the reflexive *üzä -l-* 'to long for'. Further *osm. üzän-* 'to exert oneself', and with Ablaut (vowel change) *üzün-?*

1809, 1831. *ritiwid* < Skt. Ṛg-veda. The sound crossing -*g*- > -*t*- allows a presumption of Sakish being the intermediary. Compare H. Lüders, *Zur Geschichte des ostasiatischen Tier-kreises* (On the History of the East Asian Animal), *SBAW*, 1933, p. 1017, n. 1: In three examples the Skt. *k* has disappeared and in the Sakish, in its place, a -*t*- that gets rid of the hiatus has appeared. One of these examples is the Skt. *makara* > toch. -*kuč mātār* > Uig. *madar.*

It is of importance for the Turkish religions history and that of its early literature to pay attention to further Sakish elements in our Buddhistic texts. Dr. Hansen in his forthcoming '*Tocha-rischiranischen Beziehungen,* 'Tocharien–Iranian Connections' (*ZDMG*) will explain to us the form of a whole series of foreign words in the Uigurish as Sakish.

Even the Sakish title *'Kaniṣkas: ṣaonano ṣao'* works itself into the Uigurish; it is definitely the model of the Buddha title *tängri tängrisi,* 'God of Gods' (R. Gauthiot, in his essay on this word in 1910).

1810. *iki böz* 'two cottons', that is two bales of cotton, probably of a weight as customary in commerce / trade: silk bales were legal paying material; compare this biography (*Life*, p. 40) in

---

[25]Does the use of the word *moksha* in Mokshadeva by the Theravādins (in contrast to the Mahāyānists) throw light on relationship, etymological or ideational, with Vedism (early Hinduism), and Mahāyāna's divergence from Vedism, and (very deliberately from) Theravāda.

Chinese 230 r.u. 18: for the financing of his further travels, Hsüan-tsang was presented with 500 pieces of silk and taffeta. Also from *Kao-ch'ang* we know (see O. Franke, *Tempelinschrift aus Idikutšahri*, 'Temple Inscription from Idikutšahri', p. 27) that taxes were paid in silver money or in hemp. Cotton was already cultivated at this time in Turfan, but not yet in China (ibid., p. 28). In the T'ang period it was, in China, a very wondrous article of commerce / business / trade. The cognates of this loan word can be found compiled together in P. Schmidt-riga's *Etymol. Beiträgen*, (Etymological Contributions), *JSFOu* 42, 3, p. 3.

1810. read *intin* or *äwätïn*, *ạwatïn*. There are many examples in which *intin qïdïɣ*, (is) the translation of 彼岸 *pi-an* (which means) 'the bank on the far side' (i.e. *Nirvāṇa*): **G 2** r.4 *intin qïdïɣ-nïng käčgüläg (käčügi ärür* = 237 v.o. 16

彼岸之津涉 ; **G 11**, 8 *täggülük) qïltï intin qïdïɣqa* = 235 r.u. 4 臻彼岸 ; **Y 69** r. 12 *anï üčün burχanlar bu ädgülärkä tükällig bolup oruɣlïɣ intin qïdïɣqa* = 249 v.u. 10

p. 392 是以諸佛具而昇彼岸 ; **Y 103** r. 10 *nïrwanlïɣ intin qïdïɣqa aqtïn-* = 249 r.u. 12 為彼岸之良因 ; **Y 11** r. 9 *tam tübintä olurup, intinin körmäyük täg* = 238 r.u. 12 猶百墙而靡見

In spite of these many examples I do not understand '*intin*'. Does there hide therein the third person pronoun which one looks for, for example, also in '*inčä*'?

1812. *üzä* I would like to read and not *özä*, since the Brāhmī texts write *üsä* (*TM* 318) and *üzā̄* , (*T II, S* 59; *T III D* 319; *T III M* 145 etc.). But one must realize that these texts belong to another dialect, other than that of the remaining manuscripts.

These post-positions in the inscriptions are tied up with Lok. [locative] or Kas. ind [case indicative]; in the manuscripts mostly with the Kas. ind., but sometimes also with the Instr. pronouns stand before *üzä* in the Akk. [accusative], to be sure, only in dependence on other frequently used post-positions which govern the Akk. [accusative]. Example: Inscription *I E* 1 *kiši oɣlïnda üzä*, *I E* 16 *ol törüdä üzä*; and *II E* 15 *Tarduš budun üzä*. In *A. Ind.* are many examples for the Kas. Ind. given in the manuscripts. Further also there is *töpü + n üzä*. Further *U III* 14, 5 *sizlärni üzä*, *M III* 13, 2 *uruɣ + ï + n tarïɣ + ï + n üzä saqïn-*, and finally *M III* 42, 18 *q(a)maɣurt + nï üzä*.

We have thus to assume, in spite of the few accusatives which have their origin only by analogy, an intransitive verb **üz-* with the meaning of 'to be above' or 'to be greater' as the origin.

Derivatives of this postulated root are: (tel. osm. krm.) (*üz-är* top surface, of the top; (bar.kazak.) *üz-ük* roof (old)) *üz-ür-ö* 'over inside'; (bar.) *üz-üm* 'growth' (tob. bar and also kas.!) *üs-* 'to grow, grow-up'.

To be sure the Kom. knows an *özä-* upon. And in addition to this (kar. in Kowalski, *Kar. Texte*) *öžalań-* 'to have come down from above'. That might go back to a root which is similar in meaning *ös-* (old)- 'to grow', to which belongs the above mentioned Kas. *üs-*.

The (osm.) *üslük* 'head veil / scarf' belongs to a further root **üs,* from which comes the Uigurish *üs + t + ün*, *üstürdi*, *üs + tä*.

Deny in § 897 (osm. ğaɣ) assigns *üzrä-* upon, to in this last mentioned root, **üs* and it assumes a directive. However, **üs-rä* would not have needed to become *-z-*. We can assign this word without compulsion to **üz-*, and assume a derivative from its factitive form **üz-ür-*.

One asks oneself if in Uigurish there was perhaps an *üzä* (over) and an **özä-* (by means of). However, the Osmanic binds in the one word *üzrä* both meanings (Deny, p. 606); hence I too will not assume in the Uigurish two different words of the same spelling. Can the Mongolists give us any surety over these groups? Ramstedt, *Kalm WB*, p. 460 *üzūr* 'the top end'. Castrén Schiefner, *Burj. Sprachlehre*, p. 107 (nišne-udinic and chorinic) *uzur* (selengin.) *uʒur* 'close / end', K. Golstunskij, p. 232 *üs-* to grow—but Mostaert, *Textes oraux Ordos* (Oral Texts of Ordos): *ös-* 'croître (to increase), grandir (to become big), se multiplier (to multiply)', Ramstedt, p. 301, likewise.

p. 393 **1817.** *qawzadïl-mïš* 'encircle / surround' < Chinese 合 *ho*

< B. Karlgren 71 γāp 'together' + sa- (Ishaky, p. 38; e.g. *tang* 'miracle', *tangsa-* 'to astound') *-t-il- qawsadīl-* > *qawzadïl-*; *U III* 13, 6 *qawzayu* 'crowding together in the circle', created from (out of) the same root are (osm. Uig.) *qaw* + *ïš-* 'to unite oneself' (Uig.) *qab* + *šur-* 'to lay together', (Kāš.) *qawšut* 'contract / treaty'; *qaw* + *ïr-* *U III* 44, 3 'to summarize'. The χ*awsadïlu* in *U II* 28, 1. We may, since it is there a case of block printing, identify it with our *qawzadïl-* without hesitation.

1819. *äsängü* 'intact'. Compare *M I* 27, 11 *ymä ạmtï bolzun äsängü alqïš tözü nom arqasïnga* 'and now may there be for the end of the perfect prayer a perfect blessing!' *M III* 12, 2 *qmaγ tngri yir'i-n äsängüsin birti* 'the whole land of the gods its entirety / completeness has he given' *M III* 43 Nr. 29 2 *äsängü ögrünčü* 'unimpaired joy'. This word is derived from *äsän* *U II* 64, 6 'peace'; *W* 21, *Ht V*, Kāšγ 'healthy'; WB *äsän, äzän, ezän, esän, isän* and *izän*—a similar construction is hidden in *inčkü*—'peace' (*A. Ind.*) from *inč* 'peace' (*ibid.*); *mängigü* 'blessed' (Mus. 36. p. 144; *M III* 11, 16) from *mängi* 'joy' (*A. Ind.*); *oγl(a)nγu* 'tender' (thus in place of *oγlaγu*? *A. Ind.* from *oγlan* 'boy' (*ibid.*); *tözügü* 'complete' to *tözü* 'all' (*A. Ind.*)

1826. *az-qï-a*; with respect to the intensificatory particle *qïya*, *qïna* both forms of which go back to the inscriptional *qïnya* we have said in *TT I* note 152 that we take the first to be Uigurish and last for the form of the Manichean text, perhaps even for *Oγuzisch*. I wish now to somewhat modify this observation, because not all of the Manichean texts are in fact written in the same dialect.

Apart from the older language of the inscriptions (which displayed written by hand in Thomsens *Wahrsagebuch* (A book of truthful sayings) one can ascertain the presence of three different dialects in the Central Asiatic pre-Islamic manuscripts. After the word, the inscriptional form of which is *anyïγ*, I call the one '*ayïγ*' and the other '*anïγ*' dialect. About the third dialect more below.

The indications of sporadic features of the differentiations of both the dialects are as follows:

1. The *-ny-* sound has once become *-y-*, and another time *-ṇ-*.

It comes through in the following words: *anyïγ* 'bad, very'; *qïnya*, 'an intensificatory (strengthening) particle'; *qony* 'sheep'; *köny-* 'to burn'; *qanyu* 'who'?; *qanyaq* 'butter'; *qïtany* 'china'; *čïγany* 'poor'; *yany* 'to broaden out' (spread); *tany* 'hen'(?); *könyäk* 'bucket'; *sany-* 'to pierce through', and *qunyaš* 'sun'.

Evidence: *anyïγ W* 9, *ayïγ U II* 8, 17, *anïγ M I* 6, 17. *qïnya I E* 34, *qïya U II* 9, 5, *qïna TT I* 152, *qony W* 40, *qoin* < **qoi* + (Deminut) °*n U II* 80, 60 *qon* Kāš.: Arγu and *W I* c5. **köny-*, *köi- U II* 8, 27, kön- *WI* a 6, Kāš.: Arγu. *qanyu M III* 20, 4, *TT V* A 23, *qayu U III* 73, 3, *qanu* Kāš.: In Arγu with Guzz and Qïfčaq. **qanyaq, qayaq* Kāš., *qanaq* Kāš.: Arγu Bulγar. *qïtany I E* 4, *qïtai* Kotwič-Samoilowič 17, *qïtan* testified in 契 丹 *K'i-tan čïγany W* 45, *čïγai U II* 29, 14, *čïγan* Kāš.: Guzz and Qïfčaq. *yany- I E* 23 yai- Suv. 617, 4, **yan-*. *tany* is doubtful. Compare *IOd* p. 28, and, moreover Kāš. knows a *tai* 'to fill'; here to ? *könyäk W* 88, *könäk* Kāš., *QB *sany-* and **san-* in the 5th letter p. 18, *sai- A. Ind. *qunyaš, quyaš* Kāš., **qunaš* proves itself through osm. *günäš*.)

p. 394

2. In the *ayïγ* dialect in the form in − °*p* prevails; in the *anïγ*-dialect it is used without any distinction with the form in − °*pan*. The Aorist in Guzzish has a similar extension through + °*n*: Brockelmann, *Māḥmud al-Kāšγarïs Darstellung des türkischen Verbalbaus* (Description of the Turkish verbal construction), *K. Sz.* 1919 p. 43: instead of the *käl-ir* of the other dialects they say *Kälirän*.)

3. The instrumental sounds in the *anïγ-* dialect not only in *-in*, but also in *-un* and *-an*. (This is also attested in Kāšγarī for the Arγu dialect.)

4. The *anïγ* dialect used the endings *-ta* and *-da* for the locative and ablative. The ending *-dïn*, *-tïn* is used only in the constructions like *tört-din sïngar*.

5. The perfect tense in the *ayïγ* dialect sounds *-dïm* or after round vowels *-dum*. In the 3rd person only the vowel *-ï* occurs. The other dialect also knows a *-dam*, *-dang* in the 3rd person a *u*. (Brockelmann *-Kāšγarī*, p. 36: the Guzz say *bardam*, the Arγu *bardum*). For the 2nd person singular in the *anïγ-* dialect instead of *dïng* also a *dïγ* occurs, exactly similar as in the

Yenissei inscriptions (thus also in Kāš., p. 36 attested for the Arɣu and as Brockelmann says in old-osm.- frequently / usual).

6. In the same way, the *a* predominates in the imperative of the *anïɣ* dialect: instead of *-ïng* and *-alïm*: *-ang* and *-alam*.

7. And finally also the possessive endings of the *anïɣ* dialect sounds, instead of *-imiz* and *-ingiz*: *-amaz* and *-angaz*. The accusative of the 3rd person sounds also *-an* in addition to *-ïn*.

8. The necessitative form in *-ɣuluq* is indeed in the *anïɣ* dialect only represented by means of the verbal-noun in *-sïq* (a somewhat doubtful comparison: Brockelmann *-Kāš*, p. 39) for the specifying of a duty one uses the form in ɣuluq, e.g., in the original text volume II, p. 47, 7. *ol barɣuluq ärdi*; 47, 8 *ol munda turɣuluq ärdi* (for which Brockelmann wished to read *baruɣluq* and *turuɣluq*). For that the Guzz use a form in + *s* °*q* that is, to be sure: denominal *ol mundïn barïɣsaq täkül* (he will not continue / go forth from there). Perhaps here Kāšɣarī has confused two similar forms which are not differentiated through the script: the denominal form + *saq*, which designates 'one who desires the noun' and the deverbal form + *sïq*, *-suq* that is attested in *Xuastuanift*, Bangs edition, p. 164. *išlämä-sig iš* a thing which one ought not to do. It appears to be the same as a *išlämägülük iš* in the texts of the *ayïɣ-* dialect.

There predominates in the text, no sharp division between the signs of the *ayïɣ-* and the *anïɣ-* dialects. However, we are able, at times, to establish, a preponderance of one of the two.

All Buddhist texts, including the late Hīnayānist ones from Kansu, in Swedish possession, are composed in the *ayïɣ-* dialect, with the exception of those written in Brāhmī script. In Manichean texts, for example, *TT III* and *TT II* B (both in man. letters).

p. 395 To the *anïɣ-* dialect belong: Thomsens Military passes (passports) of Miran and all further Mss. in Runen (in v. Le Coq); the *Xuastuanift*; the v. Le Coq's text a publication in Honour of Thomsen; *TT I* (the cursive written book of prophesy, with Chinese influence); in *M I* pp. 10–12 (in honour of the presbyter *Mar Niv Mani*, dated AD 798); *M I*, p. 23 (without the post-scripts pp. 29–30); it celebrates the accession to power of the Prince Arslan of *Altun-Arɣu . . . Qašu, Ordu* and *Čigil känt* and is written about the year AD 740; in *M II*, p. 7 and p. 12; in *M III*,

p. 35, no. 16, according to the handwriting there belongs to it the fragment in *TT VII*, p. 19, no. 9, which carries the date '358, after *Yezdegerd*': AD 990 and finally *M III*, p. 40, no. 25, where it is mentioned that 'we' are going to the Uigur (people), so that 'we' the writers of the *anïγ*-dialect, must belong to a different tribe.

We have thus Manichaean texts in the *anïγ* dialect which originate from the pre-Uigurish period of Turkistan (before AD 840) and even one which was written before the Uigur (people) had accepted this religion (AD 762). Also the area ruled by the Prince Arslan appears to imply that he, and therefore, surely also the composers of his panegyric were west-Turks. Nemeths inscriptions (*Körösi Csoma-Archiv I*, p. 134) from the land of seven rivers write II 4 *at-um* 'my horse' exactly as the Arγu say *bar-dam*. There remains no doubt that the *anïγ* people were a west-Turk people who independently of the Uigur people and before them had accepted Manichaeism. About AD 630, Hsüan-tsang still reports about the Turks at Talas that they were fire-worshippers (Zoroastrian). A good hundred years later a part of them had already accepted Manichaeism. At the beginning of the Turfan-Uigur period, Manichaean texts are written both by Turks of the *anïγ* as well as Turks of the *ayïγ* dialect.

Above all I do not venture to say who the *anïγ* people were. According to linguistic indications one considers that these people belonged either to the Arγu or the Guzz. However, historically, the confirmation is lacking since Kāšγarī and also the accounts in the *Ḥudūd-al-'ālam* (see Minorsky, *E.I.W. Gibb Memorial Series*, New Series, XI, 1937) are too late (in original). Since the time of the pressing forward of the Uigur to the south-west, other peoples might also have moved further to the west, so that we are not able to localize the Turkish peoples of the 8th century according to these sources. Around this time one looks for the Türgiš in Semirječie and the Basmïl around Bišbalïq; Kāšγarī seems to give us no information about what their dialect was.

A third dialect is that of the Brāhmī manuscripts. It is according to the previously mentioned pieces of evidence closer to the Uigurish. However, it had many specialities: *p* in the initial sound, *o* in the second syllable and other (specialities).

If, after these words, I shall in the future, occasionally in future, use the designation 'Uigurish' for the language of all Turkish manuscripts from Central Asia, from the pre-Islamic period, it is so because of the lack of a generally established better name.

1828. If *inčmu* is read correctly, then *-mu* is naturally dittography.

1829. *ärki* < **är-ür* and an interjection + *ki* (compare my discussion in *OLZ* 1938 no. 12, p. 755 of G. Jarring, *Uzbek Texts from Afghan Turkestan*).

p. 396 **1831.** *körünč* can hardly mean anything else than 'view' [opinion] although with Kāš it means 'scout', and 'view' is supported **[to be meant by it] in the form *körüm* in our text.

1833–34. *-ïγ tänglämäk atlγ ülgü ist die* is the translation of 比量 , *pi-liang*, meaning to 'compare and ponder upon'.

The latter serves also the purpose of expressing / rendering the skt. *anumāna* as 'logical conclusion' which however could hardly be meant here.

These two works of Prajñā-deva have [presumably] not been preserved?

1840. *Saryadati* = 口授 *ji-shou* meaning 'bestowed by the Sun'. Can it be assumed that there is a mistake in writing **Suryadata* for Skt. *Sūrya-datta*—meaning the same as in Chinese.

1842. *mn* 'I' is missing in Chinese, it is incomprehensible that the main sender is not the last mentioned but Prajñā-deva. The others mentioned send only greetings.

1843. *biläg* (Kāš. ğaγ) 'present / gift'. Likewise (ğaγ.) *bölök* (*-g*?); (kys.), *pälā* ; (soj.) *päläk*; (kys.) *pälägä*; (bar.) *piläk*; (kas. tob. tara) *büläk*; (burj.) *belek*. Does this belong to Kāš. *bilä-* 'envelop' / 'to wrap' or as 'something wrapped' / 'one that is wrapped up'? Presents were definitely (then), as nowadays according to the custom of the Chinese, Japanese and Mongols, carefully packed in silk cloth before being handed over. Actually one would compare it with (soj.) *qadaq* 'Cloth as a greeting gift'.

1844. *šong* = one could also read as *s-* and *-u-* Chinese 雙 *shuang*, compare B. Karlgren 1243 *ṣàng* < *s-*.

1846. *tangïγla-*, one could also read *tangïrla*. The first one is the more likely construction. *tang* (*Man. Erz.* 19, 55) meaning 'astounding' (Kāš.), 'miracle', **tang-ï-*; *tangï-γ U II* 11, 7 'horror'.

1855. *bišinč yïl* 'the 5th year'. At the beginning of the seventh chapter, it is said in the Chinese text, that it [Seventh chapter, i.e. the happenings recorded in it] began with the 22nd year and ended with the fifth year of ger. 'devise' [reign-title] 永 徽 Yung huei. That is the first reign-title of the emperor Kao-tsung. Already as crown prince he had given Hsüan-tsang's efforts his attention and support. He was the son of the greatest emperor of the T'ang Dynasty, of its founder who had been known before by the surname [of a citizen] Li Shĭ-min. This reign-title was valid during the years AD 650–655.

1857. *yantud* 'answer' is one of the somewhat rare nouns on *-d* of *yan-* meaning 'return', *-t-* (fact). Compare with Kāš. *yïd* 'fragrance' = **yï,* of which on the other hand (Uig.) *yïpar* and Jarring, *Afghan, Uzbek i-s + kä-* 'to give out fragrance'; Kāš. (*kid* 'the end' < **ki-*, which appears as 'after' in *ki-n*; Kāš.) *qaδ* snow-storm created from **qa-*, which has formed *qar* 'snow'; (Uig.) *toδ* 'satisfied / full' [enough to eat] < **to-*, to which *tol-* 'to fill' belongs.

1859. With *bklä-* one thinks first of all of *bk* 'tight' [firm]. However, it should be remembered that (Uig. krm tel. schor. küär) (*päk, bärk* and (QB) *päg* mean 'tie / fastening' (Uig. osm. bar. küär.)) *päklä-* 'to fasten / to tie, to lock'; (Kar. T.) *bäklȝ*- likewise (ǧaγ) *bäklän-* 'to be bound'.

1859. *angayu* was in *U II* 38, 69 taken to be an attribute and was translated as 'intelligible'. The form on *-u* denotes 1. Adverbial designations; 2. Adverbs similar to prepositions (e.g. *qod-ï in-* to climb down / descend); 3. logical main predicates which are accompanied by either modal or descriptive auxiliary verbs; and 4. precede *bol-* (vide. note. 1870 I c 1). They seldom appear as attributes. That is why I have doubts about the meaning 'intelligible'. I mention here some examples: **G 20** r. 10 *anam üčün wrγar itälim , wrγar bütmiš-dä angayu ant / / / olurdačï toyïn kigürälim.* 'Because of my mother we wish to erect a monastery. After the monastery has been completed we would also like to, . . . bring monks there' = 236 r.u. 8

奉為文德聖皇后, 即營僧寺, 寺成之曰當別度僧

G 38 r.19 *ulatï burχan nomïnga tägdüktä üč yüz yükünüp, angayu yana üč ming yüküntilär* and 'after they have got [assimilated] the teaching of the Buddhas they bow 300 times, and then again 3000 times' = Chinese. 243 v.o.6

至於經禮三百曲禮三千

G 45, 4 *ol qatun šmnanč bol / / / / kösädüktä , tngri ilig qutï anïng kösüšin qanturu yrlïqap, šmnanč qïlu yrlïqadï. angayu qaγlim si atlγ wrχar itä yrlïqap, olγurtï yrlïqadï.* 'When this princess wished to become a nun, His Majesty, the emperor was pleased to fulfil her wish; and ordered her to become a nun. Besides this it pleased him to construct the monastery of Hao-lin, and to order that she be allowed to live there' = Chinese 243 r.o.19.   帝從其志為棃中別造鶴林寺

Y 86, 4 *tägmiš bi taš üčün baščïlar wrχar yuzisintä öngdün taγdïn bulungta bi tašqa angayu äw itip anta ornatdïlar.* 'Because of the arrival of the inscription stone the highest in authority ordered a house to be built for it in front of the monastery in the north-east corner, and had it erected there' = Chinese. 246 v.o.12 **Y 84**, 12 *bi taš yaratdurmaq üzä, angayu biltürdi ädrämin taibo atlγ balïq-ta* (≑ Chinese 245 r.u. 17) 'Through the establishment of the inscription stone he also let

大 饗   his virtue / piety be recognized in the city *Ta-hiang*.'†

According to this I would like to put once more the quote in *U II*: *qayu orunta bu darnïnï körkitdäči, angayu bititdäči, tutdäči . . . bar ärsär,* . . . 'wherever there are people, who show these *Dhāraṇī* and furthermore people who get them written, hold . . .' *angayu* has therefore a similar function as *ulat-ï, ym-ä*

---

† The Uigurish *taibo* must be a spelling mistake for **taiho.* † This symbol is to distinguish the editor's notes from A. von Gabain's.

and *yan-a*, and also its construction is the same. Yet, I cannot prove any *anga*. It could also be read as *nängä-, *nanga*.

1867. *aning ara* 'in the meantime'. At first glance *ara* appears to be missing *-sï* which is referring to the genetive. The basic meaning of this post-position [suffix] *ar-a* is *ar* 'to wander through'. Inscriptions *IS 5 süčig sabïn, yumšaq aγïn ar(ï)p* 'en s'insinuant par leur doux appel et leur richesses molles; they charmed through their sweet appeal and their soft splendours. (Instr.)'; *IE 6 ar-maq + či* 'trouble maker'; *TT VII 20, 16 irin iki-n ara* 'he is between the lips'; *U III 20, 5 yirlärig käzip arïp* 'wandering through the abodes'; *U III 60, 6 anï körüp, kök qalïγ üzä ardačï uluγ küčlüg tngri kišisingä inčä tip tidi* 'when he saw that, a great powerful god who moved through the [air] spoke to his spouse in the following manner'; *M III 30, 11 dïntarqa ara* 'among the elected [chosen] ones'.

p. 398   One forgot the basic meaning of the verb which is hidden in this post-position [suffix] and finally connected *ara*, like *arqa* or *öd*, to the genitive, and finally one understood it as a substantive (noun): *U II 23, 18 quwraγ ara-sïnta* 'in the crowd'.

1870. *äšid-gäli bol-*. **Ia.** The auxiliaries *är-* and *bol-* are mostly connected with nominal verb forms, whether they serve to form the various tenses, which indicate a long-lasting action, or whether they are to express the conditional: *amrar är-, aγinayurlar är-, bultï är-, alqyuq är-, alqïnmaz mu är-*, also *yaraγai* (noun?) *är-; qïlmïš bol-; arïyur ärsär, qïldïm ärsär, umaz ärsär*, etc.

Ib. In this context the expression *ögrätin-ü ärür* (line 2010) 'they are to be learnt thereby' is striking. **Y 2** r.6 *aqtar-u ärür biz* 'we are now to translate thereby'.

Y 104 4 *išlä-yü ärälim* 'we wish to work'. This is a rare construction which I will refer to later on.

Ic. Frequent—by way of contrast—is the combination *γalï bol-*, which occurs in our piece (work) in lines 1870, 1945, 2028, 2081, 2105, 2108 and 2138.

Raquette Chapter 41, p. 166g: *anaη kessäl bolsä öydin čiqïp ketgäli bolmaïdụ(r)* 'If your mother is ill, you cannot leave home'. In many other dialects 'can' is expressed through *-°p bol-* (*pol-*, kas. *bul-*). Compare WB (kas) *aša-p bul-a mï* 'can one eat this?' *kilïp bulmaz* 'he cannot come' (schor.) ρ*is ekü ödür-üp polban—čadïr* 'we could not kill him' (schor.) *mä münüp polarzïηma?* 'Can you mount me?' /

Still a couple of more examples from this biography which illustrate well the function of -*γalï bol-* as 'can'; **G 4,** 11 *qltï bu kraža ton bir-ki-ä kädgäli bolsar, timin ök tägimlig bolγai ärdi buyanlïγ tarïγlaγ tip* // *kügülgäli* = Chinese 237 v.u. 14: 'If one could only once wear this garment (K⁺) one would at once be worthy of being called 'the field of worthiness'; **G 14** r. 15 *tïltaγ tilägäli istäsär, tüpkärgäli bolmaz tözin tüpin* 'If one wishes to search for the reason one is not able to establish its root [origin];' **G 16,** 2 *ïnanmaqïnča⁺ köngülkä inčip ötkürgäli bolmaz* = Chinese 236 v.u. 10 'So long as one does not trust one's heart (*chitta*) one cannot, however, penetrate (understand); **G 16,** 5 *qatïγ kirtgünčlüg bolmaqïnča,⁺ ongarqalï bolmaz* 'So long as one is not a firm believer one cannot improve.

Following these examples I would also like to interpret *burχan-ïγ körgäli bolγailar* as 'they will then be able to see the Buddha'.

p. 399 Ic.1. a similar, almost identical function has -*u bol-*: **G 28,** 27 *örü bolmaz* 'one cannot pick up [raise]'.

Id. -*γu är-* appears to have more neutral meaning, line 2093 *küzäd-gü ärmäz* 'One does not watch out'; **G. 108** r.19 *sinχad-iwip-qa barγu ärsär, suw yolïn barmaq krgäksiz* = Chinese 223 v.o. 16 'As far as the going to Ceylon is concerned [lit. what concerns Ceylon going] one does not have to travel by the water way'. *U II* 17, 26 *qutrulγu är-* 'to be saved'.

Ie. About -*γuluq är-* and *γuluq bol-* in a later work!

IIa. In contrast to the auxiliaries the modal auxiliaries are connected with the forms of -*u* or -*γalï* 'will be able to'; *bol-γalï u-* 'to get to understand', *ärt-gäli oγra-* 'to plan to go past'; *bošur-γalï bir-* 'to let free'; *bol-u saqïn-* 'to intend to become'.

⁺*Kraža*—F.W.K. Müller (*U III* 38, 17; 53, 4) wanted to identify i with the Skt. *kāshāya*, the garment of the monks worn for assemblies (see Soothill-Hodous 76a). Actually that is certainly correct, but sound wise the connection is still not explained. Dr. Hansen referred me to *Kr'z'kh* (*Vessantara-jātaka* 1497) '*n'ant mnγz rty Zkwh kr'z'kh* (written wrongly in the publication as *kr'n'kh*) *mrγw w'sty*'. 'Ananda raised himself and straightened his garment.'

⁺-*qïnča*, not *γinča*!

⁺See footnote 28.

In our text we have the examples 1826 *ayït-u ïd-* 'to let ask' (= 1839, 2100) [but 1850 *bit-ip ïtzun* 'he may note down and send here'; *ïd* is not modal auxiliary here] *yir-ü qïl* (2092); *sözlä-yü u-* (2146); (1890) *tükät-gäli u-*; (2136) *körkit-gäli qïlïn-*; (1972) *anïtma-γalï kösä-*.

IIb. The difference between the use of -*u* or the more pointed *γalï* is clearer with the modal verbs which express respect. *yrlïqa-, tägin-, ötün-*. meaning 'most gracious' or 'acting most devotedly' is expressed as -*u yrlïqa-*, etc. (1831, 1841, 1851); however, 'to order to do', 'to request to be allowed to do' is expressed as -*γalï yrlïqa*, etc., for example 1856 *barγalï ötün-* 'to request permission to go'. In this case, that is in connection with -*γalï*, we are not dealing with modal verbs expressing respect but with modal auxiliaries.

IIb.1. Only the verbs of speech [speaking] stand in front of modal verbs expressing respect in the rigid form of -°*p: ti-p yrlïqadï*.

III. Furthermore, the descriptive verbs may be mentioned here. The nature of these verbs is such that they lose their own meaning completely when they are subordinated under a (logical) main verb, in order to determine more closely the range of this main verb; for example: *alta-yu tur-* 'to be in the habit of cheating', *qud-u tart-* 'to languish slowly', *küy-ü tut-* 'to protect constantly', *qïlu alq-* 'to make ready', *ayu bir-* 'to communicate (in every detail?)', *unïtu ïd-* 'to forget completely',—line 1995 *äwirä tur-* 'to be translating'; 2072 *käwilü tükät-* 'to be completely weakened', etc., but also *nomla-p qod-* 'to preach thoroughly', *ölüp bar-* 'to die slowly', *ärtip qal-* 'to go past for good'.

IIIa. These descriptive verbs are also used in constructions which have a future sense: *kir-gäli tur-* 'to be about to enter'; *ölgäli yat-* 'to be about to die now' but *TT V küzäd-gü tur-*.

IV. There is yet another connection of a finite verb with a verb form,—ending in -*u* which however has nothing to do with the connections mentioned so far: *sür-ä ïlt-* 'to kidnap', *qod-ï in-* 'to descend'; *qay-a kör-* 'to glance back'. Here the finite verb retains its basic meaning and the preceding verb in the -*u* form is a regular adverb that in German would be best expressed through a preposition. In our text there is *iltü bar-* in line 1857 'to go away', a **ilt-ip bar-* would mean a juxtaposition and not subordination. Likewise, 1910 *ör -ü tik-* 'to set up'; 2008 *kingür-ü yad-* 'to spread'.

All these are common knowledge and I have used up a lot of space for their presentation. However, I considered it useful to write down the system of the close verb subordinations in order to draw attention to the fine differences of meaning, and in order to evaluate the apparent irregularities. What is then the meaning of the above mentioned *ögrätin-ü är-*? Professor R. Hartman assumes two different words for *är-* In the first instance the auxiliary verb meaning 'to be' and secondly the word which is retained even today in osm. *är-* meaning 'to reach'. If we can assume in our example a main verb for *är-* which can occasionally degenerate to a descriptive verb, then the apparent irregularities which existed in the attempt to connect an auxiliary verb to an *-u-* form disappear. We would then have instead a descriptive verb which is quite regularly accompanied by an *-u-* form.

In the following [paragraph] I give examples of *är-* in which perhaps the meaning 'to be' is not there. In this manuscript: line 1882 *ärü ärü* = Chinese 漸 *tsien* 'by and by' (further off with the same Chinese sign in **Y 1** r.8; **G 35** r.23; **G 87**, 22; **G 101** r.10; **G 105**, 19); *är-iš-* (kom.krm. ad.osm.) 'to reach, to ripen'; *är-in* (*QB*) 'firm strong'; *erü* (kazak.) 'a place of halt, rest'; *ärinč* (Käš.) 'living well'; *är-t- U II* 22, 22 'to cease'. From the inscriptions: *II E* 19 *qaɣaninga ärmiš barmiš* 'to set oneself up against one's Qaɣan'; *I N* 1 = *II E* 29 *budun ärür barur äri-kli* (really not *-gli*) 'The people, when they were free and independent, . . .'

I therefore assume for our example in question a verb *är-* meaning 'to arrive', 'to get there', similar to the verb *täg-*. In connection with this, the very basic question as to the origin of auxiliary verbs generally arises. Is the auxiliary verb to be derived from this main verb?

1875. *mχabutlar*; the Skt. *mahābhūta* means first of all the four elements; then they mean as pointed out to me by Professor Lessing 'the physical condition'; as also in mong: *maχabut* Kow. 1979.

1876. Is *anta-qï-a oq* as attribute to the subject *kör-ün-mäz*? or is it to be taken as an adverbial definition of time: 'then', 'at once'?

1879. *qalangur-dï* may well have been formed as a synonym— composite together with the defective word which stands before it. *qal* (knowledge of healing I) meaning 'frenzy', madness; *qalï-* (Kāš.) 'to jump'; (ğaγ. old. tel. kazak.) *qala-* 'to inflame, also in the metaphorical meaning'; (tel.) *qalaηi* 'drunk'; bar.leb.) *qalaηna*, (old.tel.) *qalaηda-* 'to sway, to rock'. Here we then have *qal + a-η + ur-* before us.

1879. *biir* or *piir* < Chinese 筆 *pi* < B. Karlgren 1321 *pi̯ĕt* 'paint, brush', *bitig* 'Book' are both derived from the same Chinese word; this word has been borrowed twice, from two different Chinese dialects.

p. 401 **1879.** *maka* (*mäkä*?) Chinese 墨 *mo* < B. Karlgren 68 *mək* 'water colour' has been implied following *U III*, p. 92.

1880. *kim* is taken as a demonstrative pronoun:—*täg/* is per- haps to be taken as *tägmiš,: kim anta tägmiš*, is to be taken as an attribute to *öd qolu*.

1882. *isig bašlatï*; is not a *bol-γalï* or a *bol-u* missing before *bašla*? *-isig* is the translation of 暖 *nuan* 'warm, comfortable'. Also for the Turkish word the secondary meaning should be valid here—when Hsüan-tsang still lived in India, a revolt took place after the death of Śīlabhadra. In the meantime, peace returned gradually. (Compare Chinese text 225 r.u., Julien *'Life'*, p. 216).

1884. *nätäg inč mu ärki*. I would like to interpret the *nä* in *nätäg* as a generalizing word meaning 'to some extent' since the question has already been expressed through *mu*. Well known and often occurring is *nä* and its derivative in a condi- tional form as a generalization. But even without the conditional form it often has such generalizing meaning: Kāš *nämä ädgü kiši ol* 'how good he is' *WB* 667 (old), *nälä turγanïn pärïp qoidï* 'he gave everything—whatever he had' and below line 1895 *nä ymä tang* 'how surprising'.

1886. *drmagupdaki* < Skt. Dharmaguptaka. Dharmagupta was a second name of Śīlabhadra whose instruction Hsüan-tsang had enjoyed in Nālandā, compare *Ht V* 243 and *Ft* 1110 上 :. Out of respect one did not refer to Śīlabhadra by his name and instead called him 正 法 藏 *Chêng-fa-tsang*. *Fa-tsang* in our text = Dharmaguptaka, therefore does not mean here the founder of the sect named after him, but Śīlabhadra, the student of Dharmapāla.

1888. *qïyïl-* (Kāš.) 'to go down, to cease'.

1899. / / / *imiš* = Chinese 植 *chĭ-* 'to plant'.

1901. *köwšäk*; Suv. 619, 22 *körklä köwšäk* = 端 嚴 *tuan-yen* 'correct and adorned'; **G 90** r. 27 *idiz ädrämlig, king bošγutluγ, yawaš boš, bilgä köwšäk* = Chinese 224 r.u. 17 'of high talent, far reaching scholarship, gentle and free, wise and mild, 和 ; **Y 154**, 12 *sawï köwšäk* = Chinese 252 r.o. 6 言談雅亮 'his speech was fine and clear'; **G 59**, 11 *ančulayu ymä tngri iligimz qutï tümän-kä yitdäči bilgä biliglig, üč yirtinčü-kä tökädäči tüzün köwšäk qïlïqlïγ yrlïqar* = Chinese 245 v.o. 13, 伏惟皇帝陛下,智周萬物,仁霑三界 when one most humbly considers, then the majesty of our godly emperor is wise, so that he reaches out to all living beings and as he is of a mild and noble character (仁). so that he saturates the three worlds (*tökä* = 霑 *chan*; WB ²*tökün-* (ğaγ. V.) 'to be / saturated' ¹ *tögül-* (Uig.kazak.kom.) 'to be / emptied out'—both belonging to ²*tök-* (old . . .), ³*tük-* (kāš.sag.) 'to empty out'; here an addition to the stem can be assumed following the pattern of the very similar *tükä-* 'to come to an end' Bang, in 1917, already put together the family of this word (*Aus turkischen Dialekten*—From Turkish dialects p. 10, n. 2): *'käp, käb*; (osm.) *gäwšä-* 'to become tender'; *gäwšäk* 'soft'; *gäwrä*—'to become dry, hard and breakable'; *gäwräk* 'breakable, tender'; in addition now Kāš. *käwšäk ät* 'soft flesh', with a rounding (tel.) *köpšäk* 'easily breakable . . . ', (Kāš.) *köbšäk* > *küpšäk*

p. 402

'soft'. Side by side with *käp, kip, kib* can have existed (sag.koib.) *kibräk* 'breakable'; rounded to (azeri) *küwrä-* 'to become weak', *küwräk* 'weak', (kas.) *küpšäk* 'faded tender'. Whether the Kāšyāris rounded secondary form which also appears in our text originates from *käp* or *kip* one cannot know. Therefore it remains uncertain whether we should read *köwšäk* or *küwšäk*.

1905. *diwi* < Skt. (Ārya)deva; a student of Nāgārjuna from south India; the 15th Patriarch.

1907. *nagarčuni* < Skt. Nāgārjuna; the 14th Patriarch.

1909. *yana + la* = Chinese 再 *tsai* 'again', frequently in this text. A construction like *tün + lä, birlä*.

1922. *üč külüngü* = 三車 *san-ch'ê* = Skt. *triyāna* 'the three vehicles' are that of *Śrāvaka* or of the listener, that of the *Pratyekabuddha*, that is, of the one who saves himself and that of the Bodhisattva, who is the one who strives for the salvation of the whole world. They are symbolized through an antelope-cart, a *Marāla*-cart and an ox-cart (Eitel 157). For according to the smaller or bigger degree of their striving they need a small (Hīna), a medium (Madhyama) or a big (Mahāyāna) vehicle to cross over into nirvāṇa.

1924. *adïn nomluγlar* is the literal translation of 異道 *i-tao* 'the followers of dissenting teaching'.

1925. *'üzüldäči ol', 'mängü ol' ti-gli bitig*—'the books that say "that is destruction" or "that is eternal" ' *Ft* 2833 middle. The view about the impermanence or the permanence of the body and of the soul is a heretical conception—the second of 'the 5 bad views' 五惡見 *wu-o-kien'*. According to the *Nirvāṇa-sūtra,* Ch. 27, the right path is *chung-tao* [the middle path], the concept of a 'non-existence' and of a 'non-passing away'.

1929. *muima-l-* 'to be confused'; Kāš. *boimaš-* 'to become confused'; G 38, 17 *muyum adïrtsïz* = 混 *hun* 'confused' one has to add a *muyum + a-*.

1936. *yaqa* means first of all 'collar'. In Chinese there is here 袖 *siu-* meaning 'sleeve'. This is also used to express 'highest authority'. Professor Haenisch has brought to my attention that in Chinese 領 *ling* 'collar' as well as *siu-* 'sleeve' can have the meaning of 'highest authority'.

Examples for *yaqa* with this meaning are **G 15**, r.12 *yaqalarïn yïγïnturup* = Chinese 236 v.u. 7 斂衽 'to have the highest ones gather', **G 29** r.8 *yiwäki yaqasï* = Chinese 235 r.o. 10 領袖 *ling-siu* 'collar and sleeve' that is 'leaders'.

1936. *artuqraq* to **1943** *alqïnčsïz* translated into Chinese

加以恂恂善誘、曉夜不疲、衢罇自盈、酌而不竭、

Apart from that he knew how to lead in an honest manner, day and night without fatigue. 'At the cross roads the jugs are filling themselves of their own accord; they are poured out and they never become empty'. It is obvious that this is a quotation—perhaps I have overlooked other fine allusions of the famously educated Hsüan-tsang! For the proof of these references I thank Professor Haenisch: *Lun-yü* IX 10 (Legge p. 84) 夫子循循然善誘人 'The master by orderly method skillfully leads men on.' Hsüan-tsang has written for 循 'step by step' the homonym 恂 meaning *Huai-nan Tsŭ*

聖人之道、猶中衢而設耶、過者斟酌、各得其宜、

The method of the holy ones is as if they put down jugs at the crossroads. The passers-by drink from them and everyone receives sufficient.

For the entire sequence Professor Haenisch reminds us of the refreshing drink which even today is placed in small pavilions along the sunny country of south and central China for exhausted travellers and which may have the symbolic meaning of 'spiritual refreshment'.

1948. *qamγaq* according to Kāš. and in *TT I* is interpreted as 'garlic'. For that Radloff gives the word 'salsula

p. 403

oppositifolia'; compare Le Coq *Osttürkische Pflanzennamen* (East-Turkish plant name), p. 9: 'salsola collina'—This is a favourite image in the Chinese language; compare with Haenisch / *Lehrgang der Chinesischen Schriftsprache* / Course of instruction in the Chinese written language Lektion 59: 蓬生林中不扶自直 'when weed grows in the middle of hemp, it does not need any support, but stands upright by itself.' Our word 'hemp' is probably related to *kän* (*tir*), compare V. Hehn, *Kulturpflanzen und Haustiere* / Cultivated Plants and Domesticated Animals, 8th ed., 1911, p. 192.

1961. *istä-yü saqïn* = 追惟 to pursue in thought'. This means that in *istä-* the basic meaning 'to follow' is still felt. (A derivative of *iz-* 'track'.)

1968. *yop-l-un-*; compare *yoba-* (tar.) 'to be tired'; *yobal-* (tar.) 'pain'; *yóbal-* (kir.) 'to be tortured'; *yoballïg* (koib.) 'while suffering pain'.

1973. *anït-*; Chinese 裁抑 *ts'ai-i* 'to limit / to confine' (therefore negation already in the concept of the verb); *WB aniq-* (ğay) 'to increase'. That could be an intensive verb from an **anï-* 'to continue'. From there then our causative verb.

1974. *uluɣ tuimïs* 'The great enlightened one', translated by the Chinese 大覺 *Ta kio*; that is Skt. Mahābuddha 'the great awakened one'.

1974. *yrlï* comes superfluously at the end of the line instead of the expected *kirü*.

1977. *šanawazi* < Skt. Śāṇavāsa, the third Patriarch. He came from Mathurā and is supposed to have lived 100 years after the Buddha's *nirvāṇa*.

1978. *upagupdi* < Skt. Upagupta, the 4th Patriarch, is supposed to have died in 335 BC. He also lived in Mathurā.

1981. *irt-gü*, reading uncertain, although well preserved 将 ≐ *tsiang* 'guidance'; would well belong *Kāšɣarïs ärt* 'to pass said about time' *U III* 4, 14—'to set forth / to continue'.

p. 404 **1989.** *biš taɣlar* = 五 山 Wu-shan. The Buddhist 'Five holy mountains' of China which lie in the 5 directions of the sky, only since the time of the 5 dynasties have they been counted in this way according to (*Tsŭ-yüan*). Hsüan-tsang is referring here to their honoured example, the 5 holy mountains in India, upon which important scenes in the Buddha's life took place (Southill-Hodous p. 117a).

1990. *abamu* = ˙永 *yung* 'eternal' likewise in **G 15**, 12. **Y 16**, 23: *uluɣ türlüg abamu klp-qa tägi* = Chinese 239 v.u. 11 (寂寥) 無 紀 'without counting of time (without measuring time)'.

1992. *yoog šastr* is Chinese 瑜 伽 師 地 論 *Yü-kia-shĭ-ti-lun* ˙= Skt. *Yogācārya-bhūmi śāstra*; B. Nanjio 1170. It is the basic work of the *Yogācārya* school.[26] This book incidently exists in fragments also in Uigurish in Berlin.

1994. *amtï košawrti šastr-ïɣ äwirtsär, w (?) šastr birlä äwirä turur biz* 'If we now translate the *Košawrti śāstra* we are also at the same time translating the X *śāstra*.' In Chinese it is written 'The *K'ü-shê* (and) the *Shun-chêng-li* are being translated'.

The name *košawrti* could also be read in the difficult to decipher *TT V B* line 84 *küšälun atlɣ košawrti šastr* 'the 俱 舍 論 *k'ü- shê-lun* called *košawrti śāstra*.'

Because of the unclarity surrounding -wrti < Skt. *vṛtti*, 'Commentary' one asks oneself if B. Nanjio 1267, 1269 or 1270 is meant; our text tells us that this work is supposed to have been translated by Hsüan-tsang; thus 1269 is eliminated. 1267 阿 毗 達 磨 俱 舍 論 *O-pi-ta-mo k'ü-shê-lun*, Skt. *Abhidharmakośaśāstra* is a work by Vasubandhu. 1270: *O-pi-ta-mo k'ü-shê-lun pên-sung* 阿毗達磨俱舍論本頌 skt. *Abhidharmakośakārikā* is by the same author.

---

[26]Should be *Yogāchāra-bhūmi śāstra* and *Yogāchāra*. See above p. 30n.

The work 順正理 *Shun-chêng-li*, the name of which is totally ruined in Uigurish is B. Nanjio 1265: 阿毗達磨順正理論 *o-pi-ta-mo shun-chêng-li lun*, skt. *Nyāyānusāraśāstra* by Saṅghabhadra, a contemporary of Vasubandhu. As Nanjio remarks explicitly that this work contains a polemic against the work of Vasubandhu B. Nanjio 1267 (and 1269) and as furthermore the words of the Turkish text lead us to assume a contrast between both the works mentioned with us, one should initially accept the *košawrti*, B. Nanjio 1267, especially as one would not describe *kārikā* 'verses' as *vṛtti*.

1997. *tükä-mä-gäi*, 'it will not be finished'. However in Chinese it appears as 'it will be definitely finished'.

1998. 'The emperor' is inserted according to the Chinese text. It is emperor 高宗 Kao-tsung whose first reign title commenced in 650 (line 1855).

2000. *amïrtγur-yungla-* must be, according to the Chinese 安寧 *an-ning* 'to pacify and to soothe', a synonymous composite of the verb to be. *yung + la* 'to consume' mentioned in old Indian is derived from 用 *yung* 'to use etc.'. Our *yung + la*—however could be traced back to 雍 *yung* 'harmony'.

p. 405 **2005.** An example for this double *utru*: **Y 108**, 9 *utru bulmïš* / / / *utru üläyür ärdi* = 251 v.u. 2 隨得隨散 'as soon as (they) received (the texts) they distributed them'.

2011. *qalïnču čöp öd*, Chinese 像運之末 *siang-yün-chĭ-mo* 'the end of the period of similes (or images)'. See Eitel 106a s.v. *Saddharma pratirūpaka*: The age (period in history) of each Buddha consists of 3 periods. The first of them in age of the Buddha Śākyamuni, that of the 'true teaching' lasted for 500 years counting from his *nirvāṇa*. The second period, that of the teachings of similes or images should last for 1000 years. The last, that of 'the later teachings' will last for 3000 years.

čöp (Kāš) 'yeast of wine and things like that' therefore sediments, residue (ğaɣ. kir. old. tel. leb.) 'rubbish' . . . dirt'; (kas. kūr) *čüp*—likewise (kazak.schor.) *šöp*, (küär) *tsöp* 'fish bones', (bar.) 'rubbish', (tara) *tsüp* likewise and so on. An intensive word of this is (Kāš) *čöbik* (see s.v. *čübik*) = *šöbik* (s.v. *šübik*) 'the fruit peel'; (kazak.) *šübök* 'wine disposal tubes for very small children' (schor.) *šöbäg* 'the hard cover of the hemp-stalk'. The general idea of *čöp, čöbik* etc., is therefore 'the remaining, the outer cover'.

čöbic was already covered by another technical term: *U* 14, 3 *bu kälyük bulɣanyuq biš čöbik y(a)wlaq öd* and in connection with it the explanation in *U II* p. 91. This 'present confused and bad time of the 5 empty forms' is that in which (*Ta-Ming san-tsang fa-shu* p. 167 v.) one after another living beings, their opinions, their passions, their life span, and their whole *kalpa* are being depressed (according to the Chinese version).

qalïnču 'to leave behind, to stay back'. Compare **G 23** v.6 *qalïnču nom* = Chinese 234 r.u. 16 遺法 *i-fa* 'The teachings left behind', **G 21** r.24 *qalïnču nom* = 242 v.u. 6遺 *i*; **G 37** r.19 *qalïnču söz* 餘論 'The remaining words' **Y 14** r. 9 *qalïnču nom*.

2029. yuqa = Chinese 薄 po, 'scarce' (Kāś. ğaɣ) *yuqa*, (osm. ad.) *yukha* 'thin'.

2041. *osmaq suwsamaq*; Chinese 傾渴 *k'ing-ho* 'to overthrow (or destroy; to confuse) and to thirst'. Instead of *os-, us-* one can also read *ïs-* or *is-* here. I read *os-*, because I place it with (old.tel.) *os-* 'wilt, wither away'.

2047. *qap*; Kāš. 'tube / pipe / hose, pot, hewn, (old.tel.) sack, bag / purse, sheath'.

2049. To the *uyat- aiman-* 'to be ashamed' is the dative of cause referring at the beginning of line 2050. Then *köngül-ümüz* must be a mistake for *-üngüz*.

2052. Here perhaps *öd qolu* is missing according to the Chinese 節氣 meaning 'time, period'.

2055.   *nom-luγ ät 'üzüngüz* literally 'your Law-Self'. This form of politeness is not to be traced back to Chinese.

2059.   *toquz bölüg nomlar* = 九部之經 *kiu-pu-chï-king,* 'the *Sūtra (piṭaka)* of nine sections, parts' (Soothill-Hodous:) *Sūtra* 'Buddha's sermons', *geya* 'metric texts'; *vyākaraṇa* 'prophecies'; *gāthā* 'poems', *udāna* 'unrequested / speeches', *ityukta* 'stories', *jātaka* 'stories of previous births', *vaipulya* 'long *Sūtras*', and *adbhutadharma* 'wonderous'.

p. 406   **2060.**   The highly uncertain addition *tiristirt-* < *tir-* 'to collect', *-is + i-t-ir-t-* according to the Chinese 引 *yin* 'to lead (on)'.

2062.   *küdän* 'guest' added according to the Chinese 客 *k'o.*

2064.   *qarn + ïn yawalmïs* (one could of course also read *yayal-* and *yäwäl-) yadlar* = 鍱腹之賓 *ye-fu-chï pin.* 'The strangers who have armour around the stomach'. (*Ft.* 2793, Soothill-Hodous 463): The Nirgrantha-puttra 薩遮祇 *Sa-chê-k'i* was of the opinion that the stomach was the seat of wisdom. That is why he protected it carefully against wounds with his begging bowl, even though he despised all other clothing.

The *-l-* in *yawal-* will allow no accusative construction therefore *qarnïn* must be Instr. I therefore place *yawa-l-* with Kāš. *yawra* 'to grow in strength' < *yaw-ïr + a-.* A derivative of *yawal* is the frequent *yawlaq* 'very'. G **102**, 18 *yäg-ig yawaltur-u yrlïqadï* = 降薄藥叉 'he conquered the *Yakśa*'.

2065–66.   An allusion to the embarrassment of his adversaries at the gathering in Kanyakubja, which took place in the presence of 18 kings.

2074.   *ädräm-lig ayaγ čiltäg* 'The wholly deserved adulation'; a polite form of address as in osm. *hazretleri* 'Your Excellency'.

2084.   *otγuraq qïl* = 定 *ting* 'to state / to determine' *Kāš. oδyar-* 'to realize after long consideration'. Both must (according to a note by Bangs hand in his Brockelmann- Kāš.- copy) have originated from *oδ + ïγ-ar-, oδ + ïγ-ur-. oδ:* WB ²*ot,* read *od*

(Uig.) 'thought'; *oi* (tel.schor. . . .) 'understanding'; ^2ui (kas.) 'opinion'. **Y 26**, 10 *mn huintso üč yitmiš yašatïm; otγuraq bu yïl bu sangramda ät'üz qotγai mn.* 'I Hsüan-tsang have lived for 63 years, certainly I shall this year in this monastery relinquish my body.' In the Chinese version we find 251 r.o. 15 必當 *pi tang* 'certainly'.

2087. *qïl-ïmsï-n-* 'to behave·oneself, as (if) one would do'. Compare (Kāš.) *külümsin-* 'to act as if one is laughing'; (kazak) *qïlïmsï-* 'to dress up oneself, to flirt'; (osm.) *gülümsä-* 'to smile'. Further with Rachmati *TT VII* Nr. 42, 5 *bäg + i-msin-* 'to be Beg'; *at + a-q + ï-msïn-* 'to be famous'.

2088. *yarïm nom* = 半敎 *pan-kiao* 'the half teaching' in **Y 17**, 10 we find *siošing nomï* 'Hīnayāna' (239 r.u. 18) for the same 半敎.

2091. *idiz buqai* = 高下 *kao-hia* 'the high and the' low' that is 'the measure' **Y 83a** r.7 *buqai* = 卑 *pei* 'low, mean'.

Is *-o-* to read? Doubtfully, I place the following words here as the construction is not clear to me: *boqai* (Vámbéry, *Ćagat. Sprachstudien* / Studies in Language, p. 248, that is then east Turkish; 'calf'; *boγoni* (Kowalewski) 'not raised, low'; (kir. ğaγ. V.) *baqai* 'bones above hoof'; (ğaγ. V.) likewise 'shin bone of the sheep'? *baγalaq* (kir.) 'trouser leg', *baγalčaq* (kir.) 'ankle-joint of the horse'; *paqalčaq* (ot. tar.) 'shin bone, fetlock (ankle bones) of the sheep'.

p. 407 **2095.** *urunt* translates the 解 as *cho*, which means initially 'to butt with horns', the secondary meaning is also 'to offend'.

2099. *kšanti* might have come from skt. *kṣānti* or *kṣānta*. Both share the same root *kṣam*, 'to bear'. The noun means originally 'patience, forbearance, endurance'; as techn. term, *kṣānti* is the 3rd of the 6 virtues (*pāramitā*).

a. In Uigurish *kšanti* is proven to mean *Pāramitā* in *Suv.* 322, 7. Very often the translation *särinmäk*, 'toleration', is used instead of the foreign word, for example, in the thorough discussion of the *Pāramitās* in chapter IV pp. 207, 18; 208, 1; 225, 21; 229, 9.

b1. We will disregard this basic meaning of the word here. *Kšanti* very often also means 'forgiveness' in the Uigurish texts. Different from the osm., use of the language *'afv et-* 'to make forgiveness', i.e. to forgive oneself, one says here *kšanti qïl-* with the meaning 'to make forgiveness', that is, 'to cause forgiveness', for example *ökün-ü . . . kšanti qïl-tilar* 'confessing . . . they caused forgiveness' U II 76, 10; 77, 20; TT IV A 7; 14; 18; B 34; 67; S. p. 193 note; 2; 58; 64; 78; 83; 95.

As a reply it is said about the congregation *kšanti bir dilär* 'They granted forgiveness' TT IV A 8. *tižit kšanti bol-zun* = 'Let there be confession (*tižit*) and (therewith) forgiveness (*kšanti*)'. TT IV A 33; 42; 52; 66; B 36; 40; 66; note B 1; S. A 40; U II 76, 11; 77, 20; 79, 52; 85; 19; 88, 73. 'The congregation is imploring for forgiveness': *kšanti ötün-* TT IV B 65; U II 85, 18; 85, 29; 86, 38; TT IV B footnote 42; S. 58; or *kšanti qol-* U II 88, 71.

'May they find confession and forgiveness': *tižit kšanti bul-* S. 62; 65; 67; 73; 80.

'Cherish regret and engender forgiveness': *mung kai qïlu kšanti qïl-* S. A 24.

b2. Secondarily, it then means a prayer with which one blots out all one's sins in all the prescribed forms; also *kšanti*: *kšanti nom* U II 80, 63; *kšanti qïlmaq nom* U II 79, 57; *kšanti bitit-* U II 89, 83.

b3. and finally, the confession together with the prescribed ceremonies, the official confession, is also called *kšanti:* U II 79, 53 *kšanti qïlïp, qïlïnčïm . . . qalïr ärsär*. TT IV B 37 *qltï nätäg bizing qïlïnčïmïz—kšanti qïlïp—nätäg arïyur ärsär* also 41 *ol bizing—kšanti qïlïp—arïmaduq ayïγ qïlïnčïmïz* also 49 *bu mäning kšanti qïlïp—arïmaduq tsui irinčülärim.* S. 71 *qaltï näčük . . . ayïγ qïlïnčlarïn—kšanti čamχui qïlïp—nätäg arïttïlar ärsär.* S. A 41 *öngdünki qïlïnčlarïmïn—kšanti qïlïnïp—ökünü.* S. A 48 *qïlïnčïm ärsär . . . arïzun, kšanti qïlïp—ärtgülük bolzun.*

This *kšanti* is occasionally used like a synonym composition together with *čamχui* (*S.* 64; 71, 78; 83) However these two words are not identical. *Čamχui* is always *kšanti* but *kšanti* is only occasionally *čamχui*. For *čamχui* < *ch'an-huei* 懺 悔 is confession but not forgiveness. 懺 *ch'an* is, as O. Franke has shown us in his *Tempelinschrift aus Idikutšahri* (Temple Inscription from Idikutsahri), p. 60, a sign which has been created for the transcription of an Indian word. It must not be

p. 408 translated as *kšamā* but *kṣānti* or, according to a hand-written note as *kšānta*, therefore forgiveness (F.W.K. Muller, *U II* p. 89). 悔 *huei* is 'to repent'. 懺 悔 therefore literally means 'forgiveness (which produces) repentance'.

In the same way (F.W.K. Muller, *loc. cit.* Jaschke) the Tibet. *gśog-pa sdig-pa* (*nyés-pa, ltung-ba*) is constructed 'to confess a sin and thus to expiate it'.

The confessions of laymen belonged by no means to the oldest usage of the Buddhists. 'The *Sūtra* of the Golden Gleam' contains some confessional prayers, but it surely does not originate from the pre-Kushana period. Now which are the models for the many Uigurish and Chinese lay confessional prayer songs? Where and when do *kšānti* or *kšānta* occur in the Indian language first in the meaning of 'forgiveness of (sins)' and as 'confession'?

F.W.K. Muller has already referred to the similarity in the Turkish (language) between the Manichaean and Buddhistic lay confessional mirror. As the oldest Chinese lay confessional prayer in Buddhism originated already from the middle of 2nd century, he assumed that it was borrowed by the Manichaean from the Indian religion (that text, incidentally, was translated by an Arsaked. Perhaps it is in reality his own work). Now we must not forget the Zoroastrian *patīts*, to which Bang refers in his *Manichäischen Laienbeichtspiegeln* / 'Manichaean lay confessional mirrors' on page 140. Unfortunately, they do not appear to be datable. Many of the ideas expressed therein (Spiegel, *Avesta II* pp. LVIII–LXII; *III* pp. 207 and 215) one also finds in the Manichaean and Buddhist confessional prayers. For how long was Zoroastrian religion strong enough to influence other religions? (N.S. Nyberg, *'Die Religionen des alten Iran /*

'The religion of old Iran', the German version by H.H. Schaeder, *Mitt.d. vorder-asiat.-ägypt. Gesellschaft* / Journal of the Near-Eastern-Egyptian Society, vol. 43, Leipzig 1938, p. 485) assures us that even in the 11th century under the Islamic rule the country people in the eastern part of the Caliphate professed this religion. In AD 630, Hsüan-tsang testifies that the Turks from Toqmaq were exclusively fire worshippers, although 200 years earlier in the east, in Turfan, a Hunnish prince had already been a zealous Buddhist (O. Franke, *Tempelinschrift*, p. 25). A proof of the battle against the fire cult is the Magician fragments in *UI*, see specially p. 8: The magicians had been so foolish as to hurl into a well a stone clawed out of the [sacred] crib. At that moment, from the depth of the shaft shone a fiery brilliance. Frightened, they realized that they had thrown away a priceless thing, and since then they revere fire. What it proves is that the fire cult was created out of an unfortunate delusion. The truth lies with the one who had given this priceless wonderous stone, with Christ. Such a version, would have remained without any interest in a non-Zoroastrian mission area.

The earliest translators of the Chinese Buddhist canon, those of the 2nd–4th centuries, came mostly from the originally Zoroastrian area. B. Nanjio mentions that out of 57 earliest translators 4 are from Parthia, 5 from Samarkand, 7 from Kabul and 8 from Yüë-chï. It would not have been surprising if Buddhism had been handed down to Central and East Asia with Zoroastrian colouring.

p. 409 One should remember the names of the Zoroastrian Gods which, in Uigurish, as *Qormuzda* and *Äzrua* represent the Buddhist *Brahmā* and *Indra*. Already the rule of the Kushana kings can have caused Buddhism, which was strongly promoted by them, to receive ideas from the Iranian religion. I do not feel myself to be competent in the field of religious-historical questions. With these comments I only wish to draw anew the attention of specialists to the early medieval and Central Asiatic forms of Buddhism. Can one derive all these lay confessionals from the Zoroastrian examples?

2104. *anupadat*, Chinese 阿耨達 *O-nu-ta*; compare in this manuscript **G 15** r.22 *ötrü anupudat yuul suwïn ötkürdi twγač ilining säkiz uluγ arqularïnta* = Chinese, p. 236 v.u. 9

遂使阿耨達水通神甸之八\川 'At that he
let the waters of the *A*. lake to penetrate into the eight great rivers
of the Chinese empire.' That was not a deed of water-technology
but a holy deed.

Phonetically this should refer to the Anavatapta lake in Pamir
(Julien, *Mémoirs* II, p. 23). In *Si-yü-ki* thermal springs are mentioned whose waters with medicinal properties are said to have
originated in this lake. Watters (p.35) is surely right when he
assumes that there is another supernatural blessing-giving lake,
besides the real one. It is certainly the one at which the Buddha
once stayed with disciples and gods and where he worked a
miracle.

2111.   *kip*; (Kāš.) *kib* 'pattern'; Mongolian (Ramstedt. *Kalmü-
kisches Wörter-buch / Kalmucean Dictionary*, Helsingfors 1935,
p. 222) *keв* 'form, model, pattern'.

2118.   / / / *inčlig*; completion? Chinese 恨 *hên* 'to regret /
deplore'.

2119.   *täring*, completed according to 深 *shên* 'deep'.

2123.   *sutsï*, writing mistake for *tutsï* **G 18** r.23 *tutsï*
yaruqluɣ as *t*, 'full of radiance' Chinese 水精 *shuei-tsing* is
according to *Ts'u-yüan*= 水晶 'rock crystal'.

2124.   *sparir*, according to Dr. Hansen < Toch. B Spharir < Skt.
sphaṭika 'rock crystal'.   The   Chinese transcription頗胝
p'o-chĭ (or *ti*; as the fourth listing K'ang-hi gives for this sign
the pronunciation 丁計 *ting-ki* = *ti*) goes directly back to
the sanskrit.

2150.   *huilip*, completes in spite of a defect **G 67**, 18 *üč aqïlïɣ*
nom ötkürmiš **huilip** *taisï.—huilip* < 慧文 ; *Huei-li*; 文 : B.
Karlgren 524 *lịəp*.

2152.   *kintsung*, read *g-*, *h-*? < 彦悰 *Yen-ts'ung*.— 彦 B.
Karlgren 240 *ngịän*, sino-japan. *gen*.

2156. In G 54, r.18. In another colophon the title sounds somewhat different. A fact which as far as is known, does not go back to a Chinese model: 'bodistw taito samtso ačarï-qa twɣač qan bašlap, qamaɣ bäg-lär ayamïš-ïn aɣïrlamïš-ïn uqïtmaq atlɣ . . . 'in the name of those who teach reverence for the Bodhisattva, the Tripiṭaka master of the great T'ang (dynasty) (which is) shown by the Chinese emperor at the top and all the noblemen'.

Index*

abamu eternal *1990*
  a. *-luq kič* 1990
Ablativ *birtin köröm* 1796
adïn otherwise, else
  a. *nomluɣ* heretic 1924. **1924**
adru- choose, select 1902
adverb **1870**
  ilt-ü bar- 1857
  ör-ü tik- 1910
ai o! 1896. 1918
anɣïp? 2052
angayu ('*nangayu*', '*nängäyü*'?) in future, henceforth, furthermore. **1859**. 1859
  a. *yana 1859*
angsïz restless, very (?) a. *uyat-* 1802
anït- to continue, to pursue 1973. **1973**
anta + qïa oq 1876. **1876**
antïn from there 2136
anupadat, *anupudat* < Skt. *Anavatapta*; name of a lake / sea 2104. **2104**
aqtar- to translate *1870*. 2005
aqtur- to go up, to rise 1967
ar- to wander through / to diffuse / to enter by force, invade, infiltrate *1867*
ara between **1867** *anïng a.* in between 1867
  -qa a. 1867 irin iki + n a. 1867
  barïš käliš a. -sïnta 2089
arqu river, stream, current
  säkiz uluɣ a. -lar 2104
artuq more
  otuz a. bölüg 1993
aruq to drain / to exhaust 1914
awatïn s. *intin*!
ädräm gain, profit. *uluɣ ä.-lig* = Skt. *bhadanta* 1767. 1838. 1903. 2125
äntkäk sporadic for *änätkäk* 2077
är- Auxiliary: to be / exist

-ɣu är- ought to, duty 1870 -ɣuluq är- must *1870*
är- arrive; descrip. verb *ä.-ü ä.-ü* by and by 1882. 1870 2039. 2053
är- bar-. come and go, i.e. behave **1870**
  örgrätin-ü (u.a.) *är-* (descrip.) 1870. **1870**. *1870*.
ärinügsüz indefatigable 1939
ärkän being 1790. **1790**. 2022. 2142 (in *A. Ind.* carry after, add: *TT I 124³*).
ärki welfare, prosperity 1829. **1829**. 1884. 1941. 1942. 1960. 1970. 2056. 2127.
ärt- surpass, excel (masculine locative) 2116
ärü s. *är-*!
äsän Peace, healthy 1874. 1956. 2043
äsängü undamaged, wholly, totality. **1819** *ä. bitig* 1819. *1819*. 1863. 2035. 2043.
äsängülä- to enquire about something oneself 1825
äwätin s. *intin*!
äwir- translate 1993. 1994. 1995. 2156
bal- to join, to bind oneself *üstäl- b.* 1873
barïš the departure, progress. *b. käliš* 2089
bältir cross roads. 1939
bältir cross roads. 1939
bi < 石卑 *pei* inscription stone. *b. taš 1859*
biir < 筆 *pi < pi̯ĕt* brush 1879. **1879**.
bil- to know *biš bilgä bilig b.-mäk* **1774**. 1775
biläg gift, present **1843**. 1883. 2054 *b.ötüg* 1843 *yantud b.* 1859
bilil- to become known *b.-ür* 2097
bir once *bir yangliɣ* 1781 unanimous *b.-tin körüm*

*[s – see; n – neuter; Sie – you (2nd pl. Nom. & Acc.); A. Ind. – Ancient India]

one-sidedness, partiality, narrow-mind-
edness 1796
b.wrkharlïγ toyïn co-brother 1807 *b.-kiä
adrïl-* 1866
b.-täm 1962
biš five *b. taγlar* 1989. **1989**
b. bilgä bilig bilmäk The five sciences.
1774. **1774**
b.-inč yïl 1855. **1855** *b. balïq* 2154
bitig letter, Book *äsängü b.* 1819 *taš b.*
1773. *1773*
bklä- tie up, lace 1859. **1859**
bodiram s. *mkha b.*!
bol- to become; 1870 Auxiliary verb *-γalï
b.* . . . 1870 to be able to *1870*. **1870**.
1945. 2028. 2081. 2105. 2108. 2138
-u b. to be able to *1870*
-γuluq bol- . . . must 2133
bošγun Instruction *widis b.* 1785
böz cotton cloth, bales of cotton cloth 1844
iki b. 1810. **1810**. 2047
buqai low 2091 *idiz b.* 2091
buranč fragment 2128
bügüš wisdom 2058

čal- beat 1911

čamkhui < 懺 悔 *ch'an-huei*   pardon,
repentance **2099**
čitawan < Skt. *Jetavana č. sangram* 2017
čkrawart < Skt. *cakravarttī č. ilig χanlar*
2001.
čöbik empty form and things like that *biš č.*
2011
čöp the remaining outside **2011** *qalïnču č.
öd* 2011
d- nominal 1857
da there also 2112
deskriptive verbs 1870
-u tur-, tart-, tut-, alq- etc. rarer
-°p qod-, bar-, qal- means etc.
-γalï tur- futurish *-γu tur-*
Dialekte handwriting, signature **1826**
dirgadrmi < Skt.   Dīrghadharma   1808.
1835. 1855. 1873. 2042
diwi < Skt. *Deva* **1905** *d. bodistw* Bodhisattva (Ārya) deva 1905
drmagupdaki < Skt.   Dharmaguptaka
1886. **1886**. 1897.

Denominale + *γu-Nomina. 1819*

Hilfsverben 1870 Auxiliary with nominal
connected verb form *1870*
-γalï bol- . . . to be able to *1870*. **1870**
-u bol- . . . to be able to **1870**
-γu är- **1870** *-γuluq är-, -γuluq bol-* *1870*
Höflichkeitsanrede sermon on politeness
nomluγ ät 'üzüngüz 2055
ädrämlig ayaγ čiltäg 2074
χuastuanift < parth.; Manichaean confessional prayer *2099*

huilip < 慧 立   *Huei-li* < **lip;*   Student of Hsüan-tsang 2150. **2150**

ïčïn torch 1909
ïd- to send modified auxiliary verb to let
2145
-p ïd- 1850. 2024. 2144 *-u ïd-* 1826. 1839.
2100
ïdï thoroughly (followed by Negation)
1776. 1806
ič inner *i. ta's nom*1933
ikiläyü anew, (not for the second time)
1908
inanprbi < Skt. *Jñāna-prabha* 1767 (?).
1767. 1838. 1850. 1866
inč. well being, good health 1828
intin (*äwätin, awatïn*?) 1810. **1810**
i. qïdïγ 1810
ir < 乙   *i* < *ïět* **1764**
i. tawïšqan kün 1764
irt- to continue **1981**. 1981
irtä in the mornings 1966
i.-kän betimes, early 2130
isig warm and comfortable 1882. **1882**.
1883
isil- to lessen oneself 2076
isin- treasure 1953
istä- to ponder about, traces (tell-tale
marks), to wish *1870*. 1961. **1961**

Kanyakubči < Skt. Kānyakubja, name of
a city 1799. **1799**. 2079
käčgüläg fort (mistake for *-gülük*?) *k.
käčüg 1810*
käčüg fort *1810*

käliš the coming *bariš k.* 2089

käntir hemp 1948. **1948**

käwil- to weaken 2072

kič for long 1990. 2040

kičä night 1965

kičig small *uluɣ k. külüngülär* = Mahā- and Hīnayāna 1773

kigür- to lead inwards *1859*

kim demonstrative 1880
    because 2118
    with that 2024

kimi ship 1891

king broad *k. qïsqa* length 2129

kingürt- to further, to comment 2153.

kingürü far 2008.

kintsung (*h-, g-?*) < 彦悰 *Yen-ts'ung*, commentator of this biography 2152. **2152**

kip example, sample, model **2111** *yang k.* 2111

košawrti šastr = 阿毗達磨俱舍論 *O-pi-ta-mo kü-shê-lun* < Skt. Abhi-dharmakośaśāstra, B. Nanjio Nr. 1267. 1994. **1994**

köntül- to be erected, set up, 1949

körünč view, opinion 1831. **1831**

köwšäk soft, milk, fine **1901** *king k.* 1901

kraža < soghd. *kr'z'kh* *monk's garment **1870**
    k.ton 1870

krgäksiz not necessary *1870*

kšanti < Skt. kshānta or kshānti; forgive-ness, acknowledgement, confessional prayer, confession, 3rd of the 6 virtues. 2099. **2099**

küdän guest 2062.

kügül- called, to be praised *1870*

külä- to prize 1957. 2114

külüngü vehicle, craft *üč k.* 1922. **1922** *uluɣ kičig k.-lär* 1773

küntüz daily 2030 *tünlä k.* 1939

küšälun < 俱舍論 *kü-shê-lun* = *Abhidharmakośa śāstra* B. Nanjio Nr. 1267. **1994**. °1-nominal *1929*.

lim < 懍 *lin* < **li** m rafter, beam 1921.

madar toch.-kuc. *matār* < Sak. < Skt. *makara* **1809**

magad < Skt. Magadha *m.-lïɣ* 1864

maka < 墨 *mo* < *mak* water colour 1879 (?). **1879**

mängsät- to resemble, to be comparable 1989. 2108

mängü always, eternal 1926.

mχa bodiram sangram < Skt. *Mahābodhi ārāma saṅghārāma* 1766. **1766**. 1814. 2036.

mχabut < Skt. *mahābhūta* elements, finds 1875. **1875**

mχa činatiš < Skt. *Mahācīnadeśa* the great land of China 1819.

mχakašip < Skt. Mahākāśyapa, Buddha's student 1975

Modale Auxiliaries *-u* or *-ɣalï oɣra-, bir-, u-, saqïn-* etc. **1870**. *1870*

mokšadiwi < Skt. Mokṣadeva—reveren-tial title of Hsüan-tsang from the side of the Hīnayāna 1799. 1824. 1851

°msi- do as if one . . . **2087**

muimal- to be confused 1929. **1929**

munïlayu of its kind 1854

muyum confused, muddled **1929** *m. adïrtsïz 1929*

münä- reprove, blame *yir-är m.-yür* 1798 Denominational + °n- verbs **1786**

nagarčuni < Skt. Nāgārjuna, Patriarch **1907**. 1907

***nangayu** s. *angayu*!

nä how! 1895. *1884*.

nätäg to some extent 1884. **1884**. *2099*

***nängäyü** s. *angayu*!

nikai < Skt. *nikāya* school, sects. *säkiz ygrmi* n. 1784. **1783**

nom teachings, text of teaching prayer 1784. 1795. 1991. 2005. *2099*. 2142. 2143*
    ič taš n. 1933 *n.-luɣ iliglär* 2003
    adïn n.-luɣlar 1924. **1924**
    n.-luɣ ät' üzüngüz Sie 2055. **2055**
    toquz bölüg n.-lar **2059**. 2060
    yarïm n. 2088 cleavage / schism **ny** 1826

oɣl (a) nɣu tender 1819.

oɣurt- to settle someone *1859*

olur- . . . live, to find oneself 1767.

ongar- to better *1870*

ortun mediator or medium *o. änätkäk* 1765.
1864

os- (?) wilt, languish 2041 *o. suwsa-* 2041

otɣuraq certain, sure 2084. **2084**

örlätiš- to be excited 2095

öt- to come out, force through, to be skilled
in 1793. 2040.

ötüg request, prayer *biläg ö.* A present of
reverence 1843

ptryadiwi < Skt. Prajñādeva, a monk in the
monastery of Mahābodhī 1768. **1768**.
1783. 1818. 1829. 2032

prtyadiwači < Skt. Prajñādevaja 2038
Deverbale -q- verbs *1805*

qaɣlim si < 鶏林寺 *Hao-lin ssŭ* Jungle
Monastery *1859*

qalangur- jump (for happiness), dance
1879. **1879**

qaɬincŭ leave behind, remaining **2011**
q. čöp öd 2011
q. nom 2011
q. söz. 2011

qamagurt cheeks (?) *1812*

qamɣaq garlic; salted vegetables 1948.
1948

+ qan **1790**

qantur- to pacify *1859*

qap packet **2047** *bir q. ritiwid* 2047

qawzadïl- to surround. 1817. **1817** encircle

qïl- do, modal Auxiliary: to prepare oneself
for
yirü q. 2092
-ɣu q. 2145

qïlïmsïn- to allow points to do **2087**
örü tikmäklig q. 2087

qïntur- to torture **1914**

qïyïl- to die 1888. **1888**

qonašï neighbour 2009.

quč- to cross *tiz q.-up olur-* to sit with
crossed legs (knees) **1940**
Modal Respect (honorofic) *verbs -u*
yrlïqa-, ötün-, tägin-; but *ti-p yrlïqa-*
etc. **1870**

ritiwid < sak. < Skt. Ṛgveda 1809 (?) **1809**.
1831. 2047.

saiqa- to pour out, to help 1942

Sakisches 1809

sangistwri < Skt. *sanghasthavira* the oldest
in a monastery 1818

sapïn succession, order, sequence 1983.

saryadati (wrong for **suryadati*?) < Skt.
*Sūryadatta 1840. **1840**

säkiz eight *s. ygrmi nikai* 1783. **1783**
s. uluɣ arqular 2104

särinmäk to bear, *Kshānti* (3rd of the 6
virtues) 2099

sï- . . . to win 1801

sïɣun Maral 2120

sïɣur- to take 2027

sïngqu säli translator of this biography
2154

sïq narrow *s. täring* 2084

sïqïl- to take trouble 2071

sintu Skt. *Sindhu* Indus 2021. 2141

siošing < 小乘 *Siao-shêng* = Skt. Hīnayāna small vehicle
s. säkiz ygrmi nikai 1783. **1783**.
s. nom 1792
s. nomï 2088

soq- to hide here 1928.

sparir < toch. *B spharir* < Skt. *sphaṭika*
rock crystal **2124**. 2124

sutsï s. *tutsï*!

suwsuš- drink
tuturqan s. Rice-wine 1942

sụü < 序 foreword *2007*.

šanawazi < Skt. Śānavāsa 1977. **1977**

šipqan < 十干 *shˇı-kan* the ten branches **1764.**

šong (s-, -u-?) < 雙 *shuang* pair **1844**
bir ǯ. yürüng böz 1844

šrawast < Skt. *Śrāvasti* 2016

taibo 大饗 (Haneda[†] gives the vari-

ants:) 大響 or 大嚮 Tai-hiang

[†]In his edition of this Chinese text:
Daitō daijionji Santzō hōshi den, published by *Tōhō-bunka-gakuin Kyoto
Kenkyu sho* through Utsunomiya *Shōkichi*
and Haneda *Toru* Kyōto 1932.

-1859 city name (*taibo*, mistake for *taiho*?)

taisï student s. *tïtsï*!

talui sea *tört t.* 1986

tamtur- set fire to 1908

tang astounding 1895

tangïŋla- to become a stranger 1846 (?) 1846

tarïŋlaŋ field *1870*

taš external, from outside
  t. bitig texts not belonging to the teachings. 1773. **1773**

ič taš nom 1933

tawišqan here; conforms with the Chinese
  卯 *mao:* 4. 4th member of the 12 parts of the animal cycle. **1764**
  ir. t. kün 1764

tägürd- to send out 1850.

tänglä- to compare
  sudurlarïŋ t.-mäk atlŋ ülgü 1833. **1833**

tïq- to barricade, to obstruct 1912

tïsï s. *tïtsï* !

tïtsï *t`is`ï, taisÿ* 弟子 *ti-tsï* student 1778
  1778. *1785.* 1914. 2151

til language 2151. 2154. 2155.

tirgük posts 1921

tirištirt- (?) to let oneself be gathered 2060.
  2060

tngri tngrisi, construction from Sakish
  1809.

tolu wholly independent
  yarïm-li t.-li 1923

toquz nine
  t. bölüg nomlar 2059. **2059**

tökä- to drink through *1901*. **1901**

tört four
  t. wid 1774
  t. talui **1986**

tuimïš the enlightened
  uluŋ t. Buddha 1974. **1974**

tuš- to confront (with dative) 2079.

tutsï (instead of the wrong *sutsï*) mountain
  (rock) crystal *2123*. **2123**
  t. mončuq 2123

tutung 都統 *Tu-t'ung* 2155

tuturqan suwsuš Rice-wine, 1941

tutuz- lead, conduct 1952

tükäd- descriptive verb 2072

tümkä foolish 1947

tünär- to be darkened 1931

tüpkär- to probe into, to investigate 2116.
  1870

tüš- (-ö-, -s-?) 1792. **1792**

-u -*a*, -*ï*: function of verb forms on -*u*, -*a*, -*ï*
  1859

ud bull 2121

uduz- lead
  yirčilä- u. 1785. 1938

ula- to continue 1904. 1906

ulatï and in future (conducting the sentence) 1773. 1977.

uluŋ big
  u. ädrämlig s. ädrämilig!
  u. tuimïš s. tuimïš!
  u. kičig külüngülär 1772

umun- hope 1955

upagupdi < Skt. Upagupta 1978. **1978**

urunt fjght, illness 2095. **2095**

utru face to face, against
  u ..., u ... as soon as
  ... 2005. 2005

utsuq- to be conquered, (associated form of
  -*z*- in *A. Ind.*) 1802

uzan- to be sent 1786. **1786**

üč three
  ü. külüngü = Skt. *Triyäna*, the three vehicles 1922. **1922**

üčün because of, due to
  -*mäz ü.* 1795

ükli- to increase oneself with (*ü*- as *üküš*)
  2075.

üküš rich 1941 etc.

üzä *üzā, üsā* (not *özä*) on, by means of, to
  ... 1812. 1812 etc.

üzäk- to long for 1805. **1805**

üzül- to be destroyed *ü.-däči ol, mängü ol*
  1925. **1925**

wapšï < 法師 *fa-shï < fap-ṣi* master
  2152.

wčrazan < Skt. *vajrāsana* 1813.

wid Skt. veda
  tört w. 1774

widis < parth *'bdys* instinct **1785**
  w. bir- 1785. *1785*
  w. bošɣun 1785

yailïq summer hall 1967.
yanala anew 1909. **1909**
yang sample, kind
  y. kip 2110
  bir. y.-lïɣ narrow minded, partial 1781
yantud answer **1857**
  y. bitig 1857
  y. biläg 1858
yaqa collar, head, chief 1936. **1936**
yarat- to compose 1832. 2152
yarïm half
  y. nom Hīnayāna 2088. **2088**
  y.-li tolu-li 1923
yašaɣu life 1956
yawal- to be strong 2064. **2064**
  qarnïn y.-mï̈š 2064. **2064**
yawaltur- to overcome *2064*
yawlaq very **2064**
yig fresh, good
  y. buranč 2128
yinčkä fine, exact 1823
yir- blame, to be attentive 2092
  y.-är münäyür 1798
  y.-ä yrlïqama- 2029

yirčilä- to show the way, to conduct 1786.
  1938
yiril- to separate, divide
  adrïl- y. 2039
yoog šastr = 瑜伽師地 Yü-kia-
  shǐ-ti-lun< Skt.
  Yogācāryabhūmiśāstra, B. Nanjio Nr.
  1170. 1992. **1992**
yoplun- to torture oneself 1968. **1968**
yoq not (?) 1927
yrlïqa- condescend **1974.** 1975
  y.-r ärdi he deigned to be troubled in his
  person 1936
yungla- to trouble oneself < 用 *yung*
  to use **2001.** 2114
yungla- to comfort, to give peace < 雍
  yung concord union **2001**
  amïrtɣur- y. 2001
yuqa needy. **2029**
  az y. 2029
yuul stream, lake, sea *2104.* 2105
yüüz hundred
  y. öngi šastrlar 2057

Zahlungsmittel: material of payment,
  stuff, **1810**
Zeitbestimmung: 1764 chronology

Completed on 4th March 1939.

3

Résumé of Chapters Six–Ten of the *Life*

Translated from the Histoire de la vie de Hioun-thsang et de ses Voyages dans l'Inde by S. Julien[a]*

CHAPTER SIX

p. 292   This book commences in the first month of spring of the 19th year (period Chen-kuan, AD 645) when Hsüan-tsang makes his entry into the western capital (Sianfu); it finishes in the summer of the 22nd year (AD 648), in the sixth month, when he thanks the emperor for writing a preface for the edition of the sacred books which he had just translated.

Résumé *

In the first month of spring of the 19th year of period Chen-kuan (AD 645) minister of the left, count of the kingdom of Liang, Fang Hsüan-ling and others, having learnt that the Master of the Law was arriving with a collection of sacred books and statues, sent the general Mo Chén-shih with the title of Yu-wu-hou, Li Shu-shen, commanding-officer of the cavalry of the district of Yung chow, and Li Ch'ien-yu, prefect of the region

p. 293   of Ch'ang-an, with orders to go and meet him, and to escort him from the great canal to the capital and install him in the ambassadors' residence known as Tou-t'ing-i. They were accompanied by an immense crowd.

On that day, the magistrates addressed to the monks of all the monasteries, an order to prepare tapestries, sedan-chairs, flowers, banners, etc., and to accompany the sacred books and the statues to the Monastery Hung-fu-ssǔ (of great happiness). All the monks

*Julien's footnotes from a–p are given at the end of the last, i.e. the tenth chapter. Julien's translation has been checked against the Chinese text of the *Life* published by Wang l-t'ang in 1923, reprint Kuang-wen, and published from Taiwan in 1963.

were transported with joy and vied with one another in making elaborate preparations. On the next day, they assembled in a convocation at the south of the street *Chu-ch'üeh-chieh*(Red Bird Street). They formed together several hundred groups arranged in an orderly and symmetrical manner. In this same monastery were deposited at once the objects which the Master of the Law had brought back from the western countries: namely (1) One hundred and fifty grains of *she-li* (*śarīra*) 'relics' from the body of Ju-lai (the Tathāgata); (2) A gold statue of the Buddha whose shadow remained in the *Grotto of the dragons* on the mountain *Ts'ien-cheng-chüeh-shan* (*Prāgbouddhagiri*) of the *Mo-chi'eh-t'uo*(Magadha) kingdom, with a pedestal of transparent material, 3′3″ high and resembling the statue of the Buddha which can be seen in the kingdom *P'o-luo-ni-ssŭ* (Vārāṇasī or Benaras) and which represents him turning for the first time the wheel of the Law (i.e. preaching) in the Deer Park (*Mṛgadava*); (3) A statue of

p. 294   the Buddha, carved in sandalwood, with a pedestal of transparent material 3′5″ high and resembling that in an outburst / surge of affection for *Ju-lai* (the Tathāgata), *Ch'u-ai-yuang* (*Udayana rājā*) being king of *Ch'iao-shang-mi*(Kauśāmbī) had had carved as a true replica in sandalwood; (4) A sandalwood statue, with a pedestal of transparent material, 2′9″ high resembling the one in the *Ka-pi-t'a* (*Kapitha*) kingdom which represents *Ju-lai* (the Tathāgata) just as he is coming down from the palace of the *Devas* by means of a precious flight of stairs.[b] (5) A silver statue of the Buddha with a transparent pedestal, 4′ high, similar to that which depicts him explaining *The Flower of the Law* (the *Saddharma puṇḍarīka*) and other sacred books on the Peak of Vulture (*Gṛdhrakūṭa*) in the kingdom of *Mo-chi'eh-t'uo* (Magadha); (6) A gold statue of the Buddha, with a pedestal of transparent material, 3′5″ high similar to his shadow which he left in the kingdom of *Na-kie-lo-ho* (*Nagarahāra*) and which depicts him taming a poisonous dragon.; (7) A statue of the Buddha carved in sandalwood with a pedestal of transparent material, 1′3″ high, similar to that

p. 295   in the kingdom of *Fei-she-li* (Vaiśālī) which represents him going around the town to convert the people etc.

Deposited there also (in the Monastery of great happiness were the books which the Master of the Law had obtained in the western countries; namely [1] The sacred books (*Sūtras*) of the Great Vehicle—124 works;[1] [2] *Ta-ch'eng-lun* (i.e. note / commentary upon the treatises of the *Great Vehicle*)—90 copies;[2] [3] Sacred Books, memoirs upon (the) discipline and philosophical treatises of the *Shang-tso Chang-tso pou (Sarvāsrivādas)* school—15 works; [4] Sacred books, memoirs on (the) discipline and philosophical treatises of the *San-mi-ti (Sammitīya)* school— 15 works; [5] Sacred books, memoirs on (the) discipline and philosophical treatises of the *Mi-sha-se (Mahīśāsaka)* school— 22 works; [6] Sacred books, memoirs on (the) discipline and philosophical treatises of the *Chia-yeh-pei-yen (Kāśyapīya)* school—17 works; [7] Sacred books, memoirs on (the) discipline and philosophical treatises of the *Fa-mi* (Dharmagupta) school— 42 works; [8] Sacred books, memoirs on (the) discipline and philosophical treatises of the *Shou-i-ch'ieh-yu (Sarvāstivāda)* school—67 works; [9] The treatise *Yin-ming-lun (Hetuvidyā* p. 296 *śāstra)*[3]—36 volumes; [10] The treatise *Shêng-ming-lun (Śabdavidyā śāstra)*—13 volumes.

This collection made up of 520 parts / fascicules and forming 657 works[4] was carried by 22 horses.[5]

On that day the magistrates distributed in all monasteries a decree ordering all monks to assemble on the 28th day of the month, with precious cloths, standards and banners on the street *Chu-ch'üeh-chieh* (Red Bird street), to go and meet the newly arrived books and statues that were to be deposited in the Monastery Hung-fu-ssŭ (i.e. the monastery of great happiness).

Then everybody redoubling their enthusiasm and zeal, made magnificent preparations in which they displayed an extraordinary luxury and brilliance. They came from each monastery with banners, cloths, canopies, precious tables and rich palanquins which they arranged in an orderly way. The monks and nuns walked behind them in ceremonial habits. At the head of the procession could be heard religious hymns; persons carrying perfume jars filled with perfume completed the procession. Soon it arrived at the street *Chu-ch'üeh-chieh* (Red Bird Street).

---

[1]According to the Chinese text 224 works.
[2]According to the Chinese text 192 works.
[3]This appears again in Chapter eight. The two different Sanskrit renderings are variants for the same work.
[4]The total is 14 short of 657 in the Chinese text. Julien's total falls short of 216 works.
[5]According to the Chinese text, 20 horses.

The books and statues were placed here and there in the middle of the procession which advanced at a calm and majestic pace. One could hear resounding of the belts set with precious stones; and a quantity of golden flowers which shone with a dazzling brilliance could be seen. The monks, who walked at the head or formed the escort, celebrated this extraordinary event with hymns and a crowd of lay people, forgetting the inducements of the age (worldly life?) and freeing themselves from its bonds, shared their joy and admiration. The procession commencing at the street *Chu-ch'üeh-chieh* (Red Bird Street), finished only at the door of the Monastery Hung-fu-ssŭ (of great happiness) and occupied thus a distance of (?) about thirty or so *li* (several leagues). The inhabitants of the capital, the scholars, the magistrates from within (i.e. of the palace) and without, were ranged along the two sides of the road, stood in an attitude which expressed at the same time love and admiration. Men and horses formed a compact mass of an immense size. The magistrates in charge, believing that a great number of people would be crushed in the crowd, ordered that everybody remain in his place, burning perfumes and strewing flowers. Along the whole length of the procession, one could see floating a sweetly scented cloud, and could hear from one end to the other the rhythmical sounds of the religious hymns. On that day, the whole multitude saw, at the same time, clouds of five colours which shone in the sun, and unrolled themselves in sparkling sheets over a distance of several *li*, above the books and the statues, and seemed sometimes to precede them and sometimes to accompany them. When the convent was reached, they vanished in the twinkling of an eye. On the day Jen-ch'en, the emperor received the Master of the Law in his palace at Loyang.

p. 297

On the day Chi-hai of the second month (of spring in the year AD 645) the Master of Law went to pay his respects to the emperor in the Phoenix palace where he received a most affectionate welcome.

p. 298

The emperor asked Hsüan-tsang why he had left previously without having advised him. He replied that at the time he had addressed several petitions in order to obtain permission to travel afar; but, no doubt due to the obscurity of his name having not received the authorization which he needed, and not being able moreover, to contain the outburst of his passionate zeal for the religion of the Buddha, he had left in secret and of his own accord.

The emperor, far from reproaching him, congratulated him on having put his life in peril for the well-being and happiness of all men, and expressed his astonishment, that, in spite of the obstacles which mountains and the rivers, the distance of the places and the differences in customs had placed before him, he had come happily to the object of his journey.

Hsüan-tsang replied that he who is assisted by a favourable wind arrives in an instant at the heavenly lake, and that when one has boarded a boat drawn by dragons, one is able to cross without difficulty the impetuous waves of the Kiang.[c] He added: 'Since Your Majesty holds the Talisman of Heaven (i.e. occupies the throne) he has pacified the four seas (the empire): his virtue encircles the nine countries[d], his humanity stretches as far as the eight regions, his pure instructions have refreshed like a healthy wind, the lands south of the burning disc (of the sun) and his impressive power has affected / touched the beaches situated beyond the Ts'ung-ling mountains.

p. 299

That is why when princes and chiefs of barbarian tribes see a bird which arrives from the east carried upon the wings of the clouds, they believe that it has come from your noble kingdom, and at once adopting a solemn attitude they greet it with respect. With how much greater reason was Hsüan-tsang, who has had the good fortune to receive himself your beneficial / salutary instructions / orders and who was protected moreover by the power of heaven (the power of Your Majesty), able to go and come without difficulty'.

The emperor replied that he did not dare to accept such a eulogy and attribute to himself the success of his travels. Then he questioned him in detail upon the facts (knowledge) which he had gathered; upon the climates, the products, the customs of countries situated to the south of the snowy mountains and confined within the boundaries of India, the ancient monuments of the eight kings[6] and the sacred traces of the four previous Buddhas. 'These are', he added, 'things which the count of

---

[6]i.e. the eight bodhisattvas: Vajra-sattva, Mañju-śrī, Ākāśa-garbha, Maitreya, Avaloki-teśvara, Kṣiti-garbha, Āryāchala-nātha and Viśva-bhadra.

Po-wang (general Chang Ch'ien) and the historians Pan (Pan Ku) and Ma (Ssŭ-ma Ch'ien) were not in a position to record'.

As the Master of the Law had travelled in these countries, as he had observed the territorial divisions and the state of the towns, and as with the help of ears and eyes he had enriched his memory, omitting nothing useful, he was able to reply both clearly and methodically to all the emperor's questions.

p. 300 The emperor was overcome with joy. After praising Hsüan-tsang's literary talents, the rare elegance of his speech, the energy and uprightness of his character and placing him above several famous monks such as Shih-tao-an and Siu-an, he invited him to compose a history of his travels[e] and thus to make known the customs of the distant kingdoms of the Buddha, the sacred monuments and the teaching of the Law.

The emperor, struck by the great capacity of the Master of the Law, wished to entrust him with the duties of a minister and exhorted him to leave the religious life to assist him in the direction of worldly matters.

Hsüan-tsang refused, claiming that, having entered as a child by the black door (i.e. into a monastery) and having embraced fervently the law of the Buddha, he had studied its mysterious principles, and he had never learnt of the Confucian doctrine, which is the soul of administration. If he abandoned them to follow the ideas of the age, he said, he would resemble a ship travelling under full sail which left the water of the sea to sail on the mainland on dry ground. Not only would he not succeed but he could not avoid shattering / wrecking himself and perishing. He expressed the wish to finish his days in religion so as to thank the prince for his acts of kindness.

The emperor did not insist any longer, but begged him to
p. 301 accompany him with his army, on a distant expedition which had as its object the punishing of some rebels in eastern China.

Hsüan-tsang had no doubt that the emperor would win a dazzling victory, comparable to the famous victories won at Mu-yeh and at K'un-yang; but he was convinced that he could contribute nothing to the success of his arms and that he would even be for him a cause of expense and trouble. He added that his principles based upon goodwill and affection for mankind would not allow him to be present at battles and at scenes of carnage.

Hsüan-tsang, seeing that the emperor stopped pressing him, reminded him that he had not yet translated one word of the 600 works in the Fan language (of Fan-mo-luo—Brahmā) which he had brought back from the western countries. He knew that quite near, south of Mount Sung-yüeh and north of Mount Shao-Shih, was situated the monastery of the little wood, Shao-lin-ssŭ, far from the noise of markets and villages, and in which could be found silent grottos and clear fountains. This monastery was built by the emperor Hsiao-wen-ti, of the second Wei dynasty (AD 471–99). It was in this retreat that the Indian monk P'u-t'i-liu-chih (Bodhi-ruchi) devoted himself to the translation of sacred books.

Hsüan-tsang begged the emperor to authorize him, by a decree, to make his way to this convent, in order to devote himself to the translation of the holy books; but the prince suggested that he take up his abode rather in the monastery of great happiness, p. 302   Hung-fu-ssŭ which he had had built in the western capital, and promised to provide him with all that he needed.

In the third month (of summer), on the day of Chi-ssŭ the Master of the Law had no sooner arrived at Ch'ang-an than he went to live in the Monastery Hung-fu-ssŭ. Before commencing to translate, he drafted a memorial addressed to the emperor, in which he made known in detail the number of people whom he would need to revise the translations and to polish their style, to copy the texts at his dictation and to write a fair copy, then he put it in the hands of Fang Hsüan-ling, director of public works and count of the kingdom of Liang, whom the emperor had left as governor of the western capital. The latter directed an able magistrate to write at this juncture, a petition, and sent an officer to Ting-chow to present it to the emperor. An imperial decree, returned immediately, ordering that he be provided with all which he had requested.

In the summer, on the day Meou-siu, of Wu-hsu of the sixth month, twelve monks, experienced in the explanation of sacred books and treatises of the Great and of the Little Vehicle and who enjoyed the highest reputation, arrived at the capital (of the west) and made their way to Hsüan-tsang. Here are their names:

Ling-jun and Wen-pei, of the Monastery Hung-fu-ssŭ; Hui-kui, of the Monastery of Arhan (Luo-han-ssŭ); Ming-yen, of the Monastery Shih-chi-ssŭ; Fa-hsiang, of the Monastery P'ao-ch'ang-ssŭ P'ú-hsien, of the Monastery Ching-fa-ssŭ Shen-fang, of the Monastery Fa-hai-ssŭ; Tao-shen, of the Monastery Fa-chiang of the district of Kuo-chow, Hsüan-chung, of the Monastery Yen-chüeh-ssŭ, prefecture of Pien-chow, Shen-t'ai, of the Monastery P'u-chiu-ssŭ, of the district of P'u-chow; Ching-ming, of the Monastery Chen-yin-ssŭ, of the district of Mien-chow, Tao-yin, of the Monastery Tuo-pao-ssŭ, of the district of Yi-chow, etc.

p. 303

There arrived another nine monks of distinguished ability, to improve and polish the translated texts. They were: Ch'i-hsüan, of the Monastery P'u-kuang-ssŭ, of the capital; Ming-chün, of the Monastery Hung-fu-ssŭ; Pien-chi, of the Monastery Hui-ch'ang-ssŭ; Tao-hsüan, of the Monastery Feng-teh-ssŭ, of Mount Chung-nan-shan; Ching-mai, of the Monastery Fu-chu-ssŭ, of Chien-chow; Hsing-yu, of the Monastery P'u-chiu-ssŭ of P'u-chow; Tao-chuo, of the Monastery Ch'i-yen-ssŭ; Hui-li, of the Monastery Chao-jen-ssŭ; Yu-chow; Hsüan-tse, of the Monastery T'ien-kung-ssŭ of Lo-chow.

There arrived another monk well-versed in the study of characters, Sramaṇa Hsüan-ying; then another monk skilled in the revision / examination of Indian expressions and Indian texts; his name was Sramaṇa Hsüan-mo, of the Monastery Ta-hsing-ssŭ, of the capital.

Finally he received, at the same time, other monks for whom he had asked, to copy at his dictation, as well as to write fair copies of the texts.

p. 304

On the day Ting-mao, the Master of the Law took the manuscripts on Tāla leaves, explained / elucidated their Indian text and began to translate: firstly, the *P'u-sa-tsang-ching* (*Bodhisattva piṭaka sūtra*); secondly, the *Fo-ti-ching* (*Buddha-Bhūmi sūtra*); thirdly, *Liu-men t'uo-luo-ni-ching* (*Shaṭmukhī dhāraṇī*); fourthly *Hsien-yang-sheng-chiao-lun*. In a single day he completed the book *Liu-men-ching* (*Shaṭmukhī dhāraṇī*); but the *Fo-ti-ching* (*Buddha-bhūmi sūtra*) was not completed until the day Hsin-ssŭ.[7] The book of the collection of the *P'u-sa-tsang-ching* (*Bodhisattva-piṭaka sūtra*) and the *Hsien-yang-sheng-chiao-lun* were finished in the last days of the year.

In the twenty-second year (of the period Chen-kuan in AD 648)[8] on the day Chia-tsŭ of the first month, he translated as well the *Ta-ch'eng-a-p'i-ta-mo-tsa-chi-lun*(*Mahāyānābhidharma saṅgīti śāstra*); he finished it in the second month. He also translated the *Yü-chia-shih-ti-lun* (*Yogāchārya-bhūmi śāstra*).

In autumn, on the day Hsin-mao of the 7th month, the Master of the Law presented the *sūtras* (sacred books) and the *śāstras* (*philosophical treatises*) of which he had just completed the translation.

Hsüan-tsang addressed a petition to the emperor in which he mentioned the five translations of the above mentioned forming 58 books altogether, namely: first, the sacred book of the collection of the great Bodhisattvas, 2 books; second, the sacred text of the provinces of the Buddha, 1 book; third, the Invocations of the six doors, 1 book; fourth, the treatise to illuminate the holy doctrine, 25 books;[9] and fifth, the collection of different treatises of the great Vehicle on Abhidharma, 16 books. He announced that he had collected them together in eight wrappers and that he was coming respectfully to the palace to present them to him. He begged the emperor to lower his divine (paint) brush and to write, in praise of the Buddha, a preface in which the sublime ideas would sparkle like the sun and the moon, of which the writing as precious as silver and jade, would endure as long as (the) heaven and (the) earth and would become for future generations, an object of unfailing admiration.

p. 305

He ended by saying that the Memoirs on the western countries (Si-yü-ki), which the emperor had ordered him to draw up on the day when he had received him in the Loyang palace, had just been fully completed.

In this work, in which he wrote of 128 kingdoms[10] which he had himself visited or of which he had heard tell (as told to him), he recounted things unknown before him. Although he had not reached the limits of the great Chiliocosme, he had however recounted in an exact manner all the facts relative to the countries situated beyond the Ts'ung-ling mountains. Not

---

[7]i.e. fourteen days later.

[8]According to the Chinese text twentieth year (corresponding to AD 646).

[9]According to the Chinese text, 20 volumes.

[10]'cent vingt-huit royaumes', but the Chinese text has 218 kingdoms. The actual count from Beal gives a total of 72 (vol. I) + 66 (vol. II) 138 kingdoms.

daring to emboss and embellish his stories (i.e. to add studied / affected ornamentation) he drafted them dutifully, in a true and simple style, and after dividing them in 12 books, he gave them the title *Ta-t'ang-hsi-yü-chi*. (Memoirs upon the Western Countries (composed) in the great T'ang dynasty). He complained of the small extent of his knowledge, and the lack of his skill with the brush, and expressed the fear that his work might be unworthy of the gaze of the emperor.

p. 306 On the day Keng-chin[h], the emperor himself replied, praised the book and the author, and excused himself from writing the preface requested.

On the day Ting-yu, the Master of the Law presented again a petition to the emperor that he deign to ornament with an introduction 'from his divine brush' the five translations which he had just completed.

On the day Keng-ch'en, the emperor addressed to the Master of the Law a decree which ordered him to proceed to the palace. While he was on the way, he received several messengers who invited him to travel by short stages so as to avoid fatigue.

On his arrival in the Loyang palace the emperor welcomed him most graciously, and after some minutes of conversation, he pressed him again to leave the yellow cloak of Hsü-p'u-t'i (Subhūti) and the plain garment of Wei-mo-chieh (Vimalakīrtti), in order to enter upon worldly affairs and to assist him in council and to hold office among his ministers[i].

Hsüan-tsang, by means of five arguments drawn from ancient and contemporary history, endeavoured to prove to the emperor that he had no need of the help of other men, and above all his own. He expressed the wish to remain in the religious life so as to continue to propagate the doctrine which the Buddha had left to the world, and besought the emperor to allow him to finish his days there in peace.

p. 307 The emperor consented and even promised to help him with all his power to attain such a noble goal. He wrote at last the preface so greatly desired, containing 781 characters.

[Julien reports / records in entirety, this piece of imperial eloquence, written in an ambitious style, filled with brilliant metaphors and studied allusions. This preface contains at the same time, a high sounding eulogy of the Buddhist doctrine and the heroic devotion of the traveller; but it adds no new fact, no observation of any interest to the history or geography of India.]

The sixth book concludes with the reply which Hsüan-tsang addressed to the emperor to thank him for the preface, and with a note of a few lines in which the emperor, expressing himself still with an exaggerated modesty, said that he was ashamed of his poor / common style, and that he feared that he had disfigured / spoiled the golden leaves of the traveller by strewing / spreading gravel and tile-fragments in the forest of pearls (i.e. in joining to these stylish translations an introduction in a common and careless style). On receiving his letter, he added, and on reading these magnificent words of praise with which it was filled 'he retreated within himself and felt a blush rise in his face, because he recognized that he had done nothing to merit such elaborate / fine praise; he avowed with bitter regret, that expressions were lacking to him to make fitting thanks.'

CHAPTER SEVEN

p. 308   This book commences in the sixth month of the twenty-second year of the period Chen-kuan (AD 648), in summer, when the crown prince composed a memorial entitled Shu-sheng-chi; it finishes in the second month of spring of the fifth year of the period Yung-huei (AD 654), when the Master of the Law addressed a reply to Fa-ch'ang.[11]

Résumé

In the sixth month of the twenty-second year of the period Chen-kuan (AD 648), the royal prince[12] being in the spring palace, received and examined the recently translated sacred texts. On that occasion, he composed an introduction[13] in which he praised their lofty style and moral importance and finished with an elaborate eulogy of Hsüan-tsang.

The Master of the Law sent him a letter of thanks soon, followed by a reply in which the royal prince spoke with (an) extreme modesty of his lack of skill in the art of writing and of his small

[11]According to the Chinese text, a reply (to Indian monks) 'through Fa-ch'ang'.
[12]According to the Chinese text 'celestial emperor'.
[13]To the sacred books (*Shu-sheng-chi*).

learning and intelligence which prevented him from understanding and appreciating well the sacred texts. He added that he had been overcome with embarrassment on seeing the flattering compliments which the Master of the Law had addressed to him.

When the two prefaces[k] had been published, Yüan-ting, the superior of the Monastery Hung-fu-ssŭ, and the monks of the capital begged the emperor to have them engraved upon metal and stone tablets and to deposit them in the monastery. The emperor consented to this.

p. 309

On the day Keng-ch'en, the royal prince, having lost his mother (the empress Wen-teh), had built in her honour, to the south of the imperial palace, a huge (and) magnificent monastery, in which there were ten courtyards and 1890 cells, provided with all the necessary furniture and utensils.

The emperor (T'ien-wu sheng-huang-ti) having read the *Pu sa-tsang-ching* (*Bodhisattva piṭaka sūtra*), praised it and ordered that, in the spring palace, a preface[14] for this work be composed. Our author (Yen-ts'ung) cites this preface[15] which is composed of 578 words in its entirety.

The emperor gave (to) Hsüan-tsang a religious garment and a cutting instrument for cutting the hair of those who wished to begin a religious life.

The Master of the Law addressed a letter of thanks to him.

The emperor asked him what more to do to acquire merit.

Hsüan-tsang advised him to ordain monks who could propagate the teaching of the Law.

The emperor received this advice joyfully and on the day I-mao of the ninth month he put out a decree that in each monastery in the different districts five monks be ordained, and fifty in the monastery of great happiness, the Hung-fu-ssŭ. As there were then 3716 monasteries in the whole empire, about 18,500 monks and nuns were ordained[l]. Before this time, the greater number of the monasteries and temples had been sacked during the last years of the Sui dynasty, and the monks had been almost all wiped out. This immense ordination re-established them on a

p. 310

---

[14]According to the Chinese text, epilogue.
[15]Epilogue.

flourishing footing.

The emperor asked Hsüan-tsang if the celebrated work *Chin-kang-pan-jo-po-luo-mi-tuo-ching* (*Prajñāpāramitā*) which had been translated in previous centuries was complete or not in both text and meaning.

He replied that if one examined the old translation, some omissions could be noticed. In fact, the Indian title signifies: 'The book of transcendental understanding, which can cut the diamond', *Neng-tuan-chin-kang-p'an-jo* (*Vajra chhedikā prajñā-pāramitā sūtra*), while the old edition's title was: *Chin-kang-p'an-jo* etc.... Thus the two first words *neng-tuan* (which can cut) were omitted. In the text which follows, out of three questions, one was omitted, as well as a *gāthā* (verse) out of two, and three comparisons (*avadānas*) out of nine [were omitted].

Faults of the same type are noted in the name of the kingdom of She-wei (in place of Shih-luo-p'o-hsi-ti-yen—Śrāvastī), trans-cribed by the Master Shi (Kumāra-jīva)[m]; the word p'o-chia-p'o (Bhagavat), read by Liu-chih (Bodhi-ruchi), is a little less incorrect.

p. 311 'Since you possess the Indian texts', the emperor said to him, 'it is necessary to submit them to a new translation so that the people who read them may have nothing to wish for. Now in sacred books, one values the principles which they contain; but it is not necessary to add ornamentation which can alter their meaning.'

The emperor was delighted to learn in a report which was presented to him that the title *Neng-tuan-chin-kang-p'an-jo* (the sacred book of transcendental understanding which can cut the diamond) conformed to the Indian text (*Vajra-chhedikā prajñā-pāramitā sūtra*).[16]

In winter in the tenth month the emperor returned to the capital with the Master of the Law.

Before this time, the emperor had had built to the west of the Tsŭ-wei room of the imperial palace,[17] a separate building which he had called Hung-fa-yuan (the court of the Great Law).

---

[16]The emperor was also informed that the said text had been translated.
[17]The whole phrase starting with Tsŭ-wei should be replaced by Tsŭ-wei palace.

On his arrival Hsüan-tsang took up residence there. During the day he remained near the emperor who liked to discourse with him; in the evening he returned there to devote himself to the translation of the sacred texts. He re-translated: first, the *She-ta-ch'eng-lun* (*Mahāyāna saṁparigraha śāstra*), in 10 books, elucidated by Wu-hsing-p'u-sa (Abhava bodhisattva?); second, the *She-ta-ch'eng-lun* (*Mahāyāna saṁparigraha śāstra*), elucidated by Shih-ch'in (Vasu-bandhu), in 10 books; third, the *Yuan-ch'i-sheng-tao-ching* (the sacred book of the origin of the holy doctrine) in one book; fourth, the *Pai-fa-ming-men-lun* (*Śata-dharma-prabhāvatī dvāra śāstra*?) in one book.

p. 312

On the day of Wu-shen, the royal prince published an order announcing that the Monastery Ts'ŭ-en (the monastery of Beneficence) had been completed with suitable magnificence for some time but there were still no monks. That was why, by virtue of the imperial decree, he stipulated the ordaining of 300 monks and invited another fifty persons of distinction, renowned for their virtue, to accept this pious dwelling, and to come and live there to practise the Law. He decided that the new monastery would be called Ta-ts'ŭ-en-ssŭ (The Monastery of Great Beneficence). He ordered the construction of another monastery decorated with precious paintings, stones and metals, intended for the interpreters of the sacred books, and begged[18] the Master of the Law to go and settle there to continue his translations. He named it Kang-wei-ssŭ and charged the Master of the Law with its direction.[19]

Hsüan-tsang addressed a letter to the royal prince in which, pleading the state of his health and the insufficiency of his education, he begged him to excuse him from such a difficult responsibility.

In the 12th month, on the day Meou-chin, the emperor[20] ordered the master of ceremonies, Kiang-wang, and other great personages to bring together the different bodies of musicians, to prepare banners and cloths, and to gather together on the following morning at the gate (way) 'An-fo-men' (the gate of

---

[18] According to the Chinese text, 'ordered'.

[19] The original text 'Jeng Kang-wei ssŭ-jen'—'still in-charge monastery duty' has been mistakenly translated as ' . . . named it Kang-wei-ssŭ and charged . . . '

[20] According to the Chinese text, 'crown prince'.

peaceful happiness) to precede the monks who were to enter the Monastery Ta-ts'ŭ-'en-ssŭ (the Monastery of Great Beneficence).[21] The whole procession arranged itself in good order in the streets of the town. There were 1500 wagons decorated with brocaded canopies and banners on which were painted fish and dragons, and 300 parasols of precious materials.[22] Earlier, two hundred images of the Buddha had been brought from within (the palace), embroidered or painted on silk, two gold and silver statues, and 500 banners woven with silk and gold thread which were previously kept in the Monastery of Hung-fu-ssŭ (great happiness). The sacred books, the statues, the relics, etc., which the Master of the Law had brought back from the kingdoms of the west, had in like manner been brought from the Monastery Hung-fu-ssŭ. They had been placed upon pedestals which were borne by numerous wagons, in the midst of the procession. On both sides of the statues could be seen advancing two great wagons, on each of which arose a mast surmounted by a rich banner. Behind these banners floated the image of the divine king of the lions (*Śākyasiṁha?*) who led this stately procession. As well there were fifty wagons decorated magnificently on which were seated fifty personages of eminent virtue;[23] after that came all the Śramaṇas of the capital carrying flowers and singing religious hymns.

After them walked all the civil and military magistrates drawn up in an orderly manner. Finally, the nine imperial bands of musicians, marching on both sides, closed the procession. The sounds of hand bells and drums could be heard, and one could see rich standards which unfurled in the air and intercepted the brilliance of the sun. All the inhabitants of the town who had gathered in a crowd followed with their eyes this brilliant procession without being able to discover its beginning or end. A thousand (imperial) soldiers of the eastern palace formed an imposing escort. The emperor, together with the royal prince and all the ladies of the harem, had gone up to the top of a pavilion which overlooked the An-fu gate[24] (the gate of peaceful happiness), and, holding a

p. 313

p. 314

---

[21] Julien does not state that the grand procession was organized for the specific purpose to conduct Hsüan-tsang to the Monastery Ts'ŭ-en-ssŭ of which he was ordered to take charge as the 'Lord Abbot'.

[22] Should read '300 enactments of Buddhist themes under large coloured parasols.'

[23] Including Hsüan-tsang.

perfume jar, followed with an enraptured gaze the majestic movements of this immense crowd, in which people could be counted in tens and hundreds of thousands.

At last the books and the statues arrived at the monastery gate.[25] They were put down there in a cloud of perfume and to the sound of harmonious music. Finally, games were held in the vestibule of the temple, after which the whole multitude withdrew in silence.

On the day of Ting-shen, preparations were made to ordain monks.

On the day Hsin-wei, the royal prince left with his body-guards and went to stay in his former residence. He ordered that the Master of the Law be sent for and brought back to the palace.

In the fourth month of the 23rd year (of the period of Chen-kuan—AD 649), in summer, the emperor visited the Tsui-wei-kong Palace in the company of the royal prince and the Master of the Law. As soon as he arrived, each day after attending to his duties, he liked to discourse with Hsüan-tsang on the most profound principles of doctrine, and to reason on Understanding (*bodhi*). He questioned him upon the causes (the actions) and the results (the punishments and the rewards)[26] as well as on the ancient monuments intended to preserve the memory of the holy men of the kingdoms of the west.[27] Hsüan-tsang replied to him by citing the sacred texts. The emperor listened to him confidently and often expressed his admiration for him.

p. 315

At the time when the emperor left the capital, although he was slightly indisposed, his mind had lost nothing of its usual clarity and of its vigour. But on the day Chi-ssŭ of the fifth month, he experienced slight headaches and detained the Master of the Law, inviting him to stay in the palace.

On the day Keng-wu, the emperor died in the palace Han-feng. At first this event was kept hidden; the court returned to the capital and funeral preparations were made. On that day the

[24]To see off Hsüan-tsang

[25]When they were greeted by the Duke of Chao, the Duke of Ying and the Prime Minister who had gone there on imperial orders and who, with incense in their hands, conducted the scrolls and statues of the Buddha into the halls of the monastery.

[26]Theory of Karma (causation).

[27]The holy shrines of Lord Buddha, the Holy One of the West.

royal prince assumed the supreme power beside the Hsin-kung palace,[28] and at the end of the year he gave to the first period of his reign the name of Yung-hui (AD 650). All the people mourned for the emperor as a father.

The Master of the Law returned to the monastery T'sŭ-en-ssŭ (of Great Beneficence). From that moment, he applied himself solely to the translation of the sacred books, without ever losing a single instant. Each morning he set himself a new task and if, during the day some matter prevented him from completing it, he never failed to continue it at night. If he encountered a

p. 316 difficulty, he left his brush and put down the book; then having worshipped the Buddha and performed his religious duties until the third watch, he gave some time to rest, and, at the fifth watch, he got up again, read the Indian text aloud and noted successively, in red ink, the portions which he had to translate at sunrise (the next day).

Each day, early in the morning (before sunrise), after having (had) a frugal meal, he explained for two hours (4 of our hours) a new sacred book (*sūtra*) or a treatise (*śāstra*). The monks who had gathered from the various provinces to hear his lessons came constantly to beg him to explain to them the meaning of a passage and to dispel their doubts. Moreover, knowing that he was charged with the direction of the monastery, they came many times to ask him about their particular duties.[29]

The disciples from within the monastery (more than 100 in number), who came to ask him for instructions, filled the corridors and the rooms next to his bedroom. He replied clearly to all, without even omitting anything. Despite the number of his occupations, his soul maintained constantly the same energy and nothing was able to disturb or stop him. That is not all; he discoursed moreover with the monks upon the wise men and the saints of the kingdoms of the west, on the diverse systems of all the schools, and on the distant travels of his youth, and

---

[28]The Chinese characters 梓宮 (*tsŭ-kung*) mean 'imperial coffin'. Julien is confused by the word 宮 (Kung) which denotes 'palace' in other contexts and translates it as 'Hsin-kung palace'.

[29]On top of it, messengers were dispatched to him from the imperial palace to attend to works of charity.

p. 317   the public discussions in which he had taken part. He discussed in a loud voice and spoke with warmth, never giving signs of slackening or of fatigue, so great were the strength of his body and the vigour of his mind. Often princes and ministers came to pay their respects to him. After listening to his instructions they all opened their hearts to the faith; abjuring their natural pride, they never left him without having given him evidence of admiration and respect.

In the second year (of Yung-hui) (AD 651)[30] on the day Jen-yin of the first month of spring, Chia Tun-i, governor of Ying-chou; Li Tao-yu, governor of P'u Chou; (Tu Cheng-lun, governor of Ku-chou)[31] and Hsiao Jui, governor of Heng-chou, found themselves at the capital where they had come to be present at a solemn reception. They took advantage one day of the leisure which public affairs sometimes left them by visiting the Master of the Law. They begged him then to teach them the rules of behaviour of the Bodhisattvas. He did so eagerly, showed them in detail the duties of the Bodhisattvas and exhorted them to serve the prince loyally and to behave towards the people with tender affection. These illustrious people were overjoyed. After leaving him, they together drafted a letter in which they thanked him effusively for the religious precepts which he had been kind enough to teach them, and sent him at the same time, a part of their wealth, which they begged him to accept as a small mark of their gratitude.

In the third year (AD 652) in the third month of spring, the master of the Law wished to build to the south of the gate of
p. 318   the monastery Hung-fu-ssŭ, a Fu-t'u (*stūpa*) in stone, to deposit in it the books and the statues which he had brought from the western countries. He was afraid that, owing to the frailty of successive generations, the books would be dispersed and lost, or would be exposed to the ravages of fire.

This tower was to be 300 feet[32] high that it might be worthy of the majesty of a great kingdom and become one day one of the finest monuments of the religion of Śākyamuni. Before commencing construction he addressed a petition (memorial) to the

---

[30, 31](our insertions).

[32]30 chang, i.e. 300 *Ch'ih* equivalent to more than 100 metres. But the old measurement may have been much less.

emperor who immediately sent him a favourable reply through Li Yi-fu, one of his personal secretaries. The emperor gave the necessary orders, in order that the pious intentions of the Master of the Law might be fulfilled without causing him trouble or fatigue.[33] Each face of the tower was 140 feet[34] wide and in its building the form adopted in India was faithfully imitated. It had 5 flights of stairs (storeys) and was surmounted by cupola; its total height was 180 feet.[35] At the centre of each floor there were some particles of *se-li* (*sarīras*) 'relics', in one (case) a thousand, in another 2,000; in all about 10,000.

At the highest level was built a room in stone, which on the southern face had two plates (in metal) on which were engraved the two prefaces composed by the emperor and the royal prince.[36] The writing of these inscriptions was due to the elegant brush of Chu Sui-liang, minister of state and Duke of Honan.

p. 319 The day on which the foundations of this tower were laid the Master of the Law himself drew up a document in which he set out the reasons for his travels and the results which he had obtained from them. He ended it expressing his gratitude for the two imperial prefaces which 'thanks to the solidity of this tower, will be able to exist through an infinite number of *Kalpas*; his most ardent wish was that it might be honoured by the gaze of the thousand future Buddhas; that the relics which it enclosed might be eternally surrounded with a cloud of perfume, and that their mysterious duration equal that of the sun and the moon.'

In summer, on the day I-mao of the fifth month several eminent monks from the Monastery Mo-k'o-p'u-ti-ssŭ (Mahābodhī vihāra) in Central India, namely Chih-kuang (Jñāna-prabha), Hui-t'ien (Prajñā-deva), etc. sent a letter to the Master of the Law. Kuang (Jñāna-prabha) was profoundly knowledgeable in the doctrine of the great and little Vehicle, in the esoteric books, the four Wei-t'o (Vedas), and the five treatises called Wu-ming-lun (*Pañcha vidyā śāstra*); he was the most famous disciple of the master Chieh-hsien (Śīlabhadra). All the monks of the five Indias had the greatest respect for him.

---

[33]The emperor advised Hsüan-tsang that a stone pagoda of the designed magnitude might be too difficult to complete. It should be made of bricks.

[34, 35]Ch'ih. See note 32 above.

[36]Should be 'by the emperor and his late imperial father'.

Hui-t'ien (Prajñā-deva) knew thoroughly the eighteen schools of the little Vehicle; his profound knowledge and his high virtue had equally won for him universal esteem. At the time when p. 320 the Master of the Law was in India, he often studied and discussed / debated with these monks, but seeing that they were obstinately attached to narrow, erroneous principles, he criticized them severely. When the Great assembly of the Law took place in the town Ch'u-nü-ch'eng (Kānyakubja) he (Hsüan-tsang) vigorously refuted them and subjected them to a shameful defeat. However, since Hsüan-tsang's departure, they had retained a high regard for him and they had not forgotten him for a single moment. At the time of which we speak, they sent him a Sha-men (Śramaṇa) of the same monastery called Fa-chang to offer him two pieces of cotton, and to present to him a letter full of affectionate sentiments and a document consecrated to the praises of the Buddha.

In the second month of the fifth year (AD 654) Fa-chang took his leave of the Master of the Law, and before returning asked him for a reply, which Hsüan-tsang accompanied with presents. The latter addressed a gracious letter to Hui-t'ien (Prajñā-deva) in which he thanked him, and also his colleague[37] for their presents and the flattering compliments which they had lavished on him. He ended by saying that he was sending him the list of sacred books which he had lost previously in crossing the river Hsin-tu (Sindhu, Indus) and earnestly begged him to procure them for him.

CHAPTER EIGHT

p. 321 This book commences in summer, in the fifth month of the sixth year of the period Yung-hui (AD 655) when (the Master of the Law) translated the treatise Li-men-lun; it finishes in the third month of spring of the first year Hsien-ch'ing (AD 656) when the magistrates thanked (the emperor) for having made known to them the inscription which he had composed for the Monastery (of the Great Beneficence).

[37]Chih-kuang (Jñāna-prabha)

Résumé

On the day Keng-wu of the fifth month of the 6th year (AD 655) the Master of the Law in the leisure time left to him from his normal occupations, translated again the treatise Li-men-lun (*Nyāya-praveśa tarka śāstra*).[38] Previously, in the Hung-fu-ss˘ Monastery he had translated the treatise Yin-ming-lun (*Nyāya dvāra tarka śāstra*).[39] These treatises each formed one book. Lü Ts'ai, one of the assistant translators, composed on this last work a commentary entitled In-ming chu-chieh li-p'o.[40] He added to it a table which provided a résumé of the explanations, and preceded it with a quite lengthy preface in which he spoke of the progress of Buddhism in China, of the travels of the Master of the Law, of the 700 works which he had brought back, and of the measures which had been adopted by the emperor to have them translated. This commentary ended with an analysis and eulogy of the treatise *Yin-ming-lun*.

p. 322   [Our author records / reports here some dissertations, letters and eulogies relative to Buddhism, which teach us nothing of interest concerning the travels and works of Hsüan-tsang. These different pieces, which are distinguished less by the depth of ideas than by the style which is constantly of a studied elegance, occupy the greater part of book VIII.]

On the day Wu-tsŭ of the tenth month,[41] the royal prince[42] went to the Monastery Ta-t'sŭ-en-ssŭ (of Great Beneficence), provided a repast for 5000 monks and ordered that each should receive three pieces of silk. He sent two officials of the imperial palace to ask the Master of the Law what could be done to give lustre to the translations which had been entrusted to him, and in what manner one had proceeded in former times to execute works of the same type.

---

[38]See above p. 8, foot note 20. Variant: *Hetuvidyā nyāya praveśa (tarka) śāstra, sapramāṇa śāstra.*

[39]Variants: *Nyāya-mukha; Hetuvidyā nyāya-dvāra*

[40]Meaning 'A diagram showing establishment and refutation of theories, and the annotation of *Hetuvidyā-śāstra*'.

[41]Should read 'of the first month of the first year of Hsien-ch'ing era'.

[42]The newly-proclaimed royal prince. This is important because Crown prince Chung not being born of the chief queen resigned his position as the heir apparent. The emperor thereupon made him the Prince of Liang and proclaimed Chih, the Prince of Tai, the Crown prince.

Hsüan-tsang replied that as the dynasties of the Han and Wei were too far off for him to reply with sufficient details and with precision, he would restrict himself to showing what had been done from the reigns of Fu-chien and Yao-hsing in order to translate and publish the *sūtras* and the *śāstras*[n]. As well as the monks, the princes and high officials themselves had assisted the official interpreters. In the time of Fu-chien, when T'an-mo-han-t'i (Dharma-nandi) translated the sacred books, Chao-Cheng, one of the emperor's chamberlains did the brushwork; in the time of Yao-hsing, when Chiu-mo-lo-shih (Kumāra-jīva) translated the sacred books, Yao-wang (prince Yao) and the count Yao-sung, of the town of An did the brushwork.

p. 323

'Under the second Wei (AD 386–554) while P'u-t'i-liu-chih (Bodhi-ruchi) translated the sacred books, Ts'ui Kuang, the emperor's chamberlain, did the brushwork and then drafted the preface.'

Under the dynasties of (the) Ch'i (AD 479–501), Liang (502–56), Chou (557–579) and Sui (AD 581–618) the same practice was followed.

'At the beginning of the period Chen-kuan (AD 627) when Po-p'o-lo-na (Prabhā-ratna) translated the sacred books, the emperor ordered Fang Hsüan-ling, one of his ministers, Li Hsiao-kung, prince of the Chao district, Tu Cheng-lun, steward of the royal prince's household, Hsiao Ching, keeper of the imperial treasure, to re-examine the translated texts and to look over their elegance and clarity; this practice is not in existence now.'

'The Monastery Ta-t'sŭ-en-ssŭ (of the great Beneficence)', added Hsüan-tsang, 'had been built by the care of the holy emperor in honour of the august empress Wen-teh. Through its grandeur and magnificence, it surpasses all the religious buildings of ancient and modern times; but there has not as yet been placed on it an inscription engraved upon stone to transmit its fame to future generations. If your Excellencies could speak of it to His Majesty, you would be doing a meritorious work.'

They promised to do so and withdrew in haste.

p. 324 The next day they presented a report in favour of this request which received the consent of the emperor. On the day Jen-ch'en, Chu Kuo-ku, palace secretary, steward of the royal prince's household and an historian of the empire, and Ts'ui Tun-li with the title Duke of K'ai-kuo (literally prince who has contributed to the founding of the Kingdom), published an imperial decree ordering ten of the highest officials of the empire (such as the royal prince's tutor, the presidents of the ministry, of the magistracy and of rites, etc.) to assist Hsüan-tsang in the translations, in order to give all desirable purity and elegance to the style.

After the solemn audience the emperor sent an official messenger to Hsüan-tsang, the by name Wang Chün-teh who for his part spoke to him in these terms: 'I have already named the personages who are to assist you in your translations; Yu Chih-ning and his colleagues have accordingly received the order to set out. As for the inscription which you desire, I shall endeavour to compose it myself. I trust it will meet with your approval.'

On receiving this august communication, Hsüan-tsang was deeply moved, and in the presence of the imperial messenger, he was not able to restrain his tears.

On the following day, he went to the palace at the head of the monks, in order to offer thanks to the emperor.

p. 325
The inscription, due to the imperial brush, was completed at the end of a few days, and one of the ministers of state, Chang-sun Wu-chi, was charged by decree to communicate it to the princes and great dignitaries of the court. This inscription was devoted to making, in stately terms, a eulogy of the religion of the Buddha and of the traveller Hsüan-tsang whose intrepid journeys and laborious works had as their goal the glory and propagation of the law.

On the day Keng-shen of the second[43] month, the princes and great dignitaries of the court, having received the imperial inscription, went in a crowd to the palace, to offer their thanks to the emperor.

[43]According to the Chinese text 'Third'.

CHAPTER NINE

p. 326 This book commences in the third month of the first year of the period Hsien-ch'ing (AD 656) when Hsüan-tsang thanked the emperor for having deigned to compose the inscription for the Monastery Ta-t'sŭ-en-ssŭ (of Great Beneficence); it finishes (at the time) when the Master of the Law thanks him for having issued an order that a palace doctor could enquire about the state of his health.

Résumé

In the first year of the period Hsien-ch'ing (AD 656), on the day Kui-hai of the third month of spring when the imperial inscription for the Monastery Ta-t'sŭ-'en-ssŭ was completed, Hsü Ching-tsung, president of the ministry of rites, charged a messenger to go and take it to the Master of the Law.

On the day Chia-tsŭ, the Master of the Law went to the palace at the head of the monks of the monastery to give thanks to the emperor.

On the days I-ch'ou and Ching-yin of the same month, Hsüan-tsang addressed again, with the same object, several letters inspired by gratitude, and filled with praises for the elegance and nobility of the imperial composition.

On the eighth day of the fourth month, the engraving of the inscription from the imperial brush was completed.

On the fifteenth day seven novices were ordained, and a frugal meal was served to a thousand monks, during which nine companies of musicians, drawn up before the Fo-tien palace[44] (or palace of the Buddha) played harmoniously. The crowd did not disperse until the evening.

p. 327

On the sixteenth day the Master of the Law accompanied by a crowd of his disciples went to the palace to thank the emperor for the inscription.

Hsüan-tsang had formerly been sick as a result of the glacial cold which he had experienced crossing the snow peak of Mountain Hsiu-shan (Hosour dabaghan) and the Tsung-ling

---

[44]Fo = Buddha, tien = hall i.e. hall or shrine of the Buddha. It is not the name of a palace, rather it is a reference to a temple / shrine.

mountains,[45] but he had regained his health with the assistance of medicine.

In the fifth month having sought (the) cool air to avoid the overpowering heat of the summer, he felt his former illness reviving and presenting the symptoms of an incurable ailment. The monks and the laity were profoundly distressed. At the first news of this event the emperor sent several palace doctors to care for him. Every day official couriers followed one another hour after hour to inform him of the state of his health. An affectionate father would not have shown more anxiety for his son. The palace doctors did not leave him night or day. At last after five days, the Master of the Law recovered, and then calm returned to the souls of people within and without.

Hsüan-tsang, moved by the acts of kindness of the emperor, addressed to him a letter to show him his gratitude.

p. 328   The emperor congratulated him on his happy recovery and urged him to moderate his scholarly ardour, and to rest.

Hsüan-tsang addressed a new letter of thanks to the emperor. On the first day of the tenth month, the empress made to the Master of the Law a gift of a Chia-sha (*kāshāya*) religious garment and added several dozen other gifts.

Hsüan-tsang sent her a letter of thanks in which he prayed that she have good fortune in childbirth and wished her a great number of sons, and boundless happiness.

On the fifth day of the twelfth month the emperor on the occasion of the birth of his son whom the Master of the Law had named Fo-kuang-wang (the prince with the brilliance of the Buddha) had seven novices ordained and asked Hsüan-tsang to cut their hair in the name of the king.[46] o

The Master of the Law thanked the prince for this distinguished honour.

---

[45]It is a mistake for 雪嶺 Hsuen ling i.e. snow peak. This part of the sentence should read, ' . . . which he had experienced crossing the snow-peaks of Ling mountain but he had regained . . . '

[46]This part of the sentence should read, ' . . . and asked Hsüan-tsang to shave the hair of the baby prince.'

On the same day, Hsüan-tsang congratulated the emperor on Fo-kuang-wang (i.e. the newly born) reaching the age of one month; he sent to him a letter of congratulation, and, for his son, various religious objects, namely: the text of the *Prajñā* in one book, written in gold letters and enclosed in a rich wrapper, as well as the book *Pao-en-ching-pien* (the sacred book of gratitude?); a garment called Chia-sha (*kāshāya*) i.e. a complete religious garb, a perfume jar and table, a water-jug, a cabinet (?) for sacred books, a rosary, a staff for (a) Śramaṇa and a basin for ablutions.

p. 329

In the second month of spring, in the second year, the emperor visited the Loyang palace in the company of the Master of the Law and five translators, each followed by a disciple and travelling at the expense of the state

The wagon of Fo-kuang-wang (i.e. of the young prince) was at the head of the procession. Hsüan-tsang accompanied the royal prince; the other monks followed behind. On their arrival, they took up residence in the Chi-ts'ui-kung palace.

In the fourth month, in summer, the emperor to shelter from the heat, withdrew to the Ming-teh-kung palace. The Master of the Law accompanied him again and took up residence in the Fei-hua-tien palace. To the south this palace adjoined the stream Tsao-chien, to the north it crossed the bank of the river Lo and led into the Hsien-jen-kung palace.

In the fifth month, a decree ordered the Master of the Law to return to the Chi-ts'ui-kung palace to devote himself to the translation of the sacred texts.

On receiving this order, Hsüan-tsang wrote to the emperor a letter excusing himself. He reminded the emperor, that when he was living in the capital he had found the treatise Fa-chih-lun (*Abhidharma-jñāna-prasthāna*) in 30 books, and the treatise Ta-pi-p'o-sha (*Mahā vibhāshā śāstra*), the translation of which commenced before his time, still not complete.

p. 330

A new decree recommended to Hsüan-tsang to concern himself firstly with the sacred texts and the treatises which had not yet been translated and to give second place to those of which translations already existed.

The Master of the Law replied to the emperor that the treatises

Fa-chih-lun (*Abhidharma-jñāna-prasthāna*) and Pi-p'o-sha-lun (*Vibhāshā śāstra*) formed together 200 books; that before him there were in China no more than half (of them) and that there still remained a hundred to translate of which the text was confused and full of faults. 'Now', he added, 'after having corrected them, I have begun to translate them; since last autumn I have already translated 70 books, and there remain no more than 30 to be put into Chinese. These two treatises are extremely important for students; I dare to hope that you will permit me to finish them. There are still other sacred books and treatises different from these by their length, but more incorrect and more altered. I wish to be authorized to translate them following the previous ones.'

The emperor gave him permission.

The Master of the Law was a little distant from the eastern capital (Loyang). He took advantage of this journey in the emperor's retinue to obtain the right to visit his village of birth and his former home. He made enquiries about his parents and his old friends who were approaching the end of their days, for he had only one sister left, by name Chang-chi,[47] who had gone to Ying-chou. He sent someone to inform her, went to meet her and saw her again with a feeling of sadness and of joy. He asked her where the tombs of his father and mother were. He went there himself with her and pulled with his own hands the weeds which had covered them for many years. Then he chose a spot fortunately situated and prepared a double coffin for burying them elsewhere; but although his resolution was firmly fixed, he did not dare to execute it on his own initiative. He addressed a petition to the emperor in which he recalled that 'as a result of the troubles of the last years of the *Sui* his parents were buried more than 40 years ago in great haste which only the circumstances could excuse. Now the tombs of his parents were ruined by time, and soon there would be no more traces of them. In thinking of their past goodness, he felt himself disturbed by anxiety and regret. Today, he wished, with his sister already elderly, to recover their precious remains and to take them from a narrow and ignoble spot and to transport them to the western plain. Having only his sister to assist him in the

p. 331

---

[47]*Chi* is not a part of the name. It stands for Lady / Madam.

accomplishment of this sacred task, he begged the emperor to deign to prolong for some days the leave (of absence) which he had given him so that he might fulfil with fitting dignity all the tasks which filial piety prescribes.'

The emperor acceded to this wish, and ordered by a decree that
p. 332 the costs of the obsequies be borne by the public treasury. The funeral procession, of imposing pomp, was formed by the highest personages of the empire, and it was followed by more than 10,000 monks and lay people of the town of Loyang.

The emperor Hsiao-wen-ti of the dynasty of the second Wei (AD 471–76), having transported his court to Loyang, built to the north of mount Shao-shih the monastery of the little wood (Shao-lin-chia-lan). To the east it rested upon a peak, to the south of the sacred mountain Sung-yo, and to the north upon a raised hill, and three rivers formed a belt around it. Everywhere there could be seen only steep rocks and springs falling in brilliant cascades. Narrow pines, and elegant bamboos were joined together by creepers and formed a curtain of greenery. Cinnamon trees, cypresses and willows joined their shade and gave to all the landscape, majesty, grace and freshness. It was truly one of the most delightful places in the whole empire. The western tower was distinguished by the purity and elegance of its construction. It was there that P'u-t'i-liu-chih (Bodhiruchi) translated the sacred books; it was there also that Bhadra, the celebrated master of the *Dhyāna*, devoted himself to meditation. In former times could be seen the tower which enclosed their remains but at the end of the period Ta-yeh (AD 605–17) robbers destroyed it by fire, without however burning the rich monasteries which surrounded it. At the foot of a mountain which rose to the north-west, to the south-east of the district of Hou-shih, in the valley Feng-huang-ku (the Phoenix valley) was the village of Ch'en, which was also called Ch'en-pao-ku; it was the birth place of the Master of the Law.

On the twentieth day of the ninth month (AD 657) in autumn, the Master of the Law addressed a letter to the emperor in which
p. 333 he sought permission to enter the Monastery Shao-lin-ssŭ (the monastery of the little wood), to devote himself to the translation of books and to meditation. He recalled that it was there that under the second Wei (in the years AD 471–76) the monk

Bodhiruchi translated sacred books.

The emperor replied he could not do without the support of his lights (= insights?) and that he would not allow him to go and bury himself for the rest of his days, amidst rocks and trees.

Hsüan-tsang, touched by the emperor's observations, thanked him for his gracious response and said that he would not repeat his request.

On the fifth day of the 11th month, in winter, on the day when the young prince, (sur) named Fo-kuang-wang, had completed his first year, the Master of the Law offered for (= on his behalf) him a religious robe and a letter written to his design / or specially for him, in which he wished him 'to be protected by 10,000 heavenly spirits, to be surrounded by all sorts of happiness, to remain in peace and to enjoy as he grew up all the advantages of health, to honour the "three precious ones" (*tri-ratna*) after the example of his ancestors, to vanquish demons, to practice the acts, deeds of a Bodhisattva and to continue to protect the religion of the Buddha'.

While the Master of the Law was translating the sacred books in the monastery Chi-ts'ui-kung,[48] he had worked enthusiastically, without taking a moment's rest, and excessive tiredness p. 334 had produced a serious illness. He had informed the emperor, who, anxious for a life so precious, had ordered a palace doctor by name Lü Hung-cheh, to go and take him comfort and the aid of his art.

The Master of the Law was touched to the depths of his heart by this and addressed a letter to him to express his profound gratitude.

The emperor, happy to learn of his recovery, sent messengers whom he charged to bring him back to the palace Chi-ts'ui-kung, in order that he continue his translations.

In the first month of spring of the third year (of the period Hsien-ch'ing—AD 658) the emperor returned to the western capital and the Master of the Law accompanied him.

---

[48]'Monastery' is incorrect. 'Kung' stands for palace. Hsüan-tsang was translating the books in the Chi-ts'ui palace at this time, not in a monastery.

CHAPTER TEN

This book commences in the first month (of spring) in the third year of the period Hsien-ch'ing (AD 658) when the emperor returned from Loyang to the western capital Ch'ang-an: it ends at the second month of the first year Lin-te (AD 664) when (the Master of the Law) died in the palace Yü-hua-Kung.

Résumé

In the first month of the third year Hsien-ch'ing (AD 658) the emperor left the capital (Loyang) and returned to the western capital. The Master of the Law returned with him.

In the seventh month, in autumn, the emperor issued a decree which commanded the Master of the Law to go and reside in the monastery Hsi-ming-ssŭ, the construction of which started on the nineteenth day of the eighth month of the first year (of the Hsien-ch'ing period—AD 656) and had been completed in summer, in the sixth month of this year (AD 658). The monastery had a frontage of 250 paces and a circumference of several *li*;[49] a main road led there, on the right and on the left; markets and villages could be seen in front and behind. It was surrounded outside by green acacias, and it was decorated within by streams of clear water. The capital did not possess a more beautiful and more impressive religious building. That is not all; there were pavilions, towers and palaces ornamented with galleries which soared into the sky. The gold leaf on their elegant columns dazzled the eye and shone as far as the bosom of the clouds. It had ten courts and 4000 cells. It affaced the monasteries T'ung-t'ai-ssŭ of the dynasty Liang and Yung-ning-ssŭ, of the Wei by its splendour and majesty.

p. 336

The emperor gave orders first to choose fifty monks of great virtue, and to give each a servant; then to set an examination for 150 young men destined for ordination.

On the thirteenth day of the same month, the emperor prescribed a fast on the occasion of the ordination of the monks and the Master of the Law was ordered to preside at the ceremony.

---

[49]One *li* = 360 paces = 1890 ft. (i.e. just over 1/3 of a mile) according to *Matthew's Dictionary*, p. 564. *The Hsin-hua Dictionary* (1956) equates the new *li* with 0.310 mile and old *li* with 0.868 mile.

On the fourteenth day of the seventh month, the monks who were making their entry into the monastery were met (formally).

The procession advanced with great ceremony, with banners and parasols, to the sound of musical instruments, as on the day of the entry into the monastery of great Beneficence and of the accompaniment of the imperial inscription.

The emperor commanded that the Master of the Law be given a large apartment in the monastery Hsi-ming-ssŭ, and that ten newly ordained Sha-mi (*śrāmaṇera*) be attached to him to serve him as disciples.

p. 337 As the emperor T'ai-tsung had always highly esteemed the Master of the Law, as soon as Kao-tsung had succeeded him, he redoubled his affection and respect for him. Ceaselessly he sent palace officials to enquire with kindness about him and to take him rich presents. The pieces of silk which he received thus amounted to more than 10,000 without counting several hundred(s of) *kāshāyas* (a type of religious garment). But as the Master of the Law was having a tower built and constructing buildings in order to place there the books and the statues he gave many alms to the poor and to P'o-lo-mên (brāhmaṇas) of the foreign kingdoms. Hardly had he received presents than he distributed them, without keeping anything for himself. His most ardent wish was to mould 10 *koṭi* (100 million)[50] of statuettes of the Buddha; and he succeeded in fact in this pious enterprise.

The kingdom of the east (China) felt great esteem for the book P'an-jo (the book of the *Prajñā-pāramitā*, or of Transcendental Intelligence) but although it had been translated in previous centuries, it was far from being complete. A large number of people consequently begged him to make a new translation.

Now the collection P'an-jo (i.e. of the *Prajñā*) was very long, and at the capital Hsüan-tsang was weighed down with work. On the other hand he thought of the shortness of life, and feared that he could not carry it to its conclusion. He asked then for

---

[50]The Chinese text (10.2a.3-4, Canton edition) has ten *koṭi* = *pai-wan* or 100 *wan*. As *koṭi* in old Indian counting so *wan* in Chinese counting is the highest number. Soothil (p. 261) defines *koṭi* as 'a million. Also explained by 100,000; or 100 *laksha*, i.e. ten millions'. *Pai-wan* or 100 *wan* = 100 × 10 thousand = one million. For some reason the Chinese text equates one million with ten *koṭi* (100 million, according to present day counting). But we may presume that Hsüan-tsang moulded *pai-wan*, i.e. one million statues of the Buddha.

permission to go to the Yü-hua-kung Palace, where he could devote himself calmly to the translation of this work. The emperor granted this.

p. 338   In the tenth month of the fourth year (AD 659) the Master of the Law left the capital and went, in the company of his assistant translators and disciples, to the Yü-hua-kung palace.[51] The emperor provided him, as at the capital, with all that was needed.

As soon as he arrived he resided in that part of the palace called Su-ch'eng-yuan.

On the first day of the first month of spring of the fifth year (AD 660), he started to translate the sacred book Ta-p'an-jo-ching (*Mahā-prajñā-pāramitā sūtra*); the Indian manuscript contained 200,000 *slokas*. As the text was extremely long, all his disciples begged him to abridge it. The Master of the Law was disposed to accede to their wish, and to imitate thereby the example of Lo-shih (Kumāra-jīva), who in translating was accustomed to cut out / curtail tedious passages and to suppress repetitions. On the following night he had a frightening dream which deterred him from this plan.

On awakening he recounted it to the monks and let them know he was firmly resolved to translate the work in its entirety, conforming to the Indian text, such as the Buddha explained it in four famous places: first, in the town of the House of the King (Rājagrha),[52] on the Peak of Vulture (*Grdhrakūta parvata*); second, in the garden of Chi-ku-tu (Anātha-pindika); third in the palace of the being of the Devas T'a-hua-tsu-tsai (*Paranirmita vaśa-vartitā*); fourth, in the convent of bamboos (Venuvana vihāra) of the town of the king (Rājagrha). The Buddha p. 339   held in all sixteen solemn assemblies, and the texts (of the *Prajñā*) which he had expounded there were united in a single work, forming 200,000 *slokas*.

Now, as the Master of the Law had procured three copies of it in India, when he wished to commence the translation, he noted the doubtful and altered passages; he then compared the three copies, and submitted them to a strict revision, and by dint of

---

[51] *Kung* means palace.
[52] Capital of the kingdom, literally House of the king.

care and zeal he succeeded in re-establishing / restoring the text in all its purity.

When he had penetrated a profound idea, clarified a doubtful passage or restored a corrupt passage, one might have said that a god had communicated to him the solution which he was seeking. Then his soul opened out / bloomed, like that of a man plunged in darkness who sees the sun pierce the clouds and shine in all its splendour. But distrusting always his intelligence, he attributed the merit to the mysterious inspiration of the Buddhas and the Bodhisattvas.

At the time when the Master of the Law was translating this sacred book he thought constantly of death. 'Now', he said one day to the monks 'I am 65 years old; I definitely wish to end my days in this Chia-lan (Saṅghārāma) Monastery. As the collection called Pan-jo-ching (the sacred book of the *Prajñā-pāramitā*) is extremely lengthy, I fear continually that I shall not be able to finish it. You must redouble your zeal and efforts, never allowing yourselves to be stopped by difficulties or by tiredness.'

p. 340 On the twenty-third day of the tenth month of the third year Lung-suo (AD 661) the Master of the Law completed the translation of the collecton Ta-p'an-jo-ching (*Mahā-prajñā-pāramitā sūtra*) which formed 600 books (in 120 volumes).

On the twenty-second day of the eleventh month, he charged one of his disciples, by name K'ui-chi, with carrying to the palace a petition begging the emperor to compose a preface (for the collection of the *Prajñā*).

On the seventh day of the twelfth month, Fung-i, one of the masters of the (public) ceremonies, published an edict in which the emperor deigned to promise the preface requested.

After completing the translation of the collection P'an-jo (of the *Prajñā*) the Master of the Law felt that his strength was becoming exhausted and realized that his end was approaching. Then, addressing his disciples, he said to them: 'If I came to the Yu-hua palace, it was, you understand, because of the sacred book of the *Prajñā*; now that this work is completed, I feel that my life is approaching its end. When, after my death, you take me to my last resting place, it must be in a simple, modest manner. You will wrap my body in a mat and place it in the bottom of a valley in a quiet, solitary place. Carefully avoid the neighbourhood of a palace or a monastery, a body as impure as mine must be separated from it by an immense distance.'

Hearing these words, his disciples uttered cries and sobs. Then, drying their tears: 'Master', they said to him, 'you are still strong and vigorous, and your face is as it was before; why do you suddenly utter these sad words?'

p. 341

'I know it (for) myself', the Master of the Law replied; 'how would you be able to understand my fore-bodings.'

On the first day of the first month of spring of the first year Ling-teh (AD 664) the assistant translators and all the monks of the monastery came and begged him with most earnest entreaties to translate the collection Ta-pao-chi-ching (*Ratnakūṭa sūtra*).

The Master of the Law, bowing to the eagerness of their wish, made a special effort and translated some lines; then closing the Indian text he stopped and spoke thus to them: 'This collection is as large as that of the *Prajñā*, but I feel that I lack the strength to complete such an undertaking. My last moments have arrived, and my life is to have no more than a short period left. I wish today to go to the Lan-chih valley to offer my last devotions to the statues of the innumerable Buddhas.'

He left then with his disciples; the monks, seeing him leave, could not stop weeping.

After this pious journey, he returned to the monastery. From that moment, he ceased to translate and occupied himself with his religious duties only.

On the eighth day, a monk from among his disciples, name Hsüan-chüeh, originally from Kao-ch'ang, recounted to the Master of the Law a dream which he had had. He had seen a Fu-t'u (*stūpa*) of an imposing appearance and of a prodigious height, which had suddenly collapsed. Waking with a start he had run to tell the Master of the Law. 'This event does not concern you at all', Hsüan-tsang said to him, 'it is the forewarning of my approaching end.'

p. 342

In the evening of the ninth day, as he was crossing the bridge of a canal situated behind his dwelling, he fell and grazed his leg. From that moment he took to his bed, and his strength decreased visibly. On the sixteenth day he exclaimed as if he was awaking from a dream, 'Before my eyes, I see a great lotus flower, of delightful freshness and purity.'

On the seventeenth day, he had another dream in which he saw, in hundreds and thousands, tall men, clothed in brocade, who, carrying embroidered silk hangings, with flowers of wonderful beauty and jewels of the highest value, were leaving the bedroom of the Master of the Law and going to adorn, inside and outside, the room devoted to the translation of the books. Then, going behind this room, on a wooded mountain, they planted everywhere rich banners decorated with brilliant colours, and played harmonious music. He saw, moreover, beyond the door, a countless number of dazzling wagons loaded with perfumed food, and fruits of more than a thousand varieties, equally beautiful in shape and colour: they were not products of this world. They were brought to him one after the other,

p. 343   and offered to him in profusion; but he refused them, saying: 'These delicious foods are the portion of those who have attained superior understanding. Hsüan-tsang has not yet arrived at that sublime stage; how would he dare to accept them?' Despite his energetic refusal, these foods were still brought to him without interruption.

When the disciples, who had remained near him, had made a noise, he suddenly opened his eyes, and recounted to the sub-director (Karmma-dāna), by name Hui-teh, what had occured.

'According to these portents', added the Master of the Law, 'it seems to me that the merit which I have been able to acquire during my life has not fallen into oblivion, and I believe with an unimpaired faith, that one does not practice in vain the doctrine of the Buddha.'

Immediately he ordered the Master Chia-shang to write down the titles of the sacred books and treatises which he had translated, comprising in all, 740 works, and 1335 books. He also wrote down the *koṭi* (10 million) paintings of the Buddha, as well as the thousand images of Mi-le (Maitreya bodhisattva), painted on silk, which he had had executed. He had had as well 10 *koṭi* (100 million) statuettes made in plain colour (monochrome?). He had had written a thousand copies of the following sacred books: Neng-tuan-p'an-jo-ching (*Vajra-chhedikā-prajñā-pāramitā sūtra*), Yao-shih-ju-lai-pen-yuan-kung-teh-ching (*Ārya-bhagavatī-bhaishajya-guru-pūrva-praṇidhāna-nāma mahāyāna sūtra*), Liu-men-t'o-lo-ni-ching (*Ṣat mukhī dhāraṇī*), etc. He had provided food and shown compassion to more than 20,000 persons among the faithful and heretics; he had lit 100,000 lamps and redeemed several *ouan* (tens of thousands) of creatures.

p. 344

When Chia-shang had finished writing this list of good works, he ordered him to read it aloud. After listening to it, the monks crossed their hands and heaped felicitations upon him. He then said to them: 'The moment of my death is approaching; already my spirit is sinking and seems to be leaving me. You must quickly distribute as alms my clothes and my wealth, have statues moulded, and charge the monks to recite prayers.'

On the twenty-third day, a meal was given to the poor and alms distributed. On the same day, he ordered a sculptor by name Sung-fa-chih, to build in the Chia-shou-tien palace, a statue of the Intelligence (enlightenment, *bodhi*);[53] after which he invited the people of the monastery, the assistant translators and his disciples 'to say farewell, joyously, to the impure and contemptible body of Hsüan-tsang, who having finished his role, no longer deserved to live long.' 'I wish', he added, 'to see poured out upon other men the merits which I have acquired through my good works; to be born with them in the heaven of the *Tushitas*; to be admitted into the family of Mi-le (Maitreya) and to serve this Buddha full of tenderness and affection. When I (shall) come back down again to earth, to partake of other existences, I wish, at each new birth, to fulfil; with boundless zeal my duties towards the Buddha, and to reach at last the Transcendental Intelligence (*Anuttara-samyak-sambodhi*).'

p. 345

After making these farewells, he fell silent and entered into meditation; then with his dying voice, he let escape bitter regrets,[54] feeling that he was no longer enjoying the world of

---

[53]According to the text: A statue of the Buddha in the posture of attaining *bodhi*.

[54]This whole sentence needs to be reinterpreted. Julien has misunderstood Hsüan-tsang's sentiments and the meaning of the Chinese characters. In his dying words, Hsüan-tsang is reiterating his faith in the teaching of the *Prajñā-pāramitā* school. 'Form is unverifiable (*anupalambha*)', he murmured, 'Perception, thought, action, knowledge—

the eyes (faculty of seeing); the world of thought (the faculty of thinking); the world of knowing which is born of sight (knowledge of perceptible objects); world of the knowing born of the mind (perception of spiritual things); and that he did not possess the fullness of the Intelligence. Finally, he uttered two *gāthās* which he made the people who were near him repeat.

'Adoration to Maitreya Tathāgata, endowed with sublime intelligence / understanding! I wish, with all men, to see your loving face;

Adoration to Maitreya Tathāgata! I wish, after leaving life, to be re-born into the midst of the multitude which surrounds you.

The Master of the Law after gazing for a long time upon Hui-teh, the sub-director of the monastery (Karmma-dāna), brought his right hand to his chin and the left upon his breast, then he stretched his legs, crossed them and lay on his right side.

He remained thus motionless, taking nothing, until the fifth day (of the second month). In the middle of the night, his disciples asked him: 'Master, have you at last been born in the midst of the company of Maitreya?'

p. 346   'Yes', he replied in a failing voice. At this word, his breathing weakened more and more, and at the end of some moments, his soul vanished.

His servants, having examined him gently, found that his feet were already cold; but the back of his head was still warm. His face had a pink (flesh?) hue, and all his features expressed in the highest degree joy and happiness.

---

all are unverifiable. The eye, the ear, the mind—too are unverifiable. Consciousness through the Five senses is unverifiable. All the twelve causes, from ignorance to old age and death, are unverifiable. Enlightenment is unverifiable. Unverifiability itself is unverifiable.'

Prajñā-pāramitā sūtras proclaim the identity of the contradictory opposites. The absolute thought which is 'without modification or discrimination' and to which one should aspire, is identified with no-thought. The 'self', which is the epitome of all that is unreal and false, is identified with perfect wisdom and with the Tathāgata. The Tathāgata, however, is one who has 'forsaken all thought constructions and discriminations (*sarva-kalpa-vikalpa-prahīṇo hi Tathāgatah*).'

After uttering his life-*mantra*, Hsüan-tsang offered adoration to the Maitreya Buddha among whose followers he wished to be born in the Tushita heaven and with whose guidance and compassion he wished finally to attain *samyak-sambodhi*, . . . and 'in the midst of the company of Maitreya he was born.' Also see A. Waley, *The Real Tripitaka*, pp. 129, 276.

By the seventh day (of the second month) his face did not show any alteration and his body gave off no odour.

The monks of the monastery having spent several days in prayer, it was not until the morning of the ninth day (of the second month) that the sad news arrived at the capital.

The Master of the Law was seven *chih* tall; his face was of a pale colour. His eyebrows were far apart, and his eyes gleaming. His bearing was grave and dignified, and his features were full of grace and light. The timbre of his voice was pure and penetrating, and his language distinguished at one and the same time by nobility, elegance and harmony, such that his listeners could not grow weary of hearing it. When he was either in the midst of his disciples or in the presence of an illustrious host, people often listened to him for half a day, in a motionless posture (i.e., without moving). He wore by preference, a robe of fine cotton, fitted to his size; his gait was gentle and easy; he looked directly before him and never glanced sideways. He p. 347 was majestic like the great rivers which encompass the earth, calm and shining as the lotus which grows in the midst of the waters. A strict observer of discipline, he was always the same. Nothing equalled his affectionate kindness and his tender pity, the fervour of his zeal, and his unswerving attachments to the practices of the Law. He was reserved in his friendship and did not form attachments lightly, and, once he had entered the monastery, it was only an imperial decree which could make him leave his pious retreat.

On the third day of the second month (of the period Ling-teh— AD 664) the Master of the Law had sent Hsü Hsüan-pei to the emperor to inform him of the injury which he had received and the illness which had resulted from it.

On the seventh day of the same month, the emperor ordered by decree a palace doctor to take his medicines and to go and care for him; but by the time when he arrived the Master of the Law was already dead. Toŭ Shih-lun, governor of Fang-chou, announced this dire event in a report.

At this news the emperor wept and uttered heart-rending cries, saying that he had just lost the treasure of the empire. He suspended, for several days, the solemn audiences.

At this moment, all the civil and military officials gave themselves to groans (wailing) and to tears; the emperor himself was unable to restrain his sobs and to moderate his grief. On the

p. 348 following day, he spoke thus to his chief officers / magistrates: 'What a misfortune for my empire, the loss of Hsüan-tsang, the Master of the Law. It can be said that the great Śākya family has seen its unique support shattered, and that all men remain without a master or a guide. Do they not resemble the mariner whom the abyss is going to engulf, when the tempest has destroyed his oars and his boats; or the traveller lost in the midst of darkness and whose lamp goes out at the entrance to a bottomless pit?'

On finishing these words, the emperor groaned again, and uttered great sighs.

On the twenty-sixth day of the same month, the emperor put out the following decree:

'Following the report addressed to me by Toŭ Shih-lun on the death of Hsüan-tsang, Master of the Law, of the Yü-hua-ssǔ Monastery, I order that the funeral ceremonies be at the expense of the state.'

On the sixth day of the third month, he issued a new decree worded as follows:

'By the death of Tsang, the Master of the Law, the translation of the sacred books has been stopped. In accordance with previous orders, the magistrates will have the completed translations carefully copied; as for the manuscripts (Indian) which have not yet been translated, they will be all sent to the director of the Ts'ŭ-en-ssǔ Monastery (of Great Beneficence), who will look after their preservation. The disciples of Hsüan-tsang and the assistant translators who previously did not belong to the Monastery Yü-hua-ssǔ, will each return to their respective monasteries.'

p. 349 On the fifteenth day of the third month appeared the following decree:

'On the day of the funeral ceremony for the Master of the Law, Hsüan-tsang, I permit all the monks and nuns of the capital to accompany it, with banners and *chhatras* to his last resting place. The Master of the Law was conspicuous for his noble conduct and his great virtues and he was the idol of his country. That is why, now that he is no longer, it is just that I bestow abundant blessing to honour the memory of a man who had no equal in times past.'

His disciples, obedient to his last wishes, made a litter of coarse matting, brought his body to the capital, and placed it in the Monastery of Great Beneficence in the middle of the room devoted to the translation of the books. Completely overwhelmed by the feeling of common grief, they uttered cries (sufficient) to shake the earth. The monks and the lay populace of the capital hastened there and shed tears accompanied by cries and sobs. Each day the crowd was renewed in hundreds and thousands.

On the fourteenth day of the fourth month arrangements were made to bury him in the western capital. The monks and nuns and a crowd of men from the populace prepared more than five hundred objects necessary to perform the obsequies: *chhatras* of plain silk, banners and standards, the tent and the litter of Ni-huan (Nirvāṇa), the inner coffin in gold, the outer coffin in silver, the sha-lo (śāla) trees, and set them out along the streets which would be traversed.

p. 350   The sad notes of the funeral music and the gloomy hymns of the bearers resounded to the heavens. The inhabitants of the capital and the districts situated in a radius of 500 *li*[55] (50 leagues) who formed the procession, numbered more than a million. Although these obsequies were celebrated with pomp, the coffin of the Master of the Law was carried upon a litter made of coarse matting.

The silkmakers of the eastern market had used 3000 pieces in different colours to form the Nirvāṇa wagon, which they had decorated with flowers and garlands adorned with precious stones. They asked permission to place upon the marvellous and splendid catafalque the body of the Master of the Law, but for fear of dishonouring his last wishes his disciples refused. They carried in front of it his three robes and his religious cloak,

[55]See p. 105, foot note 49.

valued at 100 *ozs* of silver; then came the litter of coarse matting. There were no spectators who did not shed tears or were not choked with grief.

On that day more than 30,000 monks and lay people passed the night near the tomb.

On the morning of the fifteenth day, the grave was closed; then at the place of burial a great distribution of alms was made and the crowd dispersed in silence.

On the eighth day of the fourth month of the second year of the period Tsung-chang (AD 669) the emperor ordered by decree, the transporting of the tomb of the Master of the Law to a plain
p. 351   situated to the north of the Fan-ch'uan valley, and to build there a tower in his honour.[p]

JULIEN'S NOTES TO HIS RÉSUMÉ OF *LIFE*

VI p. 292 1. [a] Books VI to X contain only the account of facts personal to Hsüan-tsang which took place between his return from India and his death, and, although they provide a multitude of interesting and important details, they are full of reports, petitions and letters, the translation of which would add nothing to the knowledge of the reader.

We consequently thought that it would be sufficient to give a summary of them; but in abridging this second part we have been careful not to cut out anything which could shed light on the renowned traveller and promote appreciation of his literary works and astounding devotedness.

VI p. 294 1. [b] According to a legend recorded in Hsi Yü Chi (Book XV, folio 16) this king had begged Maudgalaputtra to use his supernatural power to have a wood-carver go up to the palace of the Devas in order that he himself might see the divine face of the Tathāgata and then depict it in an exact manner.

VI p. 298 1. [c] Hsüan-tsang uses two comparisons borrowed from Chinese mythology.

VI p. 298 2. [d] That is, the nine parts of China.

VI p. 300 1. [e] This work is the *Ta T'ang Hsi Yü Chi* or Memoirs on the western kingdoms, composed in the great dynasty of the T'ang, 3 vol. in-80°.

VI p. 303 1. [f] He is the author of the first draft of the present work.

VI p. 304 1. [g] The treatise to clarify the holy doctrine.

VI p. 306 1. [h] I have marked the pronunciation of chin (l. 1 and 8) to show that Keng-chīn (ch'en) and Keng-chîn (shen) are two different days

VI p. 306 2. [i] That is, he invites him to leave the religious life.

VII p. 308 1. [j] Memoir relating to the history of the Buddha.

VII p. 308 2. [k] The emperor's preface and the royal prince's preface.

VII p. 310 1. [l] The exact number would be 18,580 and, including the 50 monks from the Hung-fu-ssŭ Monastery, 18,630.

VII p. 310 2. [m] A monk from northern India who came to China in the second year of the emperor Wu-ti of the Liang (AD 503).

VIII p. 322 1. [n] Fu-chien, prince of Ch' in, reigned from AD 358 to 383, Yao-hsing from 397 to 415.

IX p. 328 1. [o] That is, in the name of his son Fo-kuang-wang.

X p. 351 1. [p] Hui-li concludes this last book of the work with a long, elaborate panegyric on Hsüan-tsang. This portion, which forms 25 pages in the imperial edition and 10 in the edition of Nanking, provides an analysis of the life and travels of the Master of the Law; but as with the official parts, the letters and petitions whose subject-matter we have seen fit simply to indicate, there is to be found in it no new fact or matter of any interest for the history and geography of India or Buddhist literature.

4

The General Account of India in the
Ta T'ang Hsi Yü Chi

(Records of the Western Lands of the Great T'ang Period)

INTRODUCTION

The biography of Hsüan-tsang, *The Life of the Master of Law* . . . , and
the account of his journey to India, *Records of the Western Lands* . . . ,
are incomplete one without the other. This, in addition to the intrinsic
value of *Chuan II* of the *Records* containing, in the first half, a general
description of India, accounts for a retranslation of this section in the
present book. Indeed, historians turn time and again to this source not
only for a study of the 7th century but also as a counter-reference for
other periods of Indian history.

Apart from consulting Samuel Beal's English rendering (1884), we
have taken special note of the English translation and critical commentary by Thomas Watters (1904–05) who, in turn, had carefully examined
M. Stanislas Julien's French translation of the *Records* (1857–58) and
to which he constantly refers in cases of difference of opinion. But,
above all, we are grateful to the three eminent Sinologists, Professor
D.C. Lau (of SOAS, London, and the Chinese University, Hong Kong),
Professor Wang Ling (of the Australian National University, Canberra),
and Professor Tan Chung (of Delhi University and the Jawaharlal Nehru
University), whose translations of the general description of India for
us we have interpreted in the light of indigenous evidence, selecting
as discriminatingly as possible from among the alternative phrases and
nuances at our disposal. Literalness is maintained not only to retain the
Chinese flavour, but also to allow for flexibility of interpretation by
future scholars who might consult this translation.[1]

[1]The editions used for the purpose of our retranslation are: *The Taishō Shinshū
Daizōkyo*, Ed. Takakusu, J., Tokyo, 1924–35, vol. 51 and the Kyoto University edition
with a volume of collation of variants, 1911.

In an evaluation of this source, it may be appreciated that the diversity of India, even in the time of Hsüan-tsang, made the recording of general facts about the country a much more difficult task than observations of a factual nature about individual states which helpfully constitute the bulk of the *Records*. The former requires an enunciation of the theory of the prevalent practices in which Hsüan-tsang, being a foreigner, may not be expected to be very knowledgeable.

Moreover, the pilgrim sometimes chose to highlight Buddhist practices, at other times those which were dominant, (leaving it to the reader to guess whether they were) Hindu, Buddhist or otherwise. Even in the matter of theory this type of confusion occurs occasionally. Overarching these problems was the bias of a devout Buddhist which caused Hsüan-tsang to interpret personal habits, social customs or educational and political institutions in a certain light. The result is a number of anomalies and contradictions in the general description. But they do not jar; rather they dissolve in the all pervasive honesty and sincerity of purpose of the author. Moreover, they can be resolved, sometimes more than partially, in the light of evidence from other sources.

THE GENERAL DESCRIPTION OF INDIA

Contents

The various names of the country; measurements of space and time; towns, villages and houses; language and education; Buddhism; class (caste); forms of greeting; illness and death; revenue and taxation (administration); and products.

The Various Names of the Country

To go into the details of the designation *T'ien-chu*, there are many different views. Formerly it was called *Shên-tu*, also *Hsien-tou*. Now, following the correct pronunciation it is better to say *Yin-tu*.[2] The people of *Yin-tu* (India) name their 'countries' after local places and different

---

[2]None of these names has any relationship with the *paurāṇic* nomenclature for India. Hsüan-tsang gives the designations used in Chinese sources. Indeed one more name for India in a Buddhist Chinese text is Indravardhana. The three names given by the pilgrim are not variations in pronunciation in different Chinese dialects, nor are they mistaken transcriptions of *Yin-tu*. They were originally given to some border regions of India, *T'ien-chu* being used also as a generic term for Buddhist countries. Later at different times they were applied to the entire sub-continent that was India. The name *Yin-tu* became common during the T'ang period. Also see P.C. Bagchi, *'She-Kia-Fang-Che'*, pp. 11–12.

localities have different customs. Giving them a general name from this distance (i.e. from China) and describing it by what is good in it we call it *Yin-tu*. '*Yin-tu*' means '*yüeh*' (moon) in Chinese. There are many names for the moon, this is one of them. It (this name) refers to the various living creatures undergoing, without cessation, the process of *saṁsāra* (the cycle of death and re-birth), a long night of ignorance without a warden of the dawn. The sun having set, the night candles have come on. Even though there is the light of the stars, how can it be as bright as a bright moon, therefore the analogy of the moon. This is because in this land there has been a succession of holy and wise men guiding the mundane people, exercising the rule: the moon shines upon what is below. It is in this sense that it is called *Yin-tu*.[3]

There are many distinctions among the races and clans (*chung-hsing tsu-lei*) of India, of which the *p'o-lo-mên* (Brāhmaṇa) are the purest and noblest. This honourable designation has come to be a popular one and without any distinction of places,[4] the country has come to be known as 'the country of the *p'o-lo-mên*' (*p'o'lo-mên kuo*).[5]

As to the demarcation of territories we can say that the territory of the five Indias is more than 90,000 *li*[6] in circumference, three sides overlooking the sea, and one side, the north, backing on the snowy mountains[7], the north being wide and the south narrow, resembling the shape of a half moon. It is divided into more than 70 'countries'. The climate is particularly hot, the ground has many springs and low places.[8] The north is mountainous, with alkaline soil. The east is a fertile river valley with richly productive fields, the south is full of luxuriant vegetation and the west has soil which is stony. This is a brief account of the general conditions.

---

[3]*Saṁsāra* is a long night of ignorance. The Buddha was the warden of the dawn. After the sun of the Buddha set (upon his entering *nirvāṇa*) India became like the moon, the most luminous among the stars of the night which were other countries. This was owing to her long succession of holy and wise men. Bright like the moon, India was called *Yin-tu* (Skt. *indu*).

[4]The meaning of this part of the sentence becomes clear in the light of the author's earlier statement: 'the people of India name their 'countries' after local places . . .'

[5]*P'o-lo-mên-kuo* or 'Brāhmaṇa-country' for India was first used in the Sui period (AD 589–618).

[6]The *Xinhua Zidian* (New China Dictionary), Beijing, 1972, p. 605, equates the new *li* with 0.311 mile, and the old *li* with 0.868 mile.

[7]Hsüeh-shan, the 'Snowy Mountain', is the ancient Chinese translation of *Himālaya*.

[8]The Chinese character, *shih*, denotes both low places and moisture since a low place is likely to be moist. As the text has only one verb here, it would be more correct to translate it as 'low places'.

Measures of Space

As to the designation of measures of space[9] they call it *yü-shan-na* (*yojana*). Formerly, it was called *yu-hsün, yü-tu-na*, or *yu-yen*, but they are all mistakes and abbreviations. *Yü-shan-na* is one day's march (variant, transportation) for royal troops[10] from the time of the ancient sage kings (*sheng wang*). According to the old Chinese accounts, one *yü-shan-na* is 40 *li*. According to the custom of *Yin-tu* it is 30 *li*, and according to the Buddhist scriptures it is only 16 *li*. For small measurements one *yü-shan-na* is divided into eight *chü-lu-shê* (*krośa*). A *chü-lu-shê* is the utmost limit of the audibility of the mooing of a big cow. A *chü-lu-shê* is divided into 500 bows (*dhanu*), one bow is divided into 4 cubits (*hasta*), one cubit is divided into 24 fingers (*anguli*) and one finger breadth is divided into 7 barley grains (*yava*). The sub-division by sevens is carried from one grain of barley to lice (*yūka*), nits (*likshā*), crevice-dust, an ox-hair, a sheep's hair, a hare's hair, copper (variant, gold) and water[11], until one reaches a 'fine grain of dust', then 'extremely fine dust'. The last is indivisible as further division would make it void, and so it is called the smallest monad of matter (*paramāṇu*).[12]

[9]The character originally meant numbers and quantities but may also convey measurements.

[10]According to the *Artha Śāstra* (x.2.12) one *yojana* is the slowest (rate of marching), one and a half middling, two *yojanas* (just over 10 miles) fastest. The *yojana*, however, varied widely with time and place.

[11]The character for 'dust', perhaps in the sense of atom or particle, is added after all the last five divisions. The characters both for copper and gold seem to be in the sense of metal.

[12]The crevice-dust, also called window-dust or sunbeam mote, is the *trasa-reṇu*, a floating particle of dust, seen when the sun shines through a lattice (*Manu, VIII* 132). The *Divyāvadāna's* (ed. Cowell & Neil, p. 644) 'fine dust' is the *aṇu* or the ultimate atom, the minutest of all material sizes. Its 'extremely fine dust' is a monad of thought which has no separate existence in matter.

Hsüan-tsang's list does not fully correspond to either Brahmanic or Buddhist measures of space but then they do not always correspond with each other. Moreover, Hsüan-tsang might have written from memory.

The commonest table, omitting microscopic divisions, was:

8 *yava* (barley corns)	=	1 *angula* (finger's breadth, ¾ in.)
12 *angula*	=	1 *vitasti* (span, 9 inches)
2 *vitasti*	=	1 *hasta* or *aratni* (cubit, 18 inches)
4 *hasta*	=	1 *danda* (rod) or *dhanu* (bow, 6 ft.)
2000 *danda* or *dhanu**	=	1 *krośa* (cry) or *go-ruta* (cow-call, 2¼ miles)
4 *krośa* (Hindi, *kos*)	=	1 *yojana* (stage, approx. 9 miles)

*Kautilya's *krośa*, however, is of only 1000 *danda*, i.e. 1⅛ miles, his *yojana*, 4½ miles.

Measures of Time

As to the movement of the sun and the moon and their position, although they use different names for these things, the seasons are the same as ours (Chinese). Months are named after their dominant stars. The smallest time-unit is called the *Ch'a-na (kshaṇa)*. One hundred and twenty *ch'a-na* make one *ta-ch'a-na (tatkshaṇa)*. Sixty *ta-ch'a-na* make one *la-fo* (or *la-fu*) (*lava*). Thirty la-fo make one *mu-hu-li-to (muhūrta)*.

Five *mu-hu-li-to* make 'one period of time'. Six periods make a day and a night.[13] But according to the custom of the place (*chü-su*) the day and the night are divided into eight periods. The period in which the moon waxes to the full is called the white division (*śukla paksha*) while the period in which the moon wanes is called the black division (*kṛshṇa paksha*). The black division is either fourteen or fifteen days. That is because there are longer and shorter months. A black division followed by a white division together make up a month. Six months make one 'march' (*ayana*). When the sun moves in the outer part of the equator it is the southern 'march'; when it moves in the inner part of it, it is the northern 'march'. The two together make up a year. Again they divide a year into six periods. From the sixteenth day of the first moon to the fifteenth day of the third moon is the period of 'increasing warmth' (*chien-jê*) (*vasanta*). From the sixteenth day of the third moon, to the fifteenth day of the fifth moon is the period of 'heat' (*shêng-jê*) (*grīshma*). From the sixteenth day of the fifth moon, to the fifteenth day of the seventh moon is the period of rain (*varshā*). From the sixteenth day of the seventh to the fifteenth of the ninth moon is the period of luxuriant growth (*sharad*). From the sixteenth of the ninth moon to the fifteenth of the eleventh moon is the period of 'intense cold' (*chien-han*) (*hemanta*). From the sixteenth of the eleventh moon to the fifteenth of the first moon is the period of 'cold' (*shêng-han*) (*śiśira*).[14]

According to the holy teaching of the Tathāgata, the year is divided into three periods. From the sixteenth day of the first moon to the fifteenth day of the fifth moon is the period of heat. From the sixteenth day of the fifth moon to the fifteenth day of the ninth moon is the

---

[13]The note in the text gives three periods of time for the day and three periods of time for the night. Hsüan-tsang appears to follow Sangha-bhadra's division as stated in his *Abhidharma-shun-chêng-li-lun*. In actual practice, however, both Buddhists and non-Buddhists observed the four-plus-four period division.

[14]Here too Hsüan-tsang follows Sangha-bhadra and differs from most Brahmanic and Buddhist writers. Thus the *Divyāvadāna* equates 120 *tatkshaṇa* with a *kshaṇa* and not the other way around.

period of rain. From the sixteenth day of the ninth moon to the fifteenth day of the first moon is the period of cold. The year is also divided into four seasons, spring, summer, autumn and winter.

The three months of spring are called the months of *Chieh-ta-lo* (*Chaitra*), *Fei-shê-ch'ü* (*Vaiśākha*) and *Shih-sê-cha* (*Jyēshṭha*) commencing from the sixteenth of the first moon to the fifteenth of the fourth moon. The three summer months are called the months of *A-sha-t'u* (*Āshāḍha*), *Sheh-lo-fa-na* (*Śrāvaṇa*) and *Po-ta-'lo-po-to* (*Bhādrapada*) commencing from the sixteenth day of the fourth moon to the fifteenth day of the seventh moon. The three autumn months are called *A-shih-lo-yü-tu* (*Āśvayuja*), *Chia-la-ti-chia* (*Kārttika*) and *Wei-chia-shih-lo* (*Mārgaśīrsha*), commencing from the sixteenth of the seventh moon to the fifteenth of the

---

The measurements of time in general use were:

18 *nimesha* (wink)	= 1 *kāshṭhā* (3⅓ seconds)
30 *kāshṭhā*	= 1 *kalā* (1⅗ minutes)
15 *kalā*	= 1 *nādikā* or *nālikā* (24 mts.)
30 *kalā*	= 1 *muhūrta* or *kshaṇa* (48 mts.)
30 *muhūrta* or *kshaṇa*	= 1 *aho-rātra* (day and night, 24 hrs.)

3 *muhūrta* equalled 1 *yāma* making 1/10 of an *aho-rātra* according to some sources. According to others 1 *yāma* was 1/8 of an *aho-rātra* (i.e. 3 hours). However, the hour or *horā* was a Gupta-period introduction from the west. It was mainly used in astronomy.

15 *tithi* (lunar days) (approximately 14¾ solar days)	= *1 paksha*
2 *paksha* (*śukla paksha* beginning with the new moon and *kṛshṇa-pakṣha*)	= 1 lunar month
2 lunar months	= 1 *ṛtu* (season)
12 lunar months	= 1 lunar year (approximately 354 days)

Albiruni (chapters XXXIV to XLIV) quotes the various divisions of time, from the minutest fraction of a *nimesha* (wink) to *manvantara*, an enormous segment of universal time. The divisions differed from source to source but had some basic agreements.

The twelve lunar months, the first being *Chaitra*, and their corresponding *ṛtus* or seasons, are as follows:

Chaitra (March–April) and Vaiśākha (April–May)	= Vasanta (spring)
Jyaishṭha (May–June) and Āshāḍha (June–July)	= Grīshma (Summer)
Śrāvaṇa (July-August) and Bhādra-pada or Praushṭha-pada (August–September)	= Varshā (rainy season)
Āśvin or Āśva-yuja (September–October) and Kārttika (October–November)	= Sharad (autumn)
Mārga-śīrsha or Āgrahāyaṇa (November–December) and Pausha or Taisha (December–January)	= Hemanta (winter)
Māgha (January–February) and Phālguna (February–March)	= Śiśira (the cool season)

Every thirty months a new month was added to equal the solar year. The lunar calendar was and is still used for religious purposes.

tenth moon. The three winter months are called *Pao-sha*, (*Paushya*), *Mo-ch'ü* (*Māgha*) and *Po-lê-chu-na* (*Phālguna*) commencing from the sixteenth of the tenth moon to the fifteenth of the first moon. That is why the monks of India following the teaching of the Buddha observe two periods of retreat, either in the early three months or the late three months. The early three months are from the sixteenth of the fifth moon (July–August) to the fifteenth of the eighth moon (October–November) and the late three months are from the sixteenth of the sixth moon to the fifteenth of the ninth moon. Previous translators of Buddhist *sūtras* and *vinayas* mention the summer retreat or the winter retreat. That is because of the distant peoples who have different customs and do not understand the standard language or it is because of the non-harmonizing of regional dialects which caused mistakes in translation.[15] Again in reckoning the dates of the conception, the birth, the renunciation and the attainment of Buddhahood and *nirvāṇa* of Lord Buddha, there are mistakes for which I refer you to the later part of the book.

Towns, Villages and Houses

The towns and residential settlements with gates (*lü yen-*) broad and high are enclosed by walls on all four sides. The streets and lanes are winding (*ch'ü ching*). There are shops at the cross-roads, and inns on both sides of the streets. Butchers, fishermen, singers and dancers (*ch'ang yu*),[16] executioners and scavengers (*ch'ufen*) have their dwellings marked with

[15]The Buddhist retreat during the rainy season, *vassāvāsa* or *vassā* (Skt. *vārshikā*) resembled that of the other sects. The monks could observe either the longer or the shorter retreat, the former beginning at the full moon of *Āshāḍha* (June–July), and the latter a month later, both ending with the full moon of *Kārttika* (October–November) (*Mahāvaṁsa* III-2). The double period may in fact be related to the *Brāhmaṇa* and *Sūtra* injunctions concerning the Vedic festivals. The northern Buddhists usually observed a three-month retreat from the first of *Śrāvaṇa* (July–August) to the first of *Kārttika*, as attested by Hsüan-tsang.

Regarding the causes of mistranslation referred to by Hsüan-tsang, the reference is surely to the misunderstanding of the standard language of Mid-India (*madhya-deśa*). Moreover, a translator not fully conversant with Sanskrit and Chinese idioms would not be able to 'harmonize the respective provincialisms / regional dialects'. Differences in climate, thus the rainy season at the end of winter in Tokhara, Samarkand, and the fact that a strict monk observed two retreats, one in summer and the other in winter to gain precedence in status would further reinforce the linguistic misunderstanding. 'The observance of two periods of retreat, either in the earlier or the later rainy season' could thus easily become 'either the summer retreat or the winter retreat'.

[16]In Chinese society too the singers and dancers were looked down upon and their children barred from appearing in imperial examinations.

flags and must live outside the city. When they walk on the road, they keep to the side to keep out of the way. As to the construction of city walls and houses, as the land is low and damp, the city walls are built of bricks. Walls for houses are also made of bamboo or wood. Rooms, halls, and terraces, and flat-roofs are made of wooden planks, cemented by lime plaster and covered with bricks. As to the various high buildings, the construction is similar to those in China. Indian houses differ from the Chinese[17] in that whether covered with thatch, bricks, or planks, their walls are white-washed with lime, and floors plastered with cow-dung (*niu-fen*) which is considered clean and pure (*ching*). Moreover, seasonal flowers are strewn over them (the floors). The monasteries (*sanghārāmas*) are quite marvellous structures. High buildings with three storeys of towers rise up from the four corners. The pillars and beams are carved with wonderful figures. Doors, windows and walls are colourfully painted. Dwellings of the common people are sumptuous inside and frugal outside. The inner rooms and central halls vary in height and width. The multi-storeyed buildings and pavilions have no fixed pattern. Doors open to the east, the throne too faces the east.

As for sitting and resting, they all use corded beds. Royal families, nobility and officials, the gentry, commoners, and the rich adorn them differently but the style of seating is the same for all. The throne of the king is very high and wide, decorated with pearls and precious stones. It is called *simhāsana* (literally the lion's seat) and is covered with fine rugs. In addition, there is a foot-rest adorned with jewels. The officials have different carved and ornamental seats according to their own tastes.

The dresses are all one piece without tailoring. Spotless white dress commands respect; multi-coloured garments are considered inferior. The men wind it around their waists and under their arm, sideways, making bare their right shoulder. As for women, the dress hangs right down and they cover up the shoulders. They make a little bun at the top of the head, the rest of the hair hangs down. Some remove their moustache or have other odd fashions.[18] On the head they wear garlands of flowers. On their body they wear a necklace.

The clothing materials are silk (*kiao-shê-ye, kausheya*) and fine cotton

---

[17]The construction here is confusing. The description that follows has to be understood to apply to houses and not to the buildings mentioned in the preceding sentence.

[18]This may refer to men and the next two sentences either to women or not impossibly to both sexes. Hsüan-tsang's amanuenses occasionally jumbled up their material and may have done so quite innocently, expecting their readers to know what seemed to them

(*tieh-pu*).[19] *Kausheya* is made from wild silk-worms. There is *ksauma* (*ch'u-mo*) which is a kind of hemp,[20] *kambala* (*han* or *kan-po-lo*) which is woven from fine wool from goat's hair and *ho-la-li* which is woven from the hair of wild animals.[21] The latter being fine and soft can be spun into thread/yarn, hence it is a prized material for clothing. In northern India where the climate is very cold, they wear closely fitted jackets like the Tartars. The dress of the non-Buddhists (members of religious sects) is varied and extraordinary. Some wear feathers and tails of the peacock, some wear pendants made of skulls. Some are naked and without dress, some cover up their bodies with matted grass, some pluck out (*pa*) their hair and cut off (*tuan*) their moustache, some let their side-hair grow and make a top-knot of their hair. There is no uniformity in their dress and its colour, and people wear white, red and other colours. As for the costume of the śramaṇa, there are just three garments,[22] *sêng-chüeh-ch'i*

obvious or well-known. In the earlier part of this section too, one has to carefully sift and adjust the material in order to make sense of the description of architecture and of the contrasts and comparisons between Indian and Chinese buildings. There are more instances of the interruption of argument and of the flow of the narrative, as in the opening section on Buddhism, p. 129 (of this book). But if the remark regarding personal appearance refers to women as one of our Chinese translators thinks, the explanation is that Hsüan-tsang, who was familiar only with a faintly visible moustache even on men, may have found the growth on Indian women's faces conspicuous enough to make an observation about it. Although the Chinese characters *chien ts'u* stand for cutting the moustache (*ts'u*) with scissors, Hsüan-tsang may have implied tweezers. However, Indian literature contains references to cleaning of the skin and removal of unwanted hair only by the use of a stiff paste made of flour, oil, and an antiseptic herbal powder (of *haridra* (*haldī*), turmeric).

[19]Watters, I, pp.148–9 prefers to regard *tieh* and *pu* as two types of materials and translates them as muslin and calico. He also points out that the term *Kausheya* for silk from the wild silk worm was applied to mixed cotton and silk. (*Mūla-sarvāsti-vāda-nikāya-vinaya vibhāshā*), chapter 5 (Nanjio, no. 1135): *Sêng-chi lü*, chapter 9).

His observation that Hsüan-tsang makes a single group of silk and cottons because he, like other Chinese of his time and district, knew nothing of the cotton plant and the clothes derived from it, is corroborated by the fact that the monks of Bodhgaya expressed their regard for Hsüan-tsang by sending him a gift of cotton material to China along with their letters. See pp.25, 26.

[20]*Ksauma* appears to be an inclusive term for cloth derived from the plants *Kshumā*—flax, *śanā*—jute, and *bhangā*—hemp, all of which are described as the source of fibre in the Chinese translation of the Sanskrit texts. The term was used for both linen and silk textiles. See Watters, pp. 148–9.

[21]*Ho-la-li* may stand for *ral*, goat's hair in Tibetan. The Sanskrit *rallaka*, the name 'for a wild animal and for the stuff made from its hair' is probably derived from it. *Ho-la-li* seems to have been used in Assam but must have been a prized material. Kumāra (Bhāskara-varman) of Kāmarūpa presented a *ho-la-li* cape to Hsüan-tsang for use during his return journey. 'Made of coarse skin, lined with soft down it was designed to protect from rain whilst on the road'. Beal, *Life*, p. 189.

[22]*Antara-vāsaka, Samghāti* and the *uttarā-sanga*.

and the *ni-fo-so-na* (*nivāsana*). The way the three garments are styled varies with the different sects, in the matter of width or folds. *Sêng-chüeh-chi* (*sankākshikā*) meaning to cover the armpits, (previously erroneously rendered as *sêng-chih-chih*) covers the left shoulder and the two armpits. It is open on the left and closed on the right side, its length reaching just below the waist. *Ni-fo-so-na*[23] has no belt (*wu tai*). It is gathered into pleats and the folded end is secured by one of these. The pleats are worn in various ways by different sects. The colour of the dress is either yellow or red.[24]

The Kshatriya and Brāhmana live in a simple manner, clean, frugal and fond of spotless white. The robes of the king and the ministers are quite different. They wear flowers and jewel-adorned headgears and rings, bracelets and pendants. The rich merchants wear only bracelets.

The people mostly go barefoot and few use foot-wear. They stain their teeth red or black. They trim their hair and pierce their ears. They have long noses and large eyes. Such is their appearance.

Cleanliness (*chieh ch'ing*) is their conscious (self-controlled, *tzu shou*) habit, not the result of compulsion. They wash before every meal, and don't eat the left-overs of the previous day (*ts'an-ssŭ*= left over; sleep). They don't allow others to use their own eating utensils. Earthenware and wooden vessels (for food) are thrown away after use. Gold, silver, copper and iron (vessels) are polished every time (*mei-chia*). After eating they chew the willow branch[25] to clean (their mouths) and they touch each other only after they finish washing. They wash (*tsao*) each time after urination and after emptying their bowels. They smear perfumes such as *chin-tan-na* (*chandana*, sandal) and *yü-chin* (*Curcuma longa*, turmeric) on their body. The king bathes (*yü*) to the accompaniment of music. People must bathe before they attend religious ceremonies and say prayers.

Language

The script which was made by the god Brahmā has been handed down along with its rules. There are forty-seven sounds / letters whose

---

[23]Meaning skirt in Chinese.

[24]For I-tsing's observations on modes of dress see pp. 72 ff.

[25]I-tsing (pp. 34–5) tells about the various types of trees, including the willow, the branches of which were used as tooth-sticks, but he says that the willow was scarce in India. In order to guide the Chinese monks who took the willow to be the tooth-stick tree, no doubt because of its easy availability in their own country, he remarks: 'It is wrong to identify the tooth-wood with a willow branch . . . the Buddha's tooth-wood tree . . . (at Nālandā) is not the willow.'

combinations express concepts with inflexions and conjugations.[26] The language has a long tradition and wide ramifications. It varies slightly with different places and peoples, but such variations do not contradict the main features of the parent language. (Among the vernaculars) the language of Mid-India (*madhya-deśa* = Uttar Pradesh, Bihar) is particularly developed and standard. The expressions are harmonious and elegant like celestial speech. The sounds are clear and distinct to guide the manners of men (to serve as a model). But the people of neighbouring states and foreign countries are habituated to mistakes, they compete with each other in developing vulgarities and refuse to abide by standards of purity.[27]

As to records and writing, they have separate officers-in-charge. Historical documents are known by the general title *ni-lo-pi-t'u* (or *ch'a*) (*nīla-piṭa*). In these are recorded in detail both good and bad deeds, and fortunate and disastrous happenings.

They begin the education of their children with the 'twelve sections / chapters' (*Shi-êrh-chang*)[28] to lead them on to progress. After the age of seven they are gradually taught the five *vidyās* (*wu-ming-ta-lun*), the five sciences (*śāstras*). The first is *shêng-ming*, i.e. the *vidyā* of sounds.[29] It

---

[26]For a detailed enunciation of the laws of grammar in Sanskrit, See Beal, *Life*, pp. 121–5. Hsüan-tsang's admiration for the language is expressed thus: '. . . we see how a skilful writer in this language is saved from ambiguity, and also how his meaning may be expressed in the most elegant manner.'

[27]Hsüan-tsang's outpourings throw light on the process leading to the birth of dialects.

[28]I-tsing in his *Nan-hai-chi-kuei* . . . , text IV.8a, trans. by J. Takakusu, *A Record of the Buddhist Religion etc.*, p. 170, states that the beginner's small book which the child started at six and completed in six months was called *Si-t'an-chang*, i.e. *Siddha* composition. He says it is also called *Si-ti-ra-su-tu* (*Siddhirastu*: May there be success or accomplishment). Shortened to *Siddhaṁ*, this primer containing the Devanāgarī vowels, consonants and their varied combinations was used by all beginners, Buddhist as well as non-Buddhist, and in its many varieties was used by Buddhist students beyond India. The *Si-t'an-tzŭ-chi* by the monk Chih-kuang of the T'ang period was taken from the *Siddhaṁ* of Prajñā-bodhi of southern India. The *Siddha-piṭaka* or *Siddha-kosha* by the Japanese Annen is dated AD 880. According to Albiruni (10–11 centuries AD), the 'most generally known alphabet is called *Siddha-mātrikā*' (Sachau's trans., p. 173). He also informs us that the Buddhists of Udunpur called their alphabet *Bhaikshukī*. The reference is obviously to the famous Odantapuri Monastery built by a devout *upāsaka* (Tāranātha, p. 264), and patronized by the Pālas. It was especially popular with the Sthavira-vādins, the Saindhava-śrāvakas of western India who lived there in large numbers (op. cit., p. 289).

[29]We may here translate it as *śabda-vidyā* after I-tsing (Takakusu, p. 169). The Buddhist five *vidyās* are *śabda* (grammar and lexicography), *śilpa* (skill in arts and crafts), *cikitsā* (medicine in all its branches), *nyāya* (logic, reasoning), and *adhyātma* (knowledge and purity of the internal). Hsüan-tsang elsewhere uses the same word *shêng-ming* for *vyākaraṇa*.

explains the meaning of words, and classifies their distinctions. The second is *kung-chiao-ming*, i.e. the *vidyā* of skills including—techniques, machinery, astronomy, and calendar. The third is *i-fang-ming*, i.e. the *vidyā* of medicine, embracing exorcisms, charms, medicine (the use of herbs and minerals), acupuncture and ignipuncture. The fourth is *yin-ming*, i.e. logic by which one investigates and distinguishes the correct from the incorrect and the true from the false. The fifth is *nei-ming*, i.e., the *vidyā* of 'the internal' and it studies the 'five vehicles'[30] and the subtle theory of causation *(karma)*.

The Brāhmaṇas learn the four vedas (*Ssŭ-fei-t'ê-lun* = Four veda treatises). The first is called 'the span of life' (*shou* = Āyur-veda), i.e. the nourishing of life and the development of one's nature.[31] The second is called 'sacrifice' (*tzŭ* = Yajur-veda), i.e. sacrifice (*hsiang-chi*) and prayers. The third is called 'evenness / balance / peace' (*p'ing* = Sāma-veda), i.e. the rites, ceremonies, divinations, and military strategies. The fourth is called 'arts' (*shu* = Atharva-veda), i.e. extraordinary ability and skills, exorcisms and medicine.

The teacher must have profound knowledge and deep insight to be able to understand all that is abstruse in them. He enlightens the students with noble principles and intricate ideas, exhorting, admonishing and persuasively leading them, bringing wisdom and ability to the inert and less gifted. If a learner should be clever but shirks work then the teacher perseveres in his instructions until he has completed his training. A student generally matures in character and becomes accomplished in his discipline by the age of thirty. He, then, gets a position of honour

---

[30]*Upāsaka, bhikshu, pratyeka-buddha, bodhisattva, buddha*. There are also other groups of five.

[31]The faculties both of the body and of the mind in relation to the body seem to be implied. The science of good health and longevity helps to develop and use them to the best advantage.

The Āyur-veda is actually a part of the Atharva-veda and it is curious that Hsüan-tsang puts it as an independent *veda* at the head of the list of vedas. The pilgrim was no doubt familiar with the Ṛg as the first veda. Its complete omission by him in this context is not easy to explain. Watters' suggestion (I, pp. 159–60) that what was still orally communicated has probably been omitted from a list of works already written down does not seem plausible. A possible explanation is that being a Buddhist Hsüan-tsang was casual about the vedas or to take another example, about the Brahmanic, theoretical class-profession equation which he records a little later and where he assigns agriculture to the *Śūdra*. The Ṛg was the most authoritative veda for the Brahmanic schools and we know that some of its hyms were directly criticized by the Buddha. Hence Hsüan-tsang's deliberate disregard for it. Incidentally, the second passage of the Uigur version of the letter from Prajñā-deva to Hsüan-tsang becomes more intelligible in the light of this omission. See p. 26

and takes the earliest opportunity to acknowledge with gifts, his indebtedness to the teacher.

Some who are profound scholars in traditional lore, and are concerned with the refinement of learning, they lead lives of seclusion and continence. Aloof from mundane affairs, they are least moved by honour and reproach. Their reputation spreads far and wide—even kings admire them, but cannot prevail upon them to come to their courts. Nevertheless, the state holds genius in esteem and the society respects the wise and the enlightened. They receive honour and awards in good measure. This attitude exhorts people to devote themselves to learning, forgetting fatigue in the pursuit of the arts, search for truth (*tao*) and perfection of virtue. They embark on travelling regardless of distance;[32] even those who come from rich families are no exception. In their journeys they live on alms. They value the knowledge of truth (*tao*) and do not look down upon the lack of wealth. Those who are given to pleasure and leisure, neglect their careers, indulge in good food and clothing, acquire no virtue nor are prepared to practise it; (such men) earn disgrace / ill repute for themselves.

Buddhism

The teachings of the Buddha (*Tathāgata*) are grasped in different ways by different kinds (of people). As the Sage (the Buddha) has long since departed the dharma is pure or mixed. It is comprehended in varying degrees according to people's capacity to understand it. The different schools stand up like mountain peaks, and the debates and discourse among them are like surging waves. They hold on to their theories, yet through various avenues reach the same end. There are eighteen schools,[33] advocating their respective merits. There are two vehicles, the great (Mahāyāna) and the little (Hīnayāna) with quite different monastic regulations. They (the Buddhist order) ponder upon the truth, live and move in a pious way, meditate and seclude themselves from society or from noisy debates. They live together within certain rules.[34]

[32]In search of wisdom . . . 'they count not 1000 *li* a long journey' (Watters, I, p. 161). He elaborates in a footnote that the expression is from the first chapter of Mencius.

[33]These are the traditional 11 + 7 schools respectively of the *Sthavira* and *Mahāsāṅghika* divisions which formed soon after the Buddha's death.

[34]Regarding the maintenance of monasteries, the Korean pilgrim Hui Ch'ao, who travelled to India a century later, remarks: 'As there are no slaves, it is necessary to donate villages and their inhabitants (to the monasteries),' *The Hye Cho Diary*, eds. Yang, H.S. et al. (Berkeley & Seoul, 1984), p. 47 and text, p. 93 (l. 10) 4b.

If a monk is able to lecture on one work of the scripture, whether it be *Vinaya* or *Abhidharma*, he is exempted from monastic administrative duties; if on two, he is accommodated in a better chamber; if on three, he is deputed a brethren to assist him; if on four, he has lay attendants assigned to him; if on five, he rides on elephant and carriage, and if on six, he gets escorts and guards who lead and follow him in procession. As his pious attainments become higher and higher, his eminence enhances accordingly. Often the monks assemble together for public discourses, to judge quality, and to distinguish good from evil (eventually) to decide upon promotions and demotions (in the holy order). Those who can expound the subtlety of ideas, and elucidate abstruseness of philosophy, who command elegance of speech and excel in the skill of debate, they are given the honour of riding on specially decorated elephants with a host of attendants. Those whose theories are hollow and arguments blunt, who are deficient in reasoning and redundant in speech, who are contrary to truth but smooth in language, their faces are smeared with red and white plaster and their bodies with dirt, they are driven out to the wilderness or left to the gutter. In this way not only goodness and badness are shown up but also sagacity and stupidity. If people are wise and find delight in truth, are diligent in domestic duties and dedicated to learning, they are free to renounce the lay world or to remain in it. About punishment by the *Samgha*: if the transgression of the rules is light, the offender is reprimanded by his fellows, but if it is a serious violation they refuse to live with him which amounts to his expulsion. Then having nowhere to live he wanders about the roads in hardship or returns to his old occupation (laylife / is deprived of the monk's robes).

Class (Caste) (Ch. 族 = clan)

As to the different classes there are four streams. The first class is *brāhmaṇa*, i.e. of pure conduct abiding by truth (*tao*), leading continent lives. The second class is *kshatriya*, i.e. the ruling race governing for generations with benevolence and generosity as part of their nature. The third class is *vaiśya*, i.e. traders / merchants who facilitate demand and supply; pursuit of profit takes them to near and far away places. The fourth class is *śūdra*, i.e. agriculturists (*nung*). They work hard at cultivating the soil and are industrious at sowing and reaping.[35] These four

---

[35]On the matter of the class-profession equation it may be said that the aim of the Chinese travellers was to give an account of the prevailing conditions rather than to

classes differ in status of purity. Marriage takes place within the caste (*hun-chü-t'ung-ch'in-fei-fu-yi-lu*: marriages go through the kindred, flying and prostrate different ways).[36] There is no marriage between persons belonging to the different branches of the family[37]. A woman once married never marries again. The mixed classes are really very numerous, and they associate[38] according to their kind. It is difficult to give a detailed record.

The Army

The sovereignty, for many generations, has been exercised only by the *kshatriyas*. Usurpation and regicide have occasionally occurred so that the throne has gone to a different class. Men of valour are selected to be warriors.[39] As the profession is hereditary, they have been able to master the art of war. When they are garrisoned they guard the palaces. When there is war they act as a brave vanguard. There are four divisions

---

enunciate the theory of social and political behaviour of the systems that they encountered. On the question of the *śūdras* being engaged in agriculture it may be pointed out that many texts such as the *smṛtis* of Manu, Yājñavalkya, Nārada and Devala, and the *Vāyu Purāṇa, Laghu-Āśvalāyana, Vṛddha-Hārīta, Mahābhārata*, etc. permit the *śūdras* to follow the professions of the *vaiśyas* in certain circumstances. In fact, irrespective of the *smṛti* injunctions, all classes did indulge in professions other than those normally ascribed to them by the texts.

[36]Watters (I, pp.168–70) takes 'flying' and 'prostrate' to imply 'the great and the obscure', i.e. the rich and the poor. Further, he supports this by quoting Manu IX.88. Both his assumption and the interpretation of Manu's verse seem to be incorrect. In IX.88, Manu advises the choice of a distinguished (*utkṛṣṭa*), handsome (*abhi-rūpa*) and similar (suitable, befitting) (*sadṛśa*) groom; in IX.90 again of a *sadṛśa* groom. Apparently the reference is to a groom of a matching class which the *dharma-śāstras* normally held to be the same class or at least a *dvija* status class for all the three upper (*dvija*) classes. It was the class and not the financial status which was of consequence. In any case the *savarṇa* rule was continually flouted in practice and the offspring of such marriages were provided for by the *smṛtis* for inheritance, etc.

[37]The reference is again to a *dharma-śāstric* injuction against *sapiṇḍa* marriages, i.e. marriages between cousins, etc. from the father's side up to the 7th generation and from the mother's to the 5th.

[38]Variant—'intermarry'.

[39]There is an important variant: 'the brave are selected from the warriors'. If the rulers and warriors are to be identified only with the kshatriya class, the general rule which Hsüan-tsang conveys in an earlier sentence, then the variant is correct reading. But the text implies that brave men of any class were chosen to man the army (Watters, I, p. 171). The warriors are heroes of '*choice valour*' (italics ours) is an English idiom. In Chinese the character for choice 選 has the function of a verb, not an adjective as averred by Watters.

Also see p. 135–6 (last paragraph under 'administration') on recruitment of soldiers which was voluntary and was remunerated. The same was the case with labourers for public constructions.

of the army: infantry, cavalry, chariots and elephants. The war-elephant is covered with coat-of-mail and sharp spurs are attached to its tusks. The general rides and controls it with one soldier each on his left and right to manage the elephant. The chariot in which the army officer rides is drawn by four horses, with infantry guarding it on both sides. The cavalry spreads and resists attack. They chase the enemy in defeat. The infantry is light and fierce; only the brave are selected for it. They bear a large shield and hold a long spear.

Some are armed with a sword or a sabre and dash to the front of the advancing line of battle. All the weapons are very sharp and pointed. Having been drilled in them for generations they are experts in the use of spears, shields, bows, arrows, sabres, swords, battle axes, lances, halberds, long javelins, and various kinds of slings (*lun = chakra?*).[40]

Social Customs

Regarding social behaviour, generally speaking, although they are rather hot-tempered, yet they are upright and simple (sincere). About money they never take anything wrongfully but they yield to others more than fairness requires. They are afraid of retribution after life and maintain a detached attitude towards life and career. They do not practice deceit, they swear on oath and keep their promise. Their government and education advocate purity and their customs are harmonious. Occasionally when the rebels and the wicked transgress the statute law of the country and plot against the rulers and superiors they are put into prison after the facts are established. They are not given any corporal punishment, but alive or dead they are no longer considered members of the community. If the people transgress social morality and go against loyalty and filial piety then they have their nose and ears, and hands and feet cut off or are driven out of the country or banished into the wilds.[41] Other offences can be atoned for by paying fines. In the trial of criminals no torture is used. They give answers to questions and they are judged according to the facts. If they deny transgressions and try to extricate themselves, then four ordeals may be resorted to for finding out the truth. They are, water, fire, weighing and poison.[42]

[40]Also see Beal (I, p. 83, fn 28) who suggests comparison with the weapons represented in the Ajantā paintings.

[41]Because of his Chinese predisposition Hsüan-tsang exaggerates the importance of, and punishment for violation of filial piety. Kauṭilya (III, 20) and Manu (VIII, 389) impose fines for it. Murder and adultery were, of course, much more severely punished.

[42]While the text says: 凡有三條 (there are three items) actually there are four. It appears that the last two are regarded as one.

Legal matters

In the case of (trial by) water the criminal is placed in one sack and a stone in the other. The two are connected and thrown into a deep stream. If the man sinks and the stone floats then he is guilty. (If the man floats and the stone sinks then he is not guilty.) In the case of (trial by) fire the criminal is (first) made to kneel on a red hot piece of iron and then to walk on it. He is made to put his palm on it and also made to lick it. If he is innocent he will not be hurt; if he is guilty he would be burned. A weak person who cannot stand this ordeal is made to hold buds which are cast towards the fire. If he is innocent the buds will open up. If he is guilty, the buds will shrivel up. In the case of weighing, a man is balanced against a stone and judged accordingly. If he is innocent he will go down and the stone will go up; if he is guilty the stone will be heavy and the man light. In the case of (trial by) poison the right thigh of a ram is cut open; a quantity of poison which the accused is asigned to eat is put inside it. If the person is guilty the poison will take effect and the ram will die. If he is innocent the poison will take effect for a while and the ram will come round after the toxic effect subsides. These four ordeals are examples of the measures to prevent all kinds of wrong-doing.[43]

Forms of Greeting

There are nine rituals for different grades of showing respect. One, to enquire after another by means of words; two, to bow one's head respectfully; three, to raise one's arms high; four, to join one's palms on the breast and bow; five, to bend one's knees (in the standing position); six, prolonged kneeling;[44] seven, to prostrate with hands and knees on the ground;[45] eight, to bend down with knees, elbows and forehead to the ground; and nine, to prostrate by laying the whole body on the ground. Among these nine ceremonials prostration is the extreme form of reverence. To kneel and praise the other person is considered to be the utmost mark of respect. When the other is far from you, you bow with your head and join your palms. When near, you kiss his feet

---

[43]For arriving at the truth Manu (VIII, 113–15), in addition to trial by ordeal by carrying fire and diving under water, mentions oaths by touching what is most valuable for one. Albiruni (chapter LXX) mentions trial by ordeal through poison, diving under water, taking an oath before a deity, weighing, putting the hand in boiling water or on hot iron, in addition to a simple oath by one's veracity.

[44]Variant—squat.

[45]A literal translation of the original is 'to bend the five wheels'.

and rub his heels.[46] When delivering a message or receiving orders (from seniors) one holds up one's dress and kneels for long (6th type). The respected one when saluted, always has a kind word or touches the head or pats the back of the person paying respect and gives him advice in good words to show his affection. With a monk, when he receives respectful greeting he only bestows a good wish upon the other (and does not stop the other from kneeling).[47]

According to the schools[48] or according to whom they show reverence , they also circumambulate, sometimes once, sometimes three times or as often as they feel like when they have a long-cherished wish or request in mind.

Illness and Death

When they meet with illness, they fast for seven days and within the period they often get well. It is only when they fail to recover that they are given medicine. There are medicines with different kinds of properties; each one has a specific name. The skill and prognosis of the doctors also vary. When someone dies, people weep and wail around at the obsequies; they rend their clothes and tear out their hair; they strike their forehead and beat their breasts. They have no fixed period of mourning nor any regulations about clothes of mourning, etc.[49]

There are three kinds of ceremonies to dispose of the dead. The first is cremation: the body is placed on a pyre of wood and consumed by flames; the second is water-burial: the corpse is allowed to sink or be washed away to disintegrate. The third is disposal in the forest where the body is left for wild animals to feed on.

Upon the death of a king the first concern is to place a successor on the throne so that he can preside at the funeral. This also establishes precedence. Kings have meritorious appellations when alive, but are not given posthumous titles. No one eats with the bereaved family but after the funeral things return to normal and the family is not avoided.

---

[46]Variant— make a noise (the character is generally used for birds but also for making noise).

[47]All grades of reverence, one at a time, appear to have been in use among the people. In the case of very distinguished superiors like the king, the important brāhmaṇas, and the Buddha, all nine may have been gone through as 'one service of worship of reverence' as suggested by Watters (I, pp. 173–4). For I-tsing's observations on behaviour in the presence of the honoured ones, see *Buddhist Practices*, chapter II, pp. 21–2.

[48]Different religious schools may require different numbers of circumambulations around the deity.

[49]This is inaccurate; both *smṛti* and custom have rules on these matters.

Participation in a funeral is considered unclean. They all wash themselves outside the city before they return.

As to people of very old age who are approaching death, or who are suffering from an incurable illness and fear that the end of life has come, they want to take leave of the mundane world. They look upon life and death with disdain, and wish to depart from the world. Then their relatives and friends give them a farewell banquet with music. They get into boats to sail to the middle of the Ganga and drown themselves. This is said to cause rebirth in heaven. One out of ten may not act consistently with his disdain (i.e. not depart). With the monks who have renounced the world, there is no practice of wailing. When their parents die they read a service of gratitude. Their 'following of the departed' and 'earnestness about the dead' added to their (the dead parents') store of merit in the other world.[50]

Administration—Revenue and Taxation

As the government is magnanimous the official requirements are few. There is no registration of households nor taxation in the form of *corvée* (*yao k'o = corvée* cess) and kind. Of the royal land there is a broad fourfold division. One part is for the expenses of the state and for religious ceremonies (*chi-ssŭ*)[51] or *yajñas*. The second is for the endowment of the ministers and courtiers. The third part is awarded to the clever, the learned and the talented, and the fourth is for the setting up of *puṇya-kshetra* (field of merit), (*fu-t'ien*) for the sustenance of the heterodoxy (non-Buddhists). That is why taxation (*fu-lien*) is light and *corvée* (*yao-shuei = corvée* tax) is light. The people are content with their inherited occupation and all cultivate their allotted estate. Sharecropping the king's land entails the surrender of 1/6 of the harvest as rent. Merchants in search of profit go to and fro with their goods which they exchange after paying a light tax at checkposts on land and water.

Government does not enlist *corvée* labour for public constructions. Labourers are paid according to their work. Soldiers are recruited for

---

[50]On the basis of the first *chuan* of the *Lun-Yü*, Watters I, (pp. 175–6) satisfactorily explains that the first phrase meant, for a Confucianist, the keeping up of the solemn services of worship to the deceased, and the second, care in the matter of duly observing all the funeral rites. In the case of a Buddhist monk these acts further ensured for the deceased a better after-life.

[51]In China these ceremonies were performed for ancestor worship, launching of military expeditions, etc. They involved the offerings of meat and food to the deity.

stationing in far away places and expeditions, and for garrisoning the palaces.[52] They are recruited according to the tasks needed for which awards are announced and the enlistment is voluntary.[53] Ministers and officials each have their own estate and are supported by the yield / income from them.

Products

As the climate and the soil differ so the products of the land also vary accordingly. Flower plants and fruit trees are of different kinds with various names. Among fruits for instance, there are the *an-mo-lo* (*āmra*, mango), the *an-mi-lo* (*āmla*, tamarind), the *mo-tu-chia* (*madhūka, bassia latifolia*), the *pa-ta-lo* (*badara, jujube, ber*), the *chieh-pi-ta-to* (*kapittha*, woodapple), the *a-mo-lo* (*āmalaka, myrobalan*), the *chên-to-chia* (*tinduka, diospyros*), the *u-t'an-pa-lo* (*udumbara, Ficus glomerata*), the *mou-chê* (*mocha*, plantain), the *na-li-chi-lo*, (*nārikela*, coconut), and the *p'an / po-no / na-so* (*panasa*, jack-fruit). It is impossible to enumerate fruits of all kinds. I have given only a few examples of those which are valued by people. As to dates, chestnuts, green and red persimmon, they are not known in India. From Kashmir onwards pears, plums, peaches, apricots, grapes, etc. are grown here and there. Pomegranates and oranges[54] are planted in all countries (of India).

For purposes of cultivation, they plant and weed, plough and harrow according to the season, and the industry and leisure of the people. The soil is fertile and paddy and wheat are particularly plentiful. Among vegetables there are ginger, mustard, gourd, snake-gourd, the *hun-t'o* (*kunda*, the olibanum tree), and others. Onions and garlic are scarce and are rarely eaten. Any member of the family who eats them is driven

---

[52]Variant—'camp'.

[53]Neither forced labour nor slaves were used for public works or in the army. A century later, the Korean Buddhist pilgrim Hui Ch'ao (Hy Ch'o), writing about Vaiśālī in Mid-India, states: 'they have no slaves; the crime of selling people is no different from that of murder'; and further under Kaśmīr: 'As in the five regions of India, human beings are not sold.' See W. Fuchs, 'Huei-ch'ao's Pigerreise dürch Nord-west-Indian und Zentral-Asien um 726', in *SBAW*, 1938, p. 431?; p. 462?; and *The Hye Ch'o Diary*, eds Yang, H.S. *et al.* (Berkeley and Seoul, 1984), p. 39, p. 47 and text p. 93 (l. 10) 4 b. The absence of slavery in India had earlier been remarked upon by Strabo (*Geography*, XVI, 34 c, 701 and 54, C710) and Arrian (*Indica*, X, 8–9), the status and the obligations of the Indian *dāsa* being very different from those of the Greek *doulos* and the Chinese.

[54]Watters, I, p. 178 has sweet oranges, so has Beal, I, p. 88. However, the character Kan 甘 which appears in the text simply means 'sweet'. It seems to be a misprint for its homonym *kan* 柑 , which means orange. There is no such category of Chinese fruits as sweet orange. A doubling-up of pronunciation and meaning has led to the mistranslation.

out of the house. As to milk, butter, cream, 'sand' sugar (*śarkarā, shakkar*), stone-honey (*gur*), mustard oil, and pancakes (*roti*) are the ordinary diet.[55] Fish, mutton, gazelle and deer are also served as dishes. Oxen, donkeys, elephants, horses, pigs, dogs, foxes, wolves, lions and monkeys and such like hairy animals are as a rule not eaten. One who eats them is looked down upon and considered unclean by others. They are banished from the community and are hardly to be seen. As to the distinction in the use of wines and other beverages, it depends on class status. Grape and sugarcane (wine) are the drink of the *kshatriya*. Fermented and distilled liquor from grains is the drink of the *vaiśya*. The *śramaṇa* and the *brāhmaṇa* drink the syrup of the sugarcane and grapes and no wines. The mixed caste and the low tribes do not have any distinctive drinks. There are vessels and implements with various functions; they are readily available. Although they have cauldrons they do not know the use of the steaming pots.[56] Their utensils are mostly earthenware and very rarely brass. They use only one vessel for eating in which they mix all the different ingredients. They take their food with their fingers and do not use spoons or chopsticks. It is only when a person is ill that he uses a copper spoon.

Gold, silver and yellow *l'u-shih* (*tāmra*), white jade and pearls are produced in this country and are very abundant. There are many curious gems and jewels with strange names. They come from the coastal area and are traded. They use gold coins, silver coins, cowrie shells (*pei*), pearls (*chu*), and small pearls (*hsiao-chu*) for currency.

Such is the land of India, its general features within its boundaries, its climate and soil. I have roughly highlighted them under different headings. I shall relate the particular features of different Indian states under specific titles.

---

[55]The Chinese characters for the seven food items mentioned are respectively: *ju, luo, kao, su, sha-t'ang, shih-mi, chieh-tzŭ-yu* and *chu ping-ch'ao*. The lattermost may be split up to mean various (kinds of) cakes, *ch'ao* standing for wheat cakes. Although butter and cream were always used in India, Hsüan-tsang may have considered them inclusive of the invariably used *ghee* and curds also. Mustard oil has always been used more in the north, other oils in the east and south of India.

[56]Once again Hsüan-tsang's remark does not apply to cooking in southern India.

THE GENERAL ACCOUNT OF INDIA:
KIE-JO-KIO-SHE-KWŎ (KĀNYAKUBJA)*

This kingdom is about 4000 *li* in circuit; the capital,[1] on the west, borders on the river Ganges.[2] It is about 20 *li* in length and 4 or 5 *li* in breadth. The city has a dry ditch[3] round it, strong and lofty, and towers facing one another. The flowers and woods, the lakes and ponds,[4] bright and pure and shining like mirrors, (are seen on every side). Valuable merchandise is collected here in great quantities. The people are well off and contented, the families are rich and abundant. Flowers and fruits abound in every place, and the land is sown and reaped in due seasons. The climate is agreeable and soft, the customs of the people honest and sincere. They are noble and gracious in appearance. For clothing they use ornamented and bright [taken in the sense of 'vivid'] (fabrics). They apply themselves much to learning, and are very much given to discussion[5] (on religious subjects). The believers in Buddha and the heretics are about equal in number. There are more than hundred *saṅghārāmas* with over 10,000 priests. They study both the Great and Little Vehicle. There are 200 Deva temples and several thousand followers.

The old capital of Kānyakubja, where men lived for a long time,

---

*For this section Beal's translation (pp. 206–21, Book V) has been retained as the framework. Some unsatisfactory words, phrases and paragraphs have been deleted or replaced. Beal's footnotes have been retained. Devahuti's notes, marked *ᵃ, ᵇ, ᶜ*, ... appear at the end of this chapter. Additional notes / comments by Devahuti have been inserted within the text in square brackets [ ].

[1]The capital, Kānyakubja (Kie-jo-kio-she-kwŏ), now called Kanauj. The distance from Kapitha or Saṅkisa is given by Hiuen Tsiang as somewhat less than 200 *li*, and the bearing north-west. There is a mistake here as the bearing is south-east, and the distance somewhat less than 300 *li*. Kanauj was for many hundred years the Hindu capital of Northern India, but the existing remains are few and unimportant. Kanauj is mentioned by Ptolemy (lib. vii.c.2, 22) who calls it Κανόγιζα. The modern town occupies only the north end of the site of the old city, including the whole of what is now called the *Kilah* or citadel (Cunningham, *Anc. Geog. of Ind.*, p. 380). This is probably the part alluded to by Hiuen-tsiang in the context. It is triangular in shape, and each side is covered by a ditch or a dry nala, as stated in the text. Fa-hian places Kanauj 7 *yojanas* south-east of Saṅkisa.

[2]That is, borders or lies near the western bank of the Ganges. Julien translates it, 'is near the Ganges'.

[3]The reference seems to be to the inner or fortified portion (citadel) of the capital city. Julien translates as if it referred to all the cities. The symbol *hwang* means 'a dry ditch'.

[4]Or the ponds *only*.

[5]This passage, which is confused, seems to refer to their going about here and there to discuss questions relating to religion. The purity of their discourses, i.e. the clearness of their arguments, is wide-spread or renowned.

was called Kusumapura.[6] The King's name was Brahmadatta.[7] His religious merit and wisdom in former births entailed on him the inheritance of a literary and military character that caused his name to be widely reverenced and feared. The whole of Jambudvīpa resounded with his fame, and the neighbouring provinces were filled with the knowledge of it. He had 1000 sons famed for wisdom and courage, and 100 daughters of singular grace and beauty.

At this time there was a *Rshi* living on the border of the Ganges river, who, having entered a condition of ecstasy, by his spiritual power passed several myriad of years in this condition, until his form became like a decayed tree. Now it happened that some wandering birds having assembled in a flock near this spot, one of them let drop on the shoulder (*of the Rshi*) a Nyagrodha (*Ni-ku-liu*) fruit, which grew up, and through summer and winter afforded him a welcome protection and shade. After a succession of years he awoke from his ecstacy. He arose and desired to get rid of the tree, but feared to injure the nests of the birds in it. The men of the time, extolling his virtue, called him 'The great-tree (Mahāvrksha) Rshi'. The Rshi, gazing once on the river-bank as he wandered forth to behold the woods and trees, saw the daughters of the king following one another and gambolling together. Then the love of the world (*the world of desire—Kāmadhātu*), which holds and pollutes the mind, was engendered in him. Immediately he went to Kusumapura for the purpose of paying his salutations to the king and asking (*for his daughter*).

The king, hearing of the arrival of the Rshi, went himself to meet and salute him, and thus addressed him graciously: 'Great Rshi! you were reposing in peace—what has disturbed you?'[8] The Rshi answered, 'After having reposed in the forest for many years, on awaking from my trance, in walking to and fro I saw the king's daughters; a polluted and lustful heart was produced in me, and now I have come from far to request (*one of your daughters in marriage*).'

The king, hearing this, and seeing no way to escape, said to the Rshi, 'Go back to your place and rest, and let me beg you to await the happy period.' The Rshi, hearing the mandate, returned to the forest.

---

[6]Keu-su-mo-pu-lo, in Chinese Hwa-kung, flower palace.

[7]In Chinese *Fan-sheu*, 'Brahma-given'.

[8]Or it may be rendered, 'What outward matter has been able to excite for a while the composed passions of the great Rshi?' It does not seem probable that the king was acquainted with the Rshi's intention; he could not, therefore, use the words as if expostulating with him.

The king then asked his daughters in succession, but none of them consented to be given in marriage.

The king, fearing the power of the Ṛshi, was much grieved and afflicted thereat. And now the youngest daughter of the king, watching an opportunity when the king was at liberty, with an engaging manner said, "The king, my father, has his thousand sons, and on every side his dependents[9] are reverently obedient. Why, then, are you sad as if you were afraid of something?'

The king replied, 'The great-tree-Ṛshi has been pleased to look down on you[10] to seek a marriage with one of you, and you have all turned away and not consented to comply with his request. Now this Ṛshi possesses great power, and is able to bring either calamities or good fortune. If he is thwarted he will be exceedingly angry, and in his displeasure destroy my kingdom, and put an end to our religious worship, and bring disgrace on me and my ancestors. As I consider this unhappiness indeed I have much anxiety.'

The girl-daughter replied, 'Dismiss your heavy grief; ours is the fault. Let me, I pray, in my poor person promote the prosperity of the country.'

The king, hearing her words, was overjoyed, and ordered his chariot to accompany her with gifts to her marriage. Having arrived at the hermitage of the Ṛshi, he offered his respectful greetings and said, 'Great Ṛshi! since you condescended to fix your mind on external things and to regard the world with complacency, I venture to offer you my young daughter to cherish and provide for you (*water and sweep*).' The Ṛshi, looking at her, was displeased, and said to the King, 'You despise my old age, surely, in offering me this ungainly thing.'

The king said, 'I asked all my daughters in succession, but they were unwilling to comply with your request: this little one alone offered to serve you.'

The Ṛshi was extremely angry, and uttered this curse (*evil charm*), saying, 'Let the ninety-nine girls (*who refused me*) this moment become hump-backed; being thus deformed, they will find no one to marry them in all the world.' The king, having sent a messenger in haste, found that already they had become deformed. From this time the town

[9]His ten thousand kingdoms.
[10]That is, on the daughters generally.
[11]The *Purāṇas* refer this story to the curse of the sage Vaya on the hundred daughters of Kuśanābha.

had this other name of the Kuih-niu-shing (Kānyakubja), i.e. 'city of the hump-backed women'.[11]

The reigning king is of the Vaiśya[12] caste. His name is Harshavardhana (Ho-li-sha-fa-t'an-na).[13] During two generations there have been three kings. (*The king's*) father was called Po-lo-kie-lo-fa-t'an-na (Prabhākaravardhana);[14] his elder brother's name was Rājyavardhana (Ho-lo-she-fa-t'an-na).[15]

Rājyavardhana came to the throne as the elder brother, and ruled with virtue. At this time the king of Karṇasuvarṇa (Kie-lo-na-su-fa-la-na),[16]— a kingdom of Eastern India—whose name was Śaśāṅgka (She-shang-kia),[17] frequently addressed his ministers in these words: 'If a neighbour country has a virtuous ruler, this is the disaster of the (*mother*) kingdom.' On this they asked the king to a conference and murdered him.

[12]Vaiśya is here, perhaps, the name of a Rājput clan (Bais or Vaisa), not the mercantile class or caste among the Hindus (Cunningham, *op.cit.*, p. 377). Baiswāra, the country of the Bais Rajputs, extends from the neighbourhood of Lakhnau to Khara-Mānikpur, and thus comprises nearly the whole of Southern Oudh (*ibid.*)

[13]In Chinese, Hi-tsang, 'increase of joy'. This is the celebrated Śīlāditya Harshavardhana, whose reign (according to Max Muller, *Ind. Ant.*, vol. xii, p. 234) began 610 AD and ended about 650 AD. Others place the beginning of his reign earlier, 606 or 607 AD. (See Bendall's *Catalogue*, Int., p. xli.) He was the founder of an era (*Śrīharsha*) formerly used in various parts of North India. Bendall, *op. cit.*, Int., p. xl; Hall's *Vāsavadattā*, pp. 51 f; *Jour. Bom. B. R. As. Soc.*, vol. x, pp. 38 ff; *Ind. Ant.*, vol. vii, pp. 196 ff; Reinaud, *Fragm. Arab. et Pers.*, p. 139.

[14]In Chinese, Tso kwong, to cause brightness. The symbol *p'o* is omitted in the text.

[15]In Chinese, Wang tsang, kingly increase.

[16]In Chinese, Kin'rh, 'gold-ear'. The town of Rañjāmati, 12 miles north of Murshidabād, in Bengal, stands on the site of an old city called Kurusona-ka-gadh, supposed to be a Bengāli corruption of the name in the text. *J. As. S. Beng.*, vol. xxii, pp. 281 f.; *J. R. As. S.*, N.S., vol. vi, p. 248; *Ind. Ant.*, vol. vii, p. 197 n.

[17]In Chinese, Yueh, the moon. This was Śaśāṅgka Narendragupta, king of Gauḍa or Bengal.

[18]Julien restores Po-ni to Bāṇī. In Chinese it is equal to Pin-liu, 'distinguished'. Bāṇa the well-known author of the *Harshacharita*, informs us that his name was Bhaṇḍin. He is referred to in the preface to Boyd's *Nāgānanda*. I-tsing relates that Śīlāditya kept all the best writers, especially poets, at his court, and that he (*the king*) used to join in the literary recitals; among the rest that he would assume the part of Jīmūtavāhana Bodhisattva, and transform himself into a Nāga amid the sound of song and instrumental music. *Nan hae* §, 32.k.iv, p. 6. Now Jīmūtavāhana (*Shing yun* 'cloud chariot') is the hero of the *Nāgānanda*. The king Śrī Harshadeva, therefore, who is mentioned, as the author both of the *Ratnāvalī* and the *Nāgānanda*, is Śīlāditya of Kanauj; and I-tsing has left us the notice that this king himself took the part of the hero during the performance of the *Nāgānanda*. The real author, however, Professor Cowell thinks, was Dhāvaka, one of the poets residing at the court of Śrī Harsha, whilst Bāṇa composed the *Ratnāvalī*. The *Jātakamālā* was also the work of the poets of Śrī Harsha's court. *Abstract*, &c., p. 197.

The people having lost their ruler, the country became desolate. Then the great minister Po-ni (Bhandi),[18] [a] whose office/wisdom and reputation were high and of much weight, addressing the assembled ministers[b], said, 'The destiny of the nation is to be fixed today. The old king's son is dead: the brother of the prince, however, is humane and affectionate, and his disposition, heaven conferred, is filial and respectful. [Because he is strongly attached to his family, the people will trust in him.][c] I propose that he assume the royal authority: let each one give his opinion on this matter, whatever he thinks.' There was no dissension and they all admired his virtue.

On this the chief ministers and magistrates[d] all exhorted him to take authority, saying, 'Let the royal prince attend! The accumulated merit and the conspicuous virtue of the former king were so illustrious as to cause his kingdom to be most happily goverened. When he was followed by Rājyavardhana we thought he would end his years (*as king*); but owing to the fault of his ministers[e], he was led to subject his person to the hand of his enemy, and the kingdom has suffered a great affliction; but it is the fault of your ministers. The opinion of the people, as shown in their songs, proves their real submission to your eminent qualities. Reign, then, with glory over the land; conquer the enemies of your family; wash out the insult laid on your kingdom and glorify the deeds of your illustrious father. Great will your merit be in such a case. We pray you reject not our prayer.'

The prince replied, 'The importance of succession to the throne has always been a difficult matter throughout the ages. In setting up a ruler on his throne, this should be done with great circumspection. I am indeed of little virtue and my father and brother have orphaned me. Would it be any use my being the king. Although public opinion thinks me fit for the throne how dare I forget my insufficiency. Now on the banks of the Ganges there is a statue of Avalokitêśvara Boddhisattva which has witnessed many spiritual wonders. I will go to it and request a response.' Forthwith, coming to the spot where the figure of the Boddhisattva was, he remained before it fasting and praying. The Boddhisattva was moved by his sincerity and appeared in a bodily form and enquired, 'What do you seek that you are so earnest in your supplications?' The prince answered, 'I have suffered under a load of affliction. My kindly father, indeed, is dead and to add to this cruel punishment my good brother has been murdered. I am aware that I am lacking in virtue, nevertheless, the people would exalt me to the royal dignity, to glorify my illustrious father. Yet I am indeed but ignorant and foolish. In my trouble I ask the holy direction.'

The Boddhisattva replied, 'In your former existence you lived in this forest as an 'Araṇya bhiksu' (*a forest mendicant*),[19] and by your earnest diligence and unremitting attention you inherited a power of religious merit which resulted in your birth as a king's son. The law of the Buddha having been destroyed by the king of Karṇasuvarṇa, you, when you become king should revive it. Now when you succeed to the royal estate, you should in the same proportion exercise towards it the utmost love and pity.[20] If you give your mind to compassionate the condition of the distressed and to cherish them, then before long you shall rule over the Five Indies. If you would establish your authority, attend to my instruction, and by my secret power you shall receive additional enlightenment, so that not one of your neighbours shall be able to triumph over you. Ascend not the Lion-throne, and call not yourself Maharaja.'[21]

Having received these instructions, he departed and assumed the royal office. He called himself the prince (Kumāra); his title was Śilāditya. And now he commanded his various ministers, saying, 'I have not yet avenged my brother, the neighbouring countries not brought to submission; while this is so my right hand [variant—hand or hands] shall never lift food to

---

[19]'A forest mendicant' is the translation of *Araṇya Bhikshu* (lan-yo-pi-ts'u). It would appear from the text that the place where this statue of Avalôkitêśvara stood was a wild or desert spot near the Ganges.

[20]So I understand the passage as relating to a corresponding favour to the law of Buddha, in return for the persecution of Śaśaṅka.

[21]This appears to be the advice or direction given oracularly (see *Jour. R. As. Soc.*, N.S., vol. xv, p. 334):

> fi shing sse tseu che tso
> fi ching ta wang che ho.

The promise is, that if this advice is followed, then, 'by my mysterious energy (*or,* in the darkness), shall be added the benefit (*happiness*) of light, so that in the neighbouring kingdoms there shall be no one strong enough to resist (*your arms*).' Śilāditya did, in fact, conquer the whole of North India, and was only checked in the south by Pulikeśi (the Pulakeśa of Hiüen-tsiang, book xi, *infra*), whose title appears to have been Parameśvara, given him on account of his victory over Śilāditya. (See Cunningham, *Arch. Surv.*, vol. i, p. 281; *Ind. Ant.*, vol. vii, pp. 164, 219, &c.) I may here perhaps observe that I-tsing, the Chinese pilgrim, notices his own visit to a great lord of Eastern India called Jih-yueh-kun, i.e., Chandrāditya rājabhṛtya (*kwan*); this is probably the Chandrāditya, elder brother of Vikramāditya, the grandson of Pulakeśi Vallabha, the conqueror of Śrī Harsha Śilāditya (vide *Jour. R. As. Soc.*, N.S., vol. i, p. 260; and *Ind. Ant.*, vol. vii pp. 163, 219; I-tsing, *Nanhae*, k.iv, fol. 6b, and k.iv, fol. 12a). I-tsing mentions that Chandrāditya was a poet who had versified the Vessantara Jātaka.

my mouth. Therefore do you, numerous officials, unite with one heart and put out your strength.' Accordingly they assembled all the soldiers of the kingdom, made the warriors practise warfare [drill] (champions, or teachers of the art of fighting). They had a body of 5000 elephant soldiers, a body of 20,000 cavalry, and 50,000 foot soldiers. He went from west to east, subduing all who were not obedient; the elephants were not unsaddled, the men never took off their armour (*unhelmeted*). After six years he had subdued [variant—repulsed] the Five Indias. Having thus enlarged his territory, he increased his forces; he had 60,000 elephant soldiers, and 100,000 cavalry. Close on thirty years his arms reposed, and he governed everywhere in peace. He then practised to the utmost the rules of economy [opp. of extravagant],[22] and sought to plant the tree of religious merit to such an extent that he forgot to sleep or to eat. He forbade the eating of meat in the Five Indias. If there is killing of life this will be punished without pardon.ᶠ He built on the banks of the river Ganges several thousand stūpas, each over 100 feet high; in all the highways of the towns and villages throughout India he erected hospices,[23] provided with food and drink, and stationed there physicians,[24] with medicines for travellers and poor persons round about, to be given without any stint. On all spots where there were holy traces (*of Buddha*) he raised *saṇghārāmas*.

Once in five years he held the great assembly called *Moksha*. He emptied has treasuries to give all away in charity, only reserving the soldiers' arms, which were unfit to give as alms.[25] Every year he assembled the Śramaṇas from all countries, and on the third and seventh daysᵍ he bestowed on them in charity the four kinds of alms (viz. food, drink, medicine, clothing). He decorated the throne of the law (*the pulpit*) and extensively ornamented (*arranged*) the oratories.[26] He ordered the priests to carry on discussions, and himself judged of their several arguments, whether they were weak or powerful. He rewarded the good and punished the wicked, degraded the evil and promoted the men of talent. If any one (*of the priests*) walked according to the moral

---

[22]*Temperate restrictions*; but *hëen* is difficult in this sense.

[23]Punyaśālās—*Tsing-leu*, pure lodging houses, or *choultries*.

[24]There is an error in the text, as pointed out by Julien, n. 2. The text may mean he placed in these buildings 'doctor's medicines', or 'physicians and medicines'.

[25]The expression in the text is Tan-she, which as Julien has observed, is a hybrid term for giving away in *dāna*, or charity.

[26]The expression may refer to mats or seats for discussion or for religious services [or feasts of?].

precepts, and was distinguished in addition for purity in morals, he himself conducted such an one to '*the lion throne*' and received from him the precepts of the law. If any one, though distinguished for purity of life, had no distinction for learning, he was reverenced, but not highly honoured. If any one disregarded the rules of morality and was notorious for his disregard of propriety, him he banished from the country, and would neither see him nor listen to him. If any of the small princes or their chief ministers lived religiously, with earnest purpose, and aspired to a virtuous character without regarding labour, he led him by the hand to occupy the same seat with himself, and called him 'good [meaning who is good] friend'; but he disdained to look upon those of a different character. If it was neccessary to transact state business, he employed couriers who continually went and returned. The king also made visits of inspection. During the tours he had no permanent abode.[27] Only during the excessive rains of the three months of the rainy season he would not travel thus. Constantly in his travelling-palace he would provide delicious rare food[i] for men of all sorts of religion.[28] The Buddhist priests would be a thousand; the Brāhmaṇas, five hundred. He divided each day into three portions. During the first he occupied himself on matters of government; in the other two he practised himself in religious devotion (*merit*) without interruption, so that the day was not sufficiently long. When I[29] first received the invitation of Kumāra-rāja, I said I would go from Magadha to Kāmarūpa. At this time Śīlāditya-rāja was visiting different parts of his empire, and found himself at Kie-mi-ou-ki-lo,[30] when he gave the following order to Kumāra-rāja: 'I desire you to come at once to the assembly with the strange Śramaṇa you are entertaining at the Nālandā convent.' On this, coming with Kumāra-rāja, we attended the assembly. The king, Śīlāditya, having asked me about the fatigue of the journey,

[27]A hut or dwelling run up for the purpose. It seems to refer to a temporary rest-house, made probably of some light material. From the next sentence it seems that he carried about with him the materials for constructing such an abode.

[28]It will be seen from this that Śīlāditya, although leaning to Buddhism, was a patron of other religious sects.

[29]This refers to the pilgrim himself. The Kumāra-rāja who invited him was the king of Kāmarūpa, the western portion of Asam (see book x). Śīlāditya was also called Kumāra. The invitation referred to will be found in the last section of the 4th book of the life of Hiüen-tsang.

[30]Here *mi*[j] is an error for *chu*. The restoration will be Kajūghira or Kajinghara, a small kingdom on the banks of the Ganges about 92 miles from Champā (vide V. de St. Martin, *Memoire*, p. 387.)

said, 'From what country do you come and what do you want?'

He said in reply, 'I come from the great Tang country, and I ask permission to seek for the law (religious books) of Buddha.'

The king said, 'Whereabouts is the great Tang country? by what road do you travel? and is it far from this, or near?'

In reply he said, 'My country lies to the north-east from this several myriads of *li*; it is the kingdom which in India is called Mahāchīna.'

The king answered, 'I have heard that the country of Mahāchīna has a crown prince called Ts'in,[31] the son of heaven, when young distinguished for his spiritual abilities, when old then 'divine warrior'.[32] The empire in previous dynasty was in disorder and confusion, everywhere divided and in disunion; there was uprising everywhere, and all the people were afflicted with calamity. Then the king of Ts'in, son of heaven, who had conceived from the first vast purposes, brought into exercise all his pity and love; he brought about a right understanding, and pacified and settled all within the seas. His laws and instruction spread on every side. People from other countries brought under his influence declared themselves subjects. The multitude whom he nourished generously sang in their songs of the prowess of the king of Ts'in. I have learned long since his praises sung thus in verses. Are the records (*laudatory hymns*) of his great (*complete*) qualities well founded? Is this the king of the great Tang, of which you speak?'

Replying, he said, 'China is the country of our former kings, but the "great Tang" is the country of our present ruler. Our king in former times, before he came to the throne (*before the empire was established*), was called the prince of Ts'in, but now he has inherited the throne and is called the "king of heaven" (emperor). When the ordained period of

---

[31]The context and Hiuen Tsiang's reply indicate the reference to the first emperor (Hwang-ti) *She*, or *Urh she*, of the Ts'in dynasty (221 BC). It was he who broke up the feudal dependencies of China and centralised the government. He built the great wall to keep out invaders, settled the country, and established the dynasty of the Ts'in. For his conduct in destroying the books, see Mayer's Manual, §368. The reference (farther on) to the songs sung in honour of this king illustrates the character of Śīlāditya, who was himself a poet.

[32]The first Japanese emperor was called *Zin mu*, divine warrior; the allusion in the text may be to the Ts'in emperor being the first to style himself *Hwang ti*; or it may be simply that he was like a god in the art of war.

[33]This can hardly refer to the Sui dynasty, which preceded the 'great Tang', as Julien says (p. 256 n.), but to the troubles which prevailed at the end of the Chow dynasty, which preceded the Ts'in.

[34]That is, the eight regions of the empire, or of the world.

the previous dynasty expired[33] the people had no ruler, civil war raged on every hand and caused confusion, the people were destroyed, when the king of Ts'in, by his supernatural gifts, exercised his love and compassion on every hand; by his power the wicked were destroyed on every side, the eight regions[34] found rest, and the ten thousand kingdoms brought tribute. He cherished creatures of every kind, submitted with respect to the three precious ones.[35] He lightened the burdens of the people and mitigated punishment, so that the country abounded in resources and the people enjoyed complete rest. It would be difficult to recount all the great changes he accomplished.'

Śīlāditya-rāja replied, 'Very excellent indeed! the people are happy in the hands of such a holy king.'

Śīlāditya-rāja being about to return to the city of Kānyakubja, convoked a religious assembly. Followed by several hundreds of thousands of people, he took his place on the southern bank of the river Ganges, whilst Kumāra-rāja, attended by several tens of thousands, took his place on the northern bank, and thus, divided by the stream of the river, they advanced on land and water. The two kings led the way with their gorgeous staff of soldiers; some were in boats; some were on elephants, sounding drums and blowing horns, playing on flutes and harps. After ninety days they arrived at the city of Kānyakubja, on the western shore of the Ganges river, in the middle of a flowery copse.

At that time the kings[k] of over twenty countries who had received instruction from Śīlāditya-rāja assembled with the Śramanas and Brāhmaṇas, the most distinguished of their country, with officers and soldiers. The king in advance had constructed on the west side of the river a great *saṅghārāma*, and on the east of this a precious tower over hundred feet in height; in the middle he had placed a golden statue of Buddha, of the same height as the king himself. On the south of the tower he placed a precious altar, which was the place for washing the image of Buddha. From this north-east 14 or 15 *li* he erected another rest-house. It was now the second month of spring-time; from the first day of the month he had presented exquisite[l] food to the Śramanas and Brāhmaṇas till the 21st day; all along, from the temporary palace[36] to the *saṅghārāma*, there were highly decorated pavilions, and places

---

[35]It is widely believed in China that the first Buddhist missionaries arrived there in the reign of the Ts'in emperor. For the story of their imprisonment and deliverance see *Abstract of Four Lectures*, p. 3.

[36]The palace of travel, erected during a travelling excursion.

where musicians were stationed, who raised the sounds of their various instruments. The king, at the resting-hall (*palace of travel*), made them bring forth on a gorgeously caparisoned great elephant a golden statue of Buddha about three feet high, and raised aloft. On the left went the king, Śilāditya, dressed as Śakra, holding a precious canopy, whilst Kumāra-rāja, dressed as Brahmā-rāja, holding a white *chāmara*, went on the right. Each of them had as an escort 500 elephant soldiers clad in armour; in front and behind the statue of Buddha went 100 great elephants, carrying musicians, who sounded their drums and raised their music. The king, Śilāditya, as he went, scattered on every side pearls and various precious substances, with gold and silver flowers, in honour of the three precious objects of worship. Having first washed the image with scented water at the altar, the king then himself bore it on his shoulder to the western tower, where he offered to it tens, hundreds, and thousands of silken garments, decorated with precious gems. At this time there were but about twenty Śramaṇas following in the procession, the kings of various countries forming the escort. After the feast they assembled the different men of learning, who discussed in subtle language on the highest truth. At evening-tide the king retired in state to his palace of travel.

Thus every day he carried the golden statue as before, till at length on the day of separation a great fire suddenly broke out in the tower, and the pavilion over the gate of the *saṅghārāma* was also in flames. Then the king exclaimed, 'I have exhausted the wealth of my country in charity, for the sake of the deceased kings, I have built this *saṅghārāma*, and I have aimed to distinguish myself by superior deeds, but my meagre virtue has not been blessed. If there are such calamities as these, what need I of further life?'

Then with incense-burning he prayed, and with this vow (oath), 'Thanks to my previous merit, I have come to reign over various Indias; let the force of my religious conduct destroy this fire; or if not, let me die!' Then he rushed headlong towards the threshold of the gate, when suddenly, as if by a single blow, the fire was extinguished and the smoke disappeared.

The various kings beholding the strange event, were filled with redoubled reverence; but he (the king), with unaltered face and unchanged accents, addressed the princes thus: 'The fire has consumed this crowning work of my religious life. What think you of it?'

The princes, prostrate at his feet, with tears, replied, 'The work which marked the crowning act of your perfected merit, and which we hoped would be handed down to future ages, has in a moment (*a dawn*) been reduced to ashes. How can we bear to think of it? But how much more when the heretics are rejoicing thereat, and interchanging their congratulations!'

The king answered, 'By this, at least, we see the truth of what Buddha said; the heretics and others insist on the permanency[37] of things, but our great teacher's doctrine is that all things are imperman- ent. As for me, my work of charity was finished, according to my purpose; and this destructive calamity (*change*) does but strengthen my knowledge of the truth of Tathāgata's doctrine. This is a great happiness (*good fortune*), and not a subject for lamentation.'

On this, in company with the kings, he went to the east, and mounted the great stūpa. Having reached the top, he looked around on the scene, and then descending the steps, suddenly (a strange man), knife in hand, rushed on the king. The king, startled at the sudden attack, stepped back a few steps up the stairs, and then bending himself down he seized the man, in order to deliver him to the magistrates. The officers were so bewildered with fright that they did not come to the rescue of the King.

The various kings all demanded that the culprit should be instantly killed, but Śīlāditya-rāja, without the least show of anger and with unchanged countenance, commanded them not to kill him; and then he himself questioned him thus:

'What harm have I done you, that you have attempted such a deed?'

The culprit replied, 'Great King! your virtues shine without partial- ity; both at home and abroad they bring happiness. I am such a foolish person that I did not take everything into account. I was misguided by the heretics, persuaded by them to be an assassin.'

The King then asked, 'And why have the heretics conceived this evil purpose?'

He answered and said, 'Great King! you have assembled the people of different countries, and exhausted your treasury in offerings to the Śramaṇas, and cast a metal image of Buddha; but the heretics who have come from a distance have scarcely been spoken to. Their minds, therefore, have been affected with resentment, and they procured me, wretched man that I am! to undertake this cruel treachery.'

The King then straitly questioned the heretics and their followers. There were 500 Brāhmaṇas, all of singular talent, summoned before the

[37]The heretics hold the view of endurance (*shang*, the opposite of *anitya*).

king. Jealous of the Śramaṇas, whom the king had reverenced and exceedingly honoured, they had caused the precious tower to catch fire by means of burning arrows, and they hoped that in putting out the fire the crowd would disperse in confusion, and at such a moment they purposed to assassinate the king. Having been foiled in this, they had bribed this man to lay wait for the king in a narrow passage and kill him.

Then the ministers and the kings demanded the extermination[m] of the heretics. The king punished the chief of them and pardoned the rest. He banished the 500 brāhmaṇas out of India, and then returned to his capital.

DEVAHUTI'S NOTES ON KĀNYAKUBJA

[a]Po-Ni or Bā nī may mean discerning, understanding, very good at argument. Watters, I, p. 343 translated it as 'great Minister or leading man—Poni'. It is better translated as 'important or big minister'.

[b]'Ministers' is a more or less satisfactory equivalent of the Chinese. The character may be taken to mean officials, subordinates, colleagues or statesmen. 'Assembled ministers' (Beal, I, p. 211, l. 2) or 'statesmen of Kanauj' (Watters, I, p. 343) is better translated as 'officials numerous'.

[c][ ] portion not quite clear in the original.

[d]'Chief ministers and the magistrates' (Beal, I, p. 211, l. 12) or 'ministers of state' (Watters, I, p. 343) is better translated as ministers and officials (or people in charge of the affairs).

[e]'. . . but owing . . . your ministers' may also be interpreted as 'owing to the badness of ministers' or 'because he lacked good ministers?'.

[f]The Chinese 'punished' is a set phrase, whether pain without death is meant by it is not certain. (Same as exterminate?)

[g]'on the third and seventh days'. It may also mean three weeks or on the 7th, 17th and 27th. Since the Chinese means 'a period of three sevens'.

[h]See Watters, p. 344.

[i]Both Beal and Watters translate this incorrectly.

[j]'mi' should be mo—which is a variant of *chu*.

[k]The Chinese word for kings is vague.

[l]For 'exquisite' more or less the same character has been used as for 'delicious, rare food' on p. 145.

[m]'extermination'. The character for it means 'punished or killed'.

APPENDIX
Inventory of the Complete Works of Hsüan-tsang

According to the biography of Hsüan-tsang by Hui-Li and Yen-ts'ung, Hsüan-tsang returned to China with 657 Buddhist works. Of these he translated as many as 74 consisting of 1335 *chuan** in 19 years, from AD 645 to AD 664, the dates respectively of his return to China from India and his death. He also wrote the *Hsi Yü Chi*, the account of his travels to the Western World, and supplied material for his biographies by Hui-Li and Yen-ts'ung, and the newly discovered one by K'uei-chi.

Formal information regarding the translated works is preserved in several Chinese and other Asian sources, all of which do not necessarily agree with each other in every detail such as the date or the month of commencement or completion of the work or the place where it was carried out. Sometimes there is a discrepancy of several years and following it, in the venue of the composition.

We give below a list of Hsüan-tsang's works on the basis of the recently published *Korean Buddhist Canon* (KBC), a descriptive catalogue compiled by Lewis R. Lancaster and brought out by the University of California Press from Berkeley, Los Angeles and London in 1979.

The catalogue sets out the information obtained from the xylographs of 81,000 printing blocks carved in the thirteenth century and stored in the Hae-in Monastery in South Korea. It has more than 1500 titles and is one of the oldest complete collections of Buddhist works in Chinese.

With a vast amount of Buddhist bibliographical scholarship of the highest quality at its disposal, such as the Chih-yüan-lu (13th century), Snar-thaṅ catalogue (1742), Nanjio (1883), Taisho (1924–35), Hōbōgirin (1929–37), TOH (Complete catalogue of the Tibetan Buddhist Canons: *Bkaḥ-ḥgyur* and *Bstan-ḥgyur*) (1934), STP (Sanskrit texts from the Imperial palace at Peking (1966–76) and many others, the

---

*Rolls of paper used as measure, not necessarily corresponding to chapters in the case of Sanskrit texts.

Korean Buddhist Canon becomes the most updated of all available catalogues with concordances in 4 languages (Sanskrit, Tibetan, Chinese and Korean) accessible under one cover. The KBC records alternate names of works, when applicable, and provides corresponding references to Nanjio, Taisho and others.

We list below the works translated by Hsüan-tsang (1) in alphabetical order and (2) in the most likely chronological order. The catalogue numbers belong to the KBC (Lancaster, 1979).

BUDDHIST TEXTS TRANSLATED BY HSÜAN-TSANG LISTED IN CHRONOLOGICAL ORDER

K 573   *Hsien yang sheng chiao lun sung*
10th day, 6th month, 19th year of Chen-kuan, T'ang dynasty (July 8th, AD 645) in Hung-fu Monastery.

K 460   *Buddha-bhūmi (sūtra)*
15th day, 7th month, 19th year of Chen-kuan, T'ang dynasty (August 12th, AD 645) in Hung-fu Monastery.

K 447   *Shanmukhī dhāranī (sūtra)*
14th day, 7th month, 19th year of Chen-kuan, T'ang dynasty (October 11th, AD 645) in Hung-fu Monastery.

K 22 (12) *Bodhisattva Piṭaka (sūtra)*
19th year of Chen-kuan, T'ang dynasty (AD 645) in Hung-fu Monastery, Hsi-ching.

K 571   *Hsien yang sheng chiao lun*
Begun on the 1st (or 11th) day, 10th month, 19th year, and completed on the 15th day, 1st month, 20th year of Chen-kuan, T'ang dynasty (October 26th or November 5th, AD 645–February 5th, AD 646) in Hung-fu Monastery.

K 576   *Abhidharma-samuchchaya-vyākhyā*
Between the 17th day, 1st month, and the 29th day, intercalary month, 20th year of Chen-kuan, T'ang dynasty (February 7th–April 19th, AD 646) at Hung-fu Monastery.

K 1065 *Ta t'ang hsi yü chi*
Written by Hsüan-tsang and compiled by Pien-chi: 20th year of Chen-kuan, T'ang dynasty (AD 646) in Hung-fu Monastery.

K 154   *Sandhi-nirmochana-sūtra*
13th day, 7th month, 21st year of Chen-kuan, T'ang dynasty (August 18th, AD 647) in Hung-fu Monastery.

K 607   *Nyāya-praveśa*

6th day, 8th month, 21st year of Chen-kuan, T'ang dynasty (September 10th, AD 647) in Hung-fu Monastery.

K 533   *P'u sa chieh pen*

21st day, 7th month, 23rd year of Chen-kuan, T'ang dynasty (September 3rd, AD 649) in Ta Tz'ŭ-ên Monastery, or the 21st year of Chen-kuan, T'ang dynasty (AD 647) in Ts'ui-wei palace.

K 582   *Chatuḥ-śataka*

21st year of Chen-kuan (AD 647) at Ts'ui-wei palace, or between the 10th day, 6th month, and 23rd day, 12th month of the first year of Yung-hui, T'ang dynasty (July 13th, AD 650–January 30th, AD 651) in Ta Tz'ŭ-ên Monastery.

K 619   *Pañcha-skandha-prakaraṇa*

21st year of Chen-kuan, T'ang dynasty (AD 647) in Ts'ui-wei palace, or 24th day, 2nd month, 21st year of Chen-kuan, T'ang dynasty (April 4th, AD 647).

K 881   *Devatā-sūtra*

20th day, 3rd month, 22nd year of Chen-kuan, T'ang dynasty (April 17th, AD 648) in Hung-fu Monastery.

K 570   *Yogāchāra-bhūmi-śāstra*

Between the 15th day, 5th month, 20th year, and 15th day, 5th month, 22nd year of Chen-kuan, T'ang dynasty (July 3rd, AD 646–June 11th, AD 648) at Hung-fu Monastery or Ta Tz'ŭ-ên Monastery.

K 1045   *Vaiśeshika-daśa-padārtha-śāstra*

15th day, 5th month, 22nd year of Chen-kuan, T'ang dynasty (June 11th, AD 648) in Hung-fu Monastery.

K 609   *Triṁśikā (kārikā)*

29th day, 5th month, 22nd year of Chen-kuan, T'ang dynasty (June 25th, AD 648) in Hung-fu Monastery.

K 644   *Mahāyāna-śata-dharma-prakāśa-mukha-śāstra*

17th day, 11th month, 22nd year of Chen-kuan, T'ang dynasty (December 7th, AD 648) in Hung-fu Hall of the Northern Palace.

K 16   *Vajra-chhedikā-prajñā-pāramitā-sūtra*

10th month, 22nd year of Chen-kuan,T'ang dynasty (AD 648) in Yü-hua-kung Monastery, Fang Chou, or during the years of Yung-hui, T'ang dynasty (AD 650–55) in the Ta Tz'ŭ-ên Monastery, Hsi-Ching.

K 603   *Karma-siddhi-prakaraṇa*

22nd year of Chen-kuan (AD 648) or 5th day, 9th intercalary month, 2nd year of Yung-hui, T'ang dynasty (September 24, AD 651) in Ta Tz'ŭ-ên Monastery.

K 259   *Nidāna-sūtra*

1st day, 1st month, 23rd year of Chen-kuan, T'ang dynasty (February 17th, AD 649) in Hung-fa Hall, Hsi-ching.

K 258   *Raj-āvavādaka (sūtra)*

6th day, 2nd month, 23rd year of Chen-kuan, T'ang dynasty (March 24th, AD 649) in Ta Tz'ŭ-ên Monastery.

K 236   *Adbhuta-dharma-paryāya-sūtra*

18th day, 5th month, 23rd year of Chen-kuan, T'ang dynasty (July 2nd, AD 649) in Ts'ui-wei Palace on Chung Nan Mountain.

K 20   *Prajñā-pāramitā-hṛdaya-sūtra*

24th day, 5th month, 23rd year of Chen-kuan, T'ang dynasty (July 8th, AD 649) in Ts'ui-wei palace, Chung-nan Mountain.

K 592   *Mahāyāna-saṅgraha*

Between the 26th day, 12th intercalary month, 22nd year, and the 17th day, 6th month, 23rd year of Chen-kuan, T'ang dynasty (January 14th, AD 649–July 31st, AD 649) in Ta Tz'ŭ-ên Monastery.

K 595   *Mahāyāna-saṅgrahopanibandhana*

Between the 1st day, 3rd month, 21st year, and 17th day, 6th month, 23rd year of Chen-kuan, T'ang dynasty, (April 10th, AD 647–July 31st, AD 649) at Ta Tz'ŭ-ên Monastery.

K 534   *P'u sa chieh chieh mo wen*

15th day, 7th month,23rd year of Chen-kuan, T'ang dynasty (August 28th, AD 649) in Ta Tz'ŭ-ên Monastery.

K 574   *Wang fa cheng li lun*

21st year of Chen-kuan, T'ang dynasty (AD 647) in Ts'ui-wei palace or on the 18th day, 7th month, 23rd year of Chen-kuan,

T'ang dynasty (August 31st, AD 649) in Ta Tz'ǔ-ên Monastery.

K 250   *Tsui wu pi ching*

19th day, 7th month, 23rd year of Chen-kuan, T'ang dynasty (September 1st, AD 649) in Ta Tz'ǔ-ên Monastery.

K 947   *(Abhidharma) vijñāna-kāya (pāda-śāstra)*

Between the 15th day, 1st month and the 8th day, 8th month, 23rd year of Chen-kuan, T'ang dynasty (March 3rd–September 19th, AD 649) in Hung-fa hall, Northern palace and Ta Tz'ǔ-ên Monastery.

K 620   *Karatalaratna*

Between the 8th and 13th days, 9th month, 23rd year of Chen-kuan, T'ang dynasty (October 19th–24th, AD 649) in Ta Tz'ǔ-ên Monastery.

K 594   *Mahāyāna-saṅgraha-bhāshya*

Between the 22nd and 23rd years of Chen-kuan, T'ang dynasty, in the Northern palace and Ta Tz'ǔ-ên Monastery (AD 648–49).

K 554   *Buddha-bhūmi-sūtra-śāstra*

Begun on the 3rd day, 10th month, 23rd year of Chen-kuan, and completed on the 24th day, 11th month, 24th year of Chen-kuan, T'ang dynasty (November 12th, AD 649–January 2nd, AD 650).

K 604   *Nyāya-mukha*

25th day, 12th month, 23rd year of Chen-kuan, T'ang dynasty (February 1st, AD 650) in Ta Tz'ǔ-ên Monastery.

K 193   *Sukhāvatī-vyūha (sūtra)*

1st day, 1st month, 1st year of Yung-hui, T'ang dynasty (February 7th, AD 650) in Ta Tz'ǔ-ên Monastery.

K 575   *Yogāchāra-bhūmi-śāstra-kārikā*

1st day, 2nd month, 1st year of Yung-hui, T'ang dynasty (March 8th, AD 650).

K 158   *Fen pieh yüan ch'i ch'u sheng fa men ching*

3rd day, 2nd month, 1st year of Yung-hui, T'ang dynasty (10th March, AD 650) in Ta Tz'ǔ-ên Monastery.

K 177   *Bhaishajya-guru-vaiḍūrya-prabhāsa-pūrva-praṇidhāna-viśesha-vistara (sūtra).*

          5th day, 5th month, 1st year of Yung-hui, T'ang dynasty (June 9th, AD 650) in Ta Tz'ǔ-ên Monastery.

K 121   *Vimala-kīrti-nirdeśa-sūtra*

          Begun on the 8th day, 2nd month and completed on the 1st day, 8th month, 1st year of Yung-hui (March 15th–September 1st, AD 650), T'ang dynasty at Ta Tz'ǔ-ên Monastery.

K 444   *Buddha-hṛdaya-dhāraṇī (dharma-paryāya).*

          26th day, 9th month, 1st year of Yung-hui, T'ang dynasty (October 26th, AD 650) in Ta Tz'ǔ-ên Monastery.

K 803   *Itivṛttaka-sūtra*

          Between the 10th day, 9th month and the 8th day, 11th month, 1st year of Yung-hui, T'ang dynasty (October 10th– December 6th, AD 650) in Ta Tz'ǔ-ên Monastery.

K 583   *Ta ch'eng kuang pai lun shih lun*

          Between the 27th day, 6th month and 23rd day, 12th month, 1st year of Yung-hui, T'ang dynasty (July 30th, AD 650–January 30th, AD 651).

K 484   *Shou ch'ih ch'i fo ming hao so sheng kung te ching*

          9th day, 1st month, 2nd year of Yung-hui, T'ang dynasty (February 4th, AD 651) in Ta Tz'ǔ-ên Monastery.

K 954   *Abhidharma-kośa-kārikā*

          2nd year of Yung-hui, T'ang dynasty (AD 651) in Ta Tz'ǔ-ên Monastery.

K 572   *Abhidharma-samuchchaya*

          Begun on the 16th day,1st month, and completed on the 28th day, 3rd month, 3rd year of Yung-hui, T'ang dynasty (February 11th–April 23rd, AD 652) in Ta Tz'u-ên Monastery, or during the years of Hsien-ch'ing, T'ang dynasty (AD 656–61).

K 483   *Mahā-parinirvāṇa-sūtra*

          4th day, 4th month, 3rd year of Yung-hui, T'ang dynasty (May 17th, AD 652) in Ta Tz'ǔ-ên Monastery.

K 57   *Daśa-chakra-kshiti-garbha (sūtra)*

          Begun on the 23rd day, 1st month, 2nd year of Yung-hui, T'ang dynasty, (February 18th, AD 651) and finished on the 29th day, 6th month, 2nd year of Yung-hui (August 9th, AD 652).

K 957   *Abhidharma-kośa-śāstra-kārikā-vibhāshya*

Between the 5th day, 4th month, 2nd year, and the 20th day, 10th month, 3rd year of Yung-hui, T'ang dynasty (April 30th, AD 651–November 26th, AD 652).

K 1046   *Nandimitr-āvadāna*

18th day, 5th intercalary month, 5th year of Yung-hui, T'ang dynasty (June 8th, AD 654).

K 256   *Ch'eng tsan ta ch'eng kung te ching*

5th day, 6th month, 5th year of Yung-hui, T'ang dynasty (July 24th, AD 654) in Ta Tz'ŭ-ên Monastery.

K 956   *(Abhidharma) Nyāyānusāra-śāstra*

Between the 1st day, 1st month, 4th year, and the 10th day, 7th month, 5th year of Yung-hui, T'ang dynasty (February 3rd, AD 653–August 27th, AD 654).

K 955   *Abhidharma-kośa-śāstra*

Between the 10th day, 5th month, 2nd year, and the 27th day, 7th month, 5th year of Yung-hui, T'ang dynasty (June 3rd, AD 651–September 13th, AD 654) in Ta Tz'ŭ-ên Monastery.

K 446   *Pa chi k'u nan t'o lo ni ching*

10th day, 9th month, 5th year of Yung-hui, T'ang dynasty (October 25th, AD 654) in Ta Tz'ŭ-ên Monastery.

K 445   *Pa ming p'u mi t'o lo ni ching*

27th day, 9th month, 5th year of Yung-hui, T'ang dynasty (November 11th, AD 654) in Ta Tz'ŭ-ên Monastery.

K 101   *Tathāgatānāṁ-Buddha-kshetra-guṇokta-dharma-paryāya (sūtra)*

28th day, 9th month, 5th year of Yung-hui, T'ang dynasty (November 12th, AD 654) in Ta Tz'ŭ-ên Monastery.

K 332   *Sheng ch'uang pei yin t'o lo ni ching*

29th day, 9th month, 5th year of Yung-hui, T'ang dynasty (November 13th, AD 654) in Ta Tz'ŭ-ên Monastery.

K 448   *Vasudhārā-dhāraṇī (sūtra)*

10th day, 10th month, 5th year of Yung-hui, T'ang dynasty (November 24th, AD 654) in Ta Tz'ŭ-ên Monastery.

K 310   Avalokiteśvaraikādaśa-mukha-dhāraṇī (sūtra).
         28th day, 3rd month, 1st year of Hsien-ch'ing, T'ang dynasty
         (April 27th, AD 656) in Ta Tz'ŭ-ên Monastery.

K 628   Ālambana-parīkshā
         29th day, 12th month, 2nd year of Hsien-ch'ing, T'ang dy-
         nasty (AD 657) in Ta-nei-li-jih Hall, Tung-tu.

K 964   Abhidharmāvatāra-prakaraṇa
         13th day, 10th month, 3rd year of Hsien-ch'ing, T'ang dynasty
         (November 13th, AD 658) in Ta Tz'ŭ-ên Monastery.

K 289   Amogha-pāśa-hṛdaya (sūtra)
         19th day, 4th month, 4th year of Hsien-ch'ing, T'ang dynasty
         (May 15th, AD 659), at Ta Tz'ŭ-ên Monastery.

K 952   (Abhidharma) mahā-vibhāshā (śāstra).
         Between the 27th day, 7th month, 1st year and the 3rd day,
         7th month, 4th year of Hsien-ch'ing, T'ang dynasty (August
         18th, AD 656–July 27th, AD 659).

K 944   (Abhidharma) Jñāna-prasthāna (śāstra).
         Between the 26th day, 1st month, 2nd year and the 7th day,
         5th month, 5th year of Hsien-ch'ing, T'ang dynasty (February
         14th, AD 657–June 20th, AD 660) in Yü-hua Monastery.

K 614   Vijñapti-mātratā-siddhi-śāstra
         10th intercalary month, 4th year of Hsien-ch'ing, T'ang dy-
         nasty (October or November, AD 659) in Yü-hua Monastery.

K 945   (Abhidharma) dharma-skandha (pāda-śāstra)
         Between the 27th day, 7th month, and the 14th day, 9th
         month, 4th year of Hsien-ch'ing, T'ang dynasty (August
         20th–October 5th, AD 659), in Ta Tz'ŭ-ên Monastery.

K 949   (Abhidharma) prakaraṇa-pāda (śāstra)
         Between the 1st day, 9th month, and the 23rd day, 10th
         month, 5th year of Hsien-ch'ing, T'ang dynasty (October
         10th—November 30th, AD 660) in Yü-hua Monastery.

K 599   Madhyānta-vibhaṅga-kārikā
         1st day, 5th month, 1st year of Lung-shuo, T'ang dynasty
         (June 3rd, AD 661) at Yü-hua Monastery.

K 601   Madhyānta-vibhaṅga-bhāshya
         Between the 10th and 30th days, 5th month, 1st year of
         Lung-shuo, T'ang dynasty (June 12th–July 2nd, AD 661) in
         Yü-hua Monastery.

K 736   *Pratītya-samutpādādi-vibhanga-nirdeśa-sūtra*

9th day, 7th month, 1st year of Lung-shuo, T'ang dynasty (August 9th, AD 661).

K 608   *Vimśatika-vṛtti*

1st day, 6th month, 1st year of Lung-shuo, T'ang dynasty (July 3rd, AD 661) in Yü-hua Monastery.

K 977   *Samayabhedoparachana-chakra*

14th day, 7th month, 2nd year of Lung-shuo, T'ang dynasty (September 2nd, AD 662), in Yü-hua Monastery.

K 482   *Praśānta-viniśchaya-pratihārya-(samādhi) sūtra*

29th day, 12th month, 3rd year of Lung-shuo, T'ang dynasty (February 1st, AD 664) in Yü-hua Monastery, or 29th day, 12th month, 2nd year of Lung-shuo, T'ang dynasty (February 12th, AD 663) in Yü-hua Monastery.

K 948   *(Abhidharma) dhātu-kāya (pāda-śāstra)*

4th day, 6th month, 3rd year of Lung-shuo, T'ang dynasty (July 14th, AD 663) in Yü-hua Monastery.

K 970   *Pañcha-vāstuka-vibhāshā*

13th day, 10th month, 3rd year of Lung-shuo, T'ang dynasty (November 18th, AD 663) in Ta Tz'ŭ-ên Monastery.

K 1   *Mahā-prajñā-pāramitā-sūtra*

Begun on the 1st day, 1st month, 5th year of Hsien-ch'ing, T'ang dynasty (February 16th, AD 660), or in the 4th year of Hsien-ch'ing, T'ang dynasty (AD 659), and completed on the 20th day, 10th month, 3rd year of Lung-shuo, T'ang dynasty (November 25th, AD 663) in Yü-hua-kung Monastery, Fang-chou.

K 946   *(Abhidharma) sangīti-paryāya (pāda-śāstra)*

Between the 26th day, 11th month, 5th year of Hsien-ch'ing, and the 29th day, 12th month, 3rd year of Lung-shuo, T'ang dynasty (January 2nd, AD 660–February 1st, AD 664), in Yü-hua Monastery.

K 312   *Chou wu shou*

1st day, 1st month, 1st year of Lin-te, T'ang dynasty (February 2nd, AD 664) in Yü-hua Monastery.

BUDDHIST TEXTS TRANSLATED BY HSÜAN-TSANG
LISTED IN ALPHABETICAL ORDER

K 945   *(Abhidharma) dharma-skandha (pāda-śāstra).*

Between the 27th day, 7th month, and the 14th day, 9th month, 4th year of Hsien-ch'ing, T'ang dynasty (August 20th–October 5th AD 659), in Ta Tz'ŭ-ên Monastery.

K 948   *(Abhidharma) dhātu-kāya (pāda-śāstra)*

4th day, 6th month, 3rd year of Lung-shuo, T'ang dynasty (July 14th, AD 663) in Yü-hua Monastery.

K 944   *(Abhidharma) Jñāna-prasthāna (śāstra)*

Between 26th day, 1st month, 2nd year and the 7th day, 5th month, 5th year of Hsien-ch'ing, T'ang dynasty (February 14th, AD 657–June 20th, AD 660) in Yü-hua Monastery.

K 954   *Abhidharma-kośa-kārikā*

2nd year of Yung-hui, T'ang dynasty (AD 651) in Ta Tz'ŭ-ên Monastery.

K 955   *Abhidharma-kośa-śāstra*

Between the 10th day, 5th month, 2nd year, and the 27th day, 7th month, 5th year of Yung-hui, T'ang dynasty (June 3rd, AD 651– September 13th, AD 654) in Ta Tz'ŭ-ên Monastery.

K 957   *Abhidharma-kośa-śāstra-kārikā-vibhāshya*

Between the 5th day, 4th month, 2nd year, and the 20th day, 10th month, 3rd year of Yung-hui, T'ang dynasty (April 30th, AD 651–November 26th, AD 652).

K 952   *(Abhidharma) mahā-vibhāshā (śāstra)*

Between the 27th day, 7th month, 1st year and the 3rd day, 7th month, 4th year of Hsien-ch'ing, T'ang dynasty (August 18th, AD 656–July 27th, AD 659).

K 956   *(Abhidharma) Nyāyānusāra-śāstra*

Between the 1st day, 1st month, 4th year, and the 10th day, 7th month, 5th year of Yung-hui, T'ang dynasty (February 3rd, AD 653–August 27th, AD 654).

K 949   *(Abhidharma) prakaraṇa-pāda (śāstra)*

Between the 1st day, 9th month, and the 23rd day, 10th month, 5th year of Hsien-ch'ing, T'ang dynasty (October 10th–November 30th, AD 660) in Yü-hua Monastery.

K 572   *Abhidharma-samuchchaya*

Begun on the 16th day,1st month, and completed on the 28th day,3rd month, 3rd year of Yung-hui, T'ang dynasty (February 11th–April 23rd, AD 652) in Ta Tz'u-ên Monastery, or during the years of Hsien-ch'ing, T'ang dynasty (AD 656-61).

K 576   *Abhidharma-samuchchaya-vyākhyā*

Between the 17th day, 1st month, and the 29th day, intercalary month, 20th year of Chen-kuan, T'ang dynasty (February 7th–April 19th, AD 646) at Hung-fu Monastery.

K 946   *(Abhidharma) saṅgīti-paryāya (pāda-śāstra).*

Between the 26th day, 11th month, 5th year of Hsien-ch'ing, and the 29th day, 12th month, 3rd year of Lung-shuo, T'ang dynasty (January 2nd, AD 660–February 1st, AD 664), in Yü-hua Monastery.

K 947   *(Abhidharma) vijñāna-kāya (pāda-śāstra)*

Between the 15th day, 1st month and the 8th day, 8th month, 23rd year of Chen-kuan, T'ang dynasty (March 3rd–September 19th, AD 649) in Hung-fa hall, Northern palace and Ta Tz'ŭ-ên Monastery.

K 964   *Abhidharmāvatāra-prakaraṇa*

13th day, 10th month, 3rd year of Hsien-ch'ing, T'ang dynasty (November 13th, AD 658) in Ta Tz'ŭ-ên Monastery.

K 236   *Adbhuta-dharma-paryāya-sūtra*

18th day, 5th month, 23rd year of Chen-kuan, T'ang dynasty (July 2nd, AD 649) in Ts'ui-wei Palace on Chung Nan Mountain.

K 628   *Ālambana-parīkshā*

29th day, 12th month, 2nd year of Hsien-ch'ing, T'ang dynasty (AD 657) in Ta-nei-li-jih hall, Tung-tu.

K 289   *Amogha-pāśa-hṛdaya (sūtra)*

19th day, 4th month, 4th year of Hsien-ch'ing, T'ang dynasty (May 15th, AD 659), at Ta Tz'ŭ-ên Monastery.

K 310   *Avalokiteśvaraikādaśa-mukha-dhāraṇī (sūtra)*

28th day, 3rd month, 1st year of Hsien-ch'ing, T'ang dynasty (April 27th, AD 656) in Ta Tz'ŭ-ên Monastery.

K 177   *Bhaishajya-guru-vaiḍūrya-prabhāsa-pūrva-praṇidhāna-*
         viśesha-vistara-(sūtra).

         5th day, 5th month, 1st year of Yung-hui, T'ang dynasty (June
         9th, AD 650) in Ta Tz'u-ên Monastery.

K 22 (12) *Bodhisattva piṭaka (sūtra)*

         19th year of Chen-kuan, T'ang dynasty (AD 645) in Hung-fu
         Monastery, Hsi-ching.

K 460   *Buddha-bhūmi (sūtra)*

         15th day, 7th month, 19th year of Chen-kuan T'ang dynasty
         (August 12th, AD 645) in Hung-fu Monastery.

K 554   *Buddha-bhūmi-sūtra-śāstra*

         Begun on the 3rd day, 10th month, 23rd year of Chen-kuan,
         and completed on the 24th day, 11th month, 24th year of
         Chen-kuan, T'ang dynasty (November 12th, AD 649–January
         2nd, AD 650).

K 444   *Buddha-hṛdaya-dhāraṇī (dharma-paryāya)*

         26th day, 9th month, 1st year of Yung-hui, T'ang dynasty
         (October 26th, AD 650) in Ta Tz'ŭ-ên Monastery.

K 582   *Chatuḥ-śataka*

         21st year of Chen-kuan (AD 647) at Ts'ui-wei palace, or
         between the 10th day, 6th month, and 23rd day, 12th month
         of the first year of Yung-hui, T'ang dynasty (July 13th, AD
         650–January 30th, AD 651) in Ta Tz'ŭ-ên Monastery.

K 256   *Ch'eng tsan ta ch'eng kung te ching*

         5th day, 6th month, 5th year of Yung-hui, T'ang dynasty
         (July 24th, AD 654) in Ta Tz'ŭ-ên Monastery.

K 312   *Chou wu shou*

         1st day, 1st month, 1st year of Lin-te, T'ang dynasty (Feb-
         ruary 2nd, AD 664) in Yü-hua Monastery.

K 57   *Daśa-chakra-kshiti-garbha (ṣūtra)*

         Begun on the 23rd day, 1st month, 2nd year of Yung-hui,
         T'ang dynasty, (February 18th, AD 651) and finished on the
         29th day, 6th month, 2nd year of Yung-hui (August 9th, AD
         652).

K 881   *Devatā-sūtra*

         20th day, 3rd month, 22nd year of Chen-kuan, T'ang dynasty
         (April 17th, AD 648) in Hung-fu Monastery.

K 158   *Fen pieh yüan ch'i ch'u sheng fa men ching*
3rd day, 2nd month, 1st year of Yung-hui, T'ang dynasty (10th March, AD 650) in Ta Tz'ŭ-ên Monastery.

K 571   *Hsien yang sheng chiao lun*
Begun on the 1st (or 11th) day, 10th month, 19th year, and completed on the 15th day, 1st month, 20th year of Chen-kuan, T'ang dynasty (October 26th or November 5th, AD 645–February 5th, AD 646) in Hung-fu Monastery.

K 573   *Hsien yang sheng chiao lun sung*
10th day, 6th month,19th year of Chen-kuan, T'ang dynasty (July 8th, AD 645) in Hung-fu Monastery.

K 803   *Itivṛttaka-sūtra*
Between the 10th day, 9th month and the 8th day, 11th month, 1st year of Yung-hui, T'ang dynasty (October 10th–December 6th, AD 650) in Ta Tz'ŭ-ên Monastery.

K 620   *Karatala-ratna*
Between the 8th and 13th days, 9th month, 23rd year of Chen-kuan, T'ang dynasty (October 19th–24th, AD 649) in Ta Tz'ŭ-ên Monastery.

K 603   *Karma-siddhi-prakaraṇa*
22nd year of Chen-kuan (AD 648) or 5th day, 9th intercalary month, 2nd year of Yung-hui, T'ang dynasty (September 24, AD 651) in Ta Tz'u-ên Monastery.

K 601   *Madhyānta-vibhaṅga-bhāshya*
Between the 10th and 30th days, 5th month, 1st year of Lung-shuo, T'ang dynasty (June 12th–July 2nd, AD 661) in Yü-hua Monastery.

K 599   *Madhyānta-vibhaṅga-kārikā*
1st day, 5th month, 1st year of Lung-shuo, T'ang dynasty (June 3rd, AD 661) at Yü-hua Monastery.

K 483   *Mahā-parinirvāṇa-sūtra*
4th day, 4th month, 3rd year of Yung-hui, T'ang dynasty (May 17th, AD 652) in Ta Tz'ŭ-ên Monastery.

K 1   *Mahā-prajñā-pāramitā-sūtra*
Begun on the 1st day, 1st month, 5th year of Hsien-ch'ing, T'ang dynasty (February 16th, AD 660), or in the 4th year of Hsien-ch'ing, T'ang dynasty (AD 659), and completed on the 20th day, 10th month, 3rd year of Lung-shuo, T'ang dynasty

(November 25th, AD 663) in Yü-hua-kung Monastery, Fang-chou.

K 592   *Mahāyāna-saṅgraha*

Between the 26th day, 12th intercalary month, 22nd year, and the 17th day, 6th month, 23rd year of Chen-kuan, T'ang dynastry (January 14th, AD 649–July 31st, AD 649) in Ta Tz'ŭ-ên Monastery.

K 594   *Mahāyāna-saṅgraha-bhāshya*

Between the 22nd and 23rd years of Chen-kuan, T'ang dynasty, in the Northern palace and Ta Tz'ŭ-ên Monastery (AD 648–49).

K 595   *Mahāyāna-saṅgrahopanibandhana*

Between the 1st day, 3rd month, 21st year, and 17th day, 6th month, 23rd year of Chen-kuan, T'ang dynasty, (April 10th, AD 647–July 31st, AD 649) at Ta Tz'ŭ-ên Monastery.

K 644   *Mahāyāna-śata-dharma-prakāśa-mukha-śāstra*

17th day, 11th month, 22nd year of Chen-kuan, T'ang dynasty (December 7th, AD 648) in Hung-fu hall of the Northern palace.

K 1046   *Nandimitr-āvadāna*

18th day, 5th intercalary month, 5th year of Yung-hui, T'ang dynasty (June 8th, AD 654).

K 259   *Nidāna-sūtra*

1st day, 1st month, 23rd year of Chen-kuan, T'ang dynasty (February 17th, AD 649) in Hung-fa Hall, Hsi-ching.

K 604   *Nyāya-mukha*

25th day, 12th month, 23rd year of Chen-kuan, T'ang dynasty (February 1st, AD 650) in Ta Tz'ŭ-ên Monastery.

K 607   *Nyāya-praveśa*

6th day, 8th month, 21st year of Chen-kuan, T'ang dynasty (September 10th, AD 647) in Hung-fu Monastery.

K 446   *Pa chi k'u nan t'o lo ni ching*

10th day, 9th month, 5th year of Yung-hui, T'ang dynasty (October 25th, AD 654) in Ta Tz'ŭ-ên Monastery.

K 445   *Pa ming p'u mi t'o lo ni ching*

27th day, 9th month, 5th year of Yung-hui, T'ang dynasty (November 11th, AD 654) in Ta Tz'ŭ-ên Monastery.

K 619   *Pañcha-skandha-prakaraṇa*

21st year of Chen-kuan, T'ang dynasty (AD 647) in Ts'ui-wei palace, or 24th day, 2nd month, 21st year of Chen-kuan, T'ang dynasty (April 4th, AD 647).

K 970   *Pañcha-vāstuka-vibhāsha*

13th day, 10th month, 3rd year of Lung-shuo, T'ang dynasty (November 18th, AD 663) in Ta Tz'ŭ-ên Monastery.

K 20   *Prajñā-pāramitā-hṛdaya-sūtra*

24th day, 5th month, 23rd year of Chen-kuan, T'ang dynasty (July 8th, AD 649) in Ts'ui-wei palace, Chung-nan Mountain.

K 482   *Praśānta-viniśchaya-prātihārya-(samādhi) sūtra*

29th day, 12th month, 3rd year of Lung-shuo, T'ang dynasty (February 1st, AD 664) in Yü-hua Monastery, or 29th day, 12th month, 2nd year of Lung-shuo, T'ang dynasty (February 12th, AD 663) in Yü-hua Monastery.

K 736   *Pratītya-samutpādādi-vibhaṅga-nirdeśa-sūtra*

9th day, 7th month, 1st year of Lung-shuo, T'ang dynasty (August 9th, AD 661).

K 534   *P'u sa chieh chieh mo wen*

15th day, 7th month, 23rd year of Chen-kuan, T'ang dynasty (August 28th, AD 649) in Ta Tz'ŭ-ên Monastery.

K 533   *P'u sa chieh pen*

21st day, 7th month, 23rd year of Chen-kuan, T'ang dynasty (September 3rd, AD 649) in Ta Tz'ŭ-ên Monastery, or the 21st year of Chen-kuan, T'ang dynasty (AD 647) in Ts'ui-wei palace.

K 258   *Rāj-āvavādaka (sūtra)*

6th day, 2nd month, 23rd year of Chen-kuan, T'ang dynasty (March 24th, AD 649) in Ta Tz'ŭ-ên Monastery.

K 977   *Samayabhedoparachana-chakra*

14th day, 7th month, 2nd year of Lung-shuo, T'ang dynasty (September 2nd, AD 662), in Yü-hua Monastery.

K 154   *Sandhi-nirmochana-sūtra*

13th day, 7th month, 21st year of Chen-kuan, T'ang dynasty (August 18th, AD 647) in Hung-fu Monastery.

K 447   Shanmukhī dhāraṇī (sūtra)

         14th day, 7th month, 19th year of Chen-kuan, T'ang dynasty
         (October 11th, AD 645) in Hung-fu Monastery.

K 332   Sheng ch'uang pei yin t'o lo ni ching

         29th day, 9th month, 5th year of Yung-hui, T'ang dynasty
         (November 13th, AD 654) in Ta Tz'ŭ-ên Monastery.

K 484   Shou ch'ih ch'i fo ming hao so sheng kung te ching

         9th day, 1st month, 2nd year of Yung-hui, T'ang dynasty
         (February 4th, AD 651) in Ta Tz'ŭ-ên Monastery.

K 193   Sukhāvatī-vyūha (sūtra)

         1st day, 1st month, 1st year of Yung-hui, T'ang dynasty
         (February 7th, AD 650) in Ta Tz'ŭ-ên Monastery.

K 583   Ta ch'eng kuang pai lun shih lun

         Between the 27th day, 6th month and 23rd day, 12th month,
         1st year of Yung-hui, T'ang dynasty (July 30th, AD 650–Janu-
         ary 30th, AD 651).

K 1065   Ta t'ang hsi yü chi

         Written by Hsüan-tsang and compiled by Pien-chi: 20th year
         of Chen-kuan, T'ang dynasty (AD 646) in Hung-fu Monastery.

K 101   Tathāgatānām-Buddha-kshetra-guṇokta-dharma-paryāya
         (sūtra).

         28th day, 9th month, 5th year of Yung-hui, T'ang dynasty
         (November 12th, AD 654) in Ta Tz'ŭ-ên Monastery.

K 609   Trimśikā (kārikā)

         29th day, 5th month, 22nd year of Chen-kuan, T'ang dynasty
         (June 25th, AD 648) in Hung-fu Monastery.

K 250   Tsui wu pi ching

         19th day, 7th month, 23rd year of Chen-kuan, T'ang dynasty
         (September 1st, AD 649) in Ta Tz'ŭ-ên Monastery.

K 1045   Vaiśeshika-daśa-padārtha-śāstra

         15th day, 5th month, 22nd year of Chen-kuan, T'ang dynasty
         (June 11th, AD 648) in Hung-fu Monastery.

K 614   Vijñapti-mātratā-siddhi-śāstra

         10th intercalary month, 4th year of Hsien-ching, T'ang
         dynasty (October or November, AD 659) in Yü-hua Monas-
         tery.

K 16   *Vajra-chhedikā-prajñā-pāramitā-sūtra*
       10th month, 22nd year of Chen-kuan, T'ang dynasty (AD 648)
       in Yü-hua-kung Monastery, Fang Chou, or during the years
       of Yung-hui, T'ang dynasty (AD 650–55) in the Ta Tz'ŭ-ên
       Monastery, Hsi-Ching.

K 121 *Vimala-kīrti-nirdeśa-sūtra*
       Begun on the 8th day, 2nd month and completed on the 1st
       day, 8th month, 1st year of Yung-hui (March 15th—Septem-
       ber 1st, AD 650), T'ang dynasty at Ta Tz'ŭ-ên Monastery.

K 608 *Vimśatikā-vṛtti*
       1st day, 6th month, 1st year of Lung-shuo, T'ang dynasty
       (July 3rd, AD 661) in Yü-hua Monastery.

K 448 *Vasudhārā-dhāraṇī (sūtra)*
       10th day, 10th month, 5th year of Yung-hui, T'ang dynasty
       (November 24th, AD 654) in Ta Tz'ŭ-ên Monastery.

K 574 *Wang fa cheng li lun*
       21st year of Chen-kuan, T'ang dynasty (AD 647) in Ts'ui-wei
       Palace or on the 18th day, 7th month, 23rd year of Chen-kuan,
       T'ang dynasty (August 31st, AD 649) in Ta Tz'ŭ-ên Monas-
       tery.

K 570 *Yogāchāra-bhūmi-śāstra*
       Between the 15th day, 5th month, 20th year, and 15th day,
       5th month, 22nd year of Chen-kuan, T'ang dynasty (July 3rd,
       AD 646–June 11th, AD 648) at Hung-fu Monastery or Ta
       Tz'ŭ-ên Monastery.

K 575 *Yogāchāra-bhūmi-śāstra-kārikā*
       1st day, 2nd month, 1st year of Yung-hui, T'ang dynasty
       (March 8th, AD 650).

Bibliography

al-Bīrūnī, Abū Raihān Muhammad Ibn Ahmad, *Tahqīq mā li 'l-Hind*, tr. E.C. Sachau, as *Alberuni's India*, London, 1880, Delhi: S. Chand, 2 vols, 1964.

Bagchi, P.C., *She-kia-fang-che*, Santiniketan: Santiniketan Press, 1959.

Beal, Samuel, *Si Yu Ki: Buddhist Records of the Western World (translated from the Chinese of Hiuen Tsiang: AD 629)*, London: Kegan Paul, Trench, Trübner & Co. Ltd., 1884.

————— , *The Life of Hiuen-tsiang by the Shaman Hwui-Li*, (with an introduction containing an account of the works of I-tsing; with a preface by L. Cranmer-Byng), London: Kegan Paul, Trench, Trubner & Co. Ltd, 1911. First published 1888.

Bira, S, *Chen-po Thaṅygur duskyi rgya-gar zhiṅgi bkodpahi kar-Chag bZhugsSo*, (*Mgon-po-Skyabs, c.* 1690–1750), Ulan Bator, 1973.

Chandra, Lokesh and Sudarshana Devi Singhal, *Acharya Raghuvira Ka Cheena Abhiyana* (Prof. Raghuvira's Expedition to China, Part I: Travel Diary and Photographs), New Delhi: International Academy of Indian Culture, 1969.

Cowell, E.B. & R.A. Neil (eds), *Divyavadana: A Collection of Early Buddhist Legends*, Amsterdam: Oriental Press (Repr. of Cambridge 1886 edition), 1970.,

Eitel, E.J., *Handbook of Chinese Buddhism*, A Sanskrit–Chinese Dictionary, 2nd edn., London, 1888.

————— , *Hsien-hua Dictionary*, 1956

Hui-li, *The life of Hsuan-tsang—The Tripiṭaka Master of the Great Tzu En Monastery*, translated from Chinese by Li Yung-hsi (Translated under the auspices of the San Shih Buddhist Institute), Peking: The Chinese Buddhist Association, 1959.

Hui-li And Yen-ts'ung, *Ta-T'ang Ta-Tz'ŭ-ên Ssŭ San-tsang Fa-shih Chuan (Life of the Master of the Law etc.)*, pub. by Chih-na nei-hsueh yuan (China Academy), 1923, repr., Taipei, 1963.

I-tsing, *Nan-hai-chi-kuei-nai-fa-ch'uan (A record of Buddhist practices sent home from the Southern sea)*,

Julien, M. Stanislas, *Histoire de la vie de Hiouen-thsang et de ses voyages dans l'Inde*, Paris, 1853.

Kangle, R.P., *The Kautilīya Arthaśāstra*, University of Bombay, 3 vols, 1960.

Lancaster, Lewis R., *Korean Buddhist Canon (KBC)*: a descriptive catalogue, Berkeley: University of California Press, 1979.

————, *Mathews Dictionary*

Lévi, S., 'Les missions de Wang Hieuen Ts'e dans l'Inde', *Journal asiatique*, IXᵉ sér., tome xv, 1900, pp. 297 ff. and pp. 401 ff. It is a most erudite article based on Ma Tuan-lin's work, certain passages of the Old and the New T'ang histories, and the *Fa-yüan chu-lin*.

Liu Hsü (ed.), *Chiu t'ang-shu*, Ssü-pu Pei-yao edition.

Ming-Hsiang, *Ta-t'ang K'u San-tsang Hsüan-tsang Fa-shih Hsing-chuang* (Report on the career of the late Master of the Law, Hsüan-tsang of Great T'ang) (*c.* A.D. 664). *Taishō Shinshū Daizōkyo*, ed. Takakusu, J., 50, 214, Tokyo, 1924–35.

Monier-Williams, *A Sanskrit–English Dictionary*, Oxford: Clarendon Press, 1888–1899.

Nanjio, Bunyiu, (Compiler), *A Catalogue of the Chinese translation of the Buddhist Tripiṭaka, the sacred canon of the Buddhists in China and Japan*, Oxford, 1883 (repr. with additions and corrections by Lokesh Chandra, New Delhi, 1980).

Takakusu, J. (ed.), *Ta-t'ang K'u San-tsang Hsüan-tsang Fa-shih Hsing-chuang (Report on the career of the later Master of the Law, Hsuan-tsang of Great T'ang) (c. AD 664)*, Tokyo, 1924–35.

————, *The Taisho Shinshu Daizokyo*, 85 vols, 51; Tokyo and the Kyoto University edition with a volume of collation of variants, 1911.

———— (trs.), *A record of the Buddhist religion as practised in India and the Malay Archipelago (AD 671–695)*, Oxford, 1896.

Takakusu, J., and Lévi, S., *Hōbōgirin. Dictionaire encyclopédique du Boudisme* . . . , Tokyo-Paris, 1929–37.

Tao-hsüan, *Chi ku-chin fo tao lun-heng*, Takakusu, vol. 52.

————, *Hsü Kao-sêng Chuan* (The continuation of the lives of eminent monks) (A.D. 645; added to until 667), *Taishō Shinshū Daizōkyo*, Takakusu, J., 50, 446, and 458b, Tokyo, 1924–35.

————, *Shih-chia Fang-chih* (A record of the country of Śākya-muni [The Buddha.]) (A.D. 650), Shih-na nei-hsueh-yuan, ed. 1924, and *Taishō Shinshū Daizōkyo*, Takakusu, J., 51, Tokyo, 1924–35.

Taranātha's History of Buddhism in India, tr. from Tibetan by Lama Chimpa and Alaka Chattopadhyaya, ed. Debiprasad Chattopadhyaya, Simla: Indian Institute of Advanced Studies, 1970.

Utsunomiya, K., *Shirin*, 12.4, 1932.

Utsonomiya, Sho Ki-chi and Haneda Toru, Kyoto, 1932.

Von Gabain, Annamarie, 'Briefe der uigerischen Huen-tsang biographie' (translation of letters of the biography of Hsuan-tsang in Uigurish), *Philosophische-historische klasse, Sitzung sberichte* (SBAW), Deutsche Akademie der Wissenschaften, 1938.

Waley, Arthur, *The Real Tripitaka and other Pieces*, London: George Allen & Unwin, 1952.

————, *The Secret History of the Mongols and other Pieces*, London: Allen & Unwin, 1963.

Watters, Thomas, *On Yuan Chwang's Travels in India (AD 629–645)* (edited after his death by T.W, Rhys Davids and S.W. Bushell), 2nd edn., New Delhi: Munshiram Manoharlal, 1973.

————, Xinhua Zidian (New China Dictionary), Beijing, 1972.

Yang, Han-Sung et al., *The Hye Ch'o Diary: Memoir of the Pilgrimage to the Five Regions of India*, trans. and ed. by Han Sung-Yang, Yun-Hua Jan and Shotaro Iida; Laurence W. Preston, Asian Humanities Press, Berkeley, California and Seoul, Korea.

Index

178 / *The Unknown Hsüan-tsang*

玄奘
三蔵

Hsüan-tsang in the Kosozo 'illustrations of eminent monks' dated
AD 1163.
Courtesy: Professor Lokesh Chandra

寶應善薩憂治□□一刀八千歲

唐朝三藏玄芊

Hsüan-tsang among the Buddhist patriarchs of three countries (namely India, China, and Japan) in a 14th century album.
Courtesy: Professor Lokesh Chandra

Hsüan-tsang and the God of the Deep Sands in Central Asia. The pilgrim is dressed as a mendicant with a staff and a scroll. The Deep Sand God wears a garland of serpents and a loin cloth of tiger skin, as he wields the trident to smite the dragons. The monkey, companion to the pilgrim in Chinese folklore, is above the God.

(From a 12th century scroll.)

Courtesy: Professor Lokesh Chandra

Hsüan-tsang

Rubbing of the relief of Hsüan-tsang at Xian.
Courtesy: Professor Lokesh Chandra

The Hsing-chiao-ssü stupa on the outskirts of Sian which was built in 669 to preserve the relics of Hsüan-tsang.